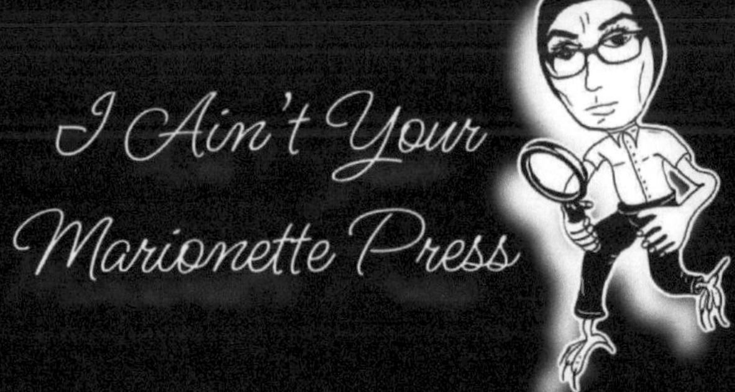
I Ain't Your
Marionette Press

Shattered Psyche

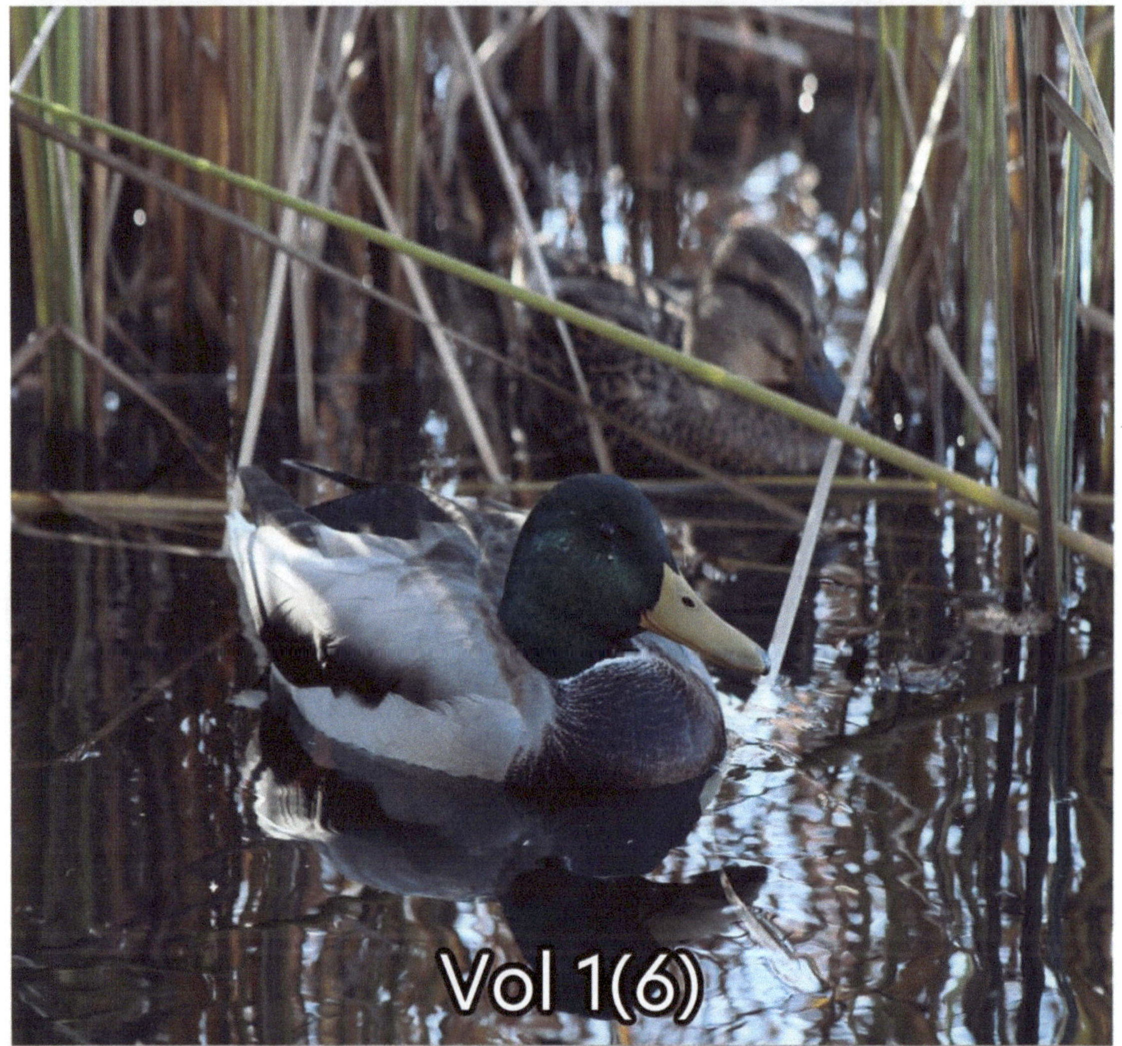

Vol 1(6)

I Ain't Your Marionette

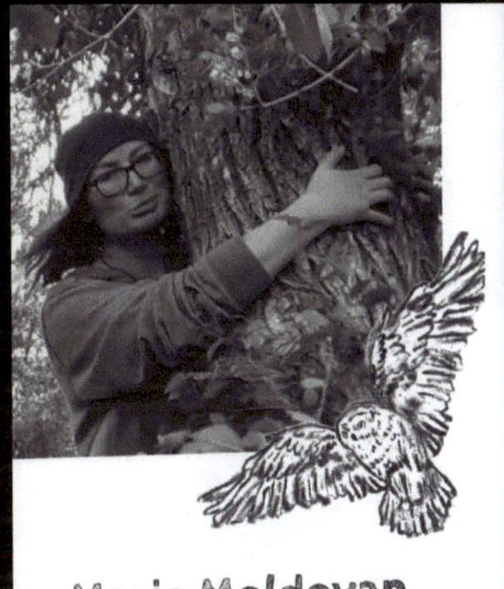

Marie Moldovan

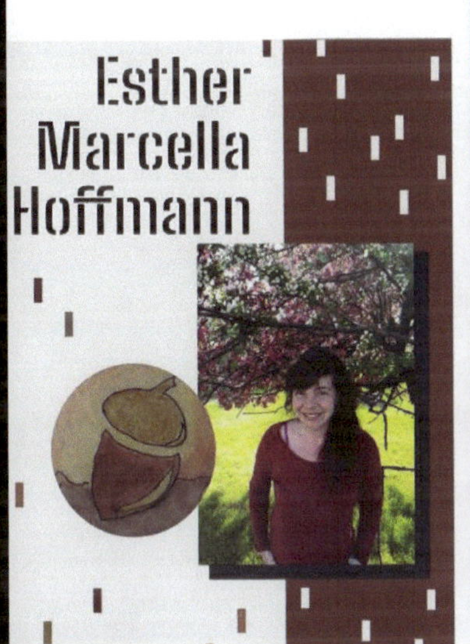

Esther Marcella Hoffmann

A behind the lens statement about Shattered Psyche 1(6) by Artist Joe Mykut:

From the shattered PSYCHE to the basis of all observed reality, at least according to Buddhism, the artists in this volume have evoked the four elements: Earth, Wind, Fire, and Water. In a most genuine and literal way, they have imitated life with art as the expression goes. The imagery is spellbinding as it calls upon the power of the elements that are represented within each collection. The anthology marries beautifully, the imaginary with realism. A matrimony between the mythical and realistic. Prepare yourself for a dual experience, where imagination is anchored in the fabric of reality, and the make believe is crafted using the very elements that make up our physical existence.

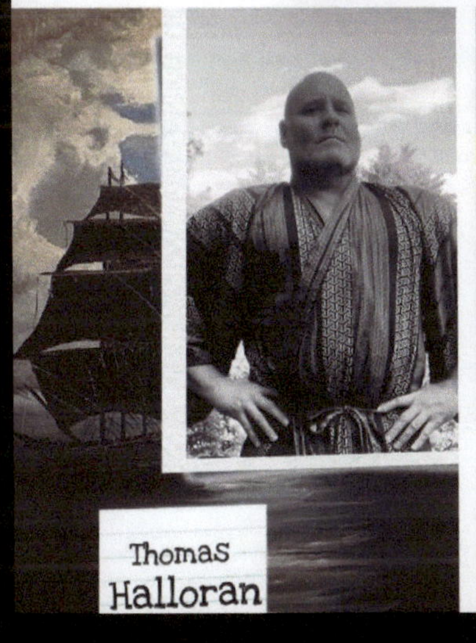

Thomas Halloran

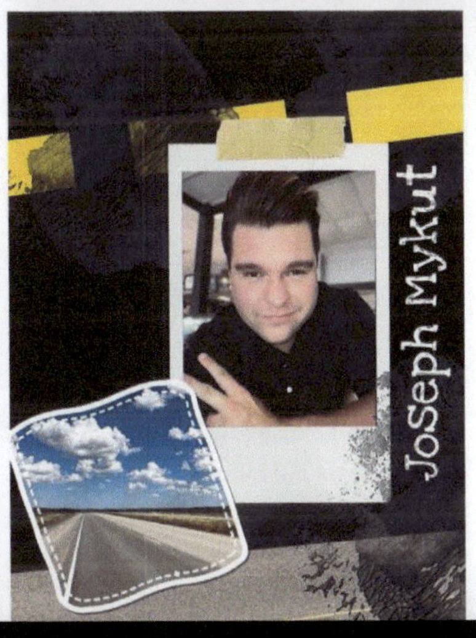

Joseph Mykut

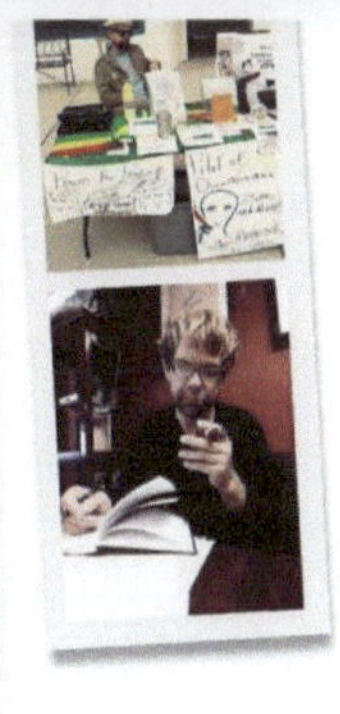

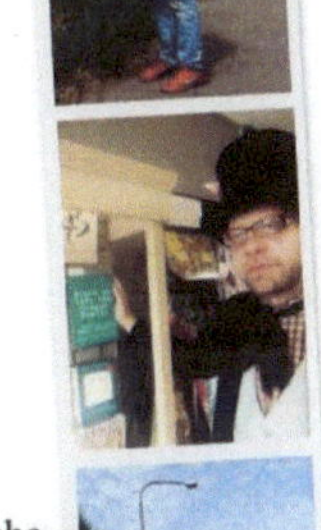

Lucas Alan Dietsche

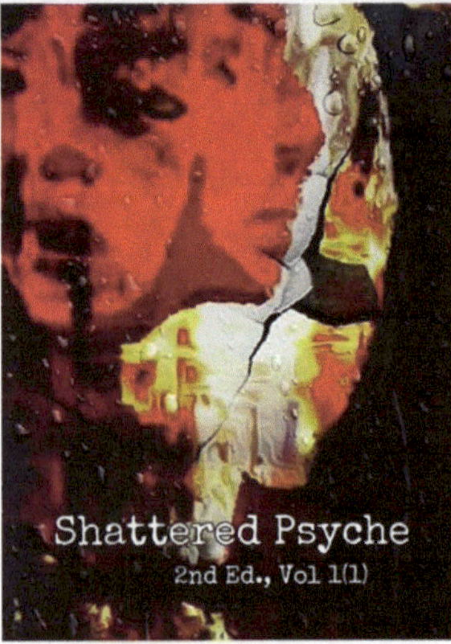

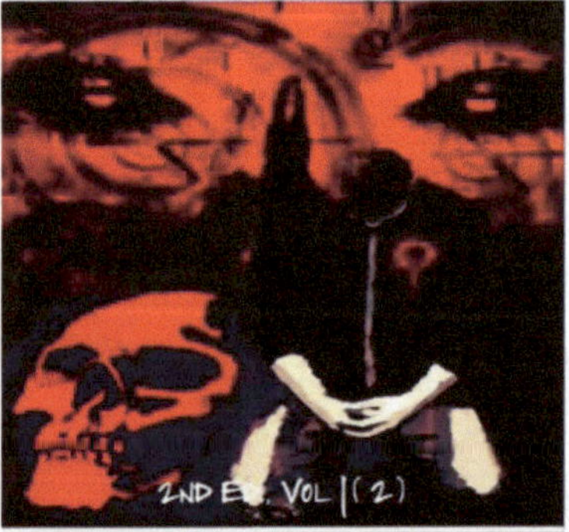

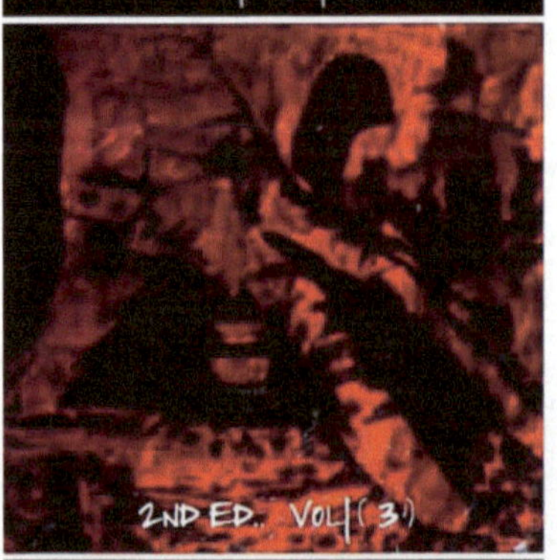

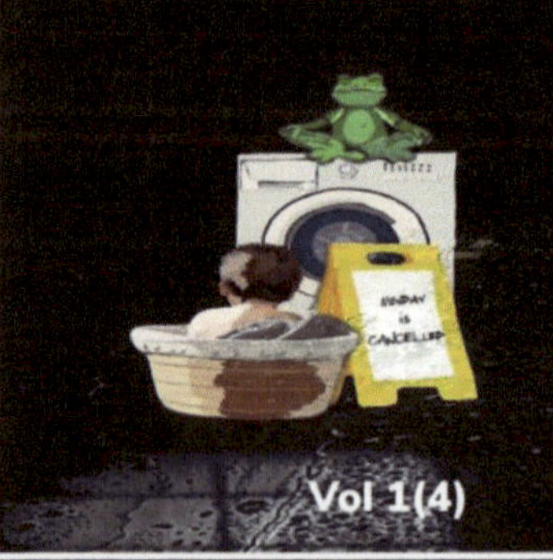

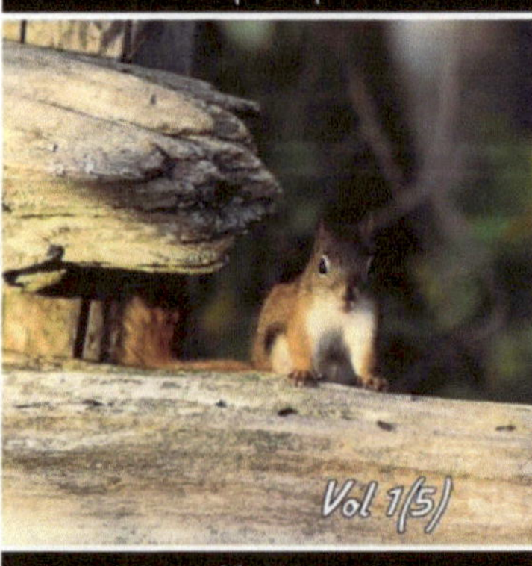

Dedicated to those seeking inner peace

TABLE OF CONTENTS

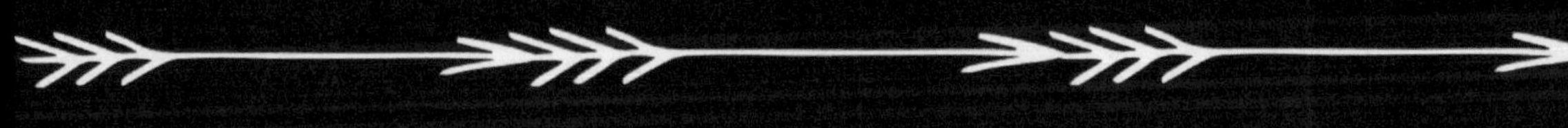

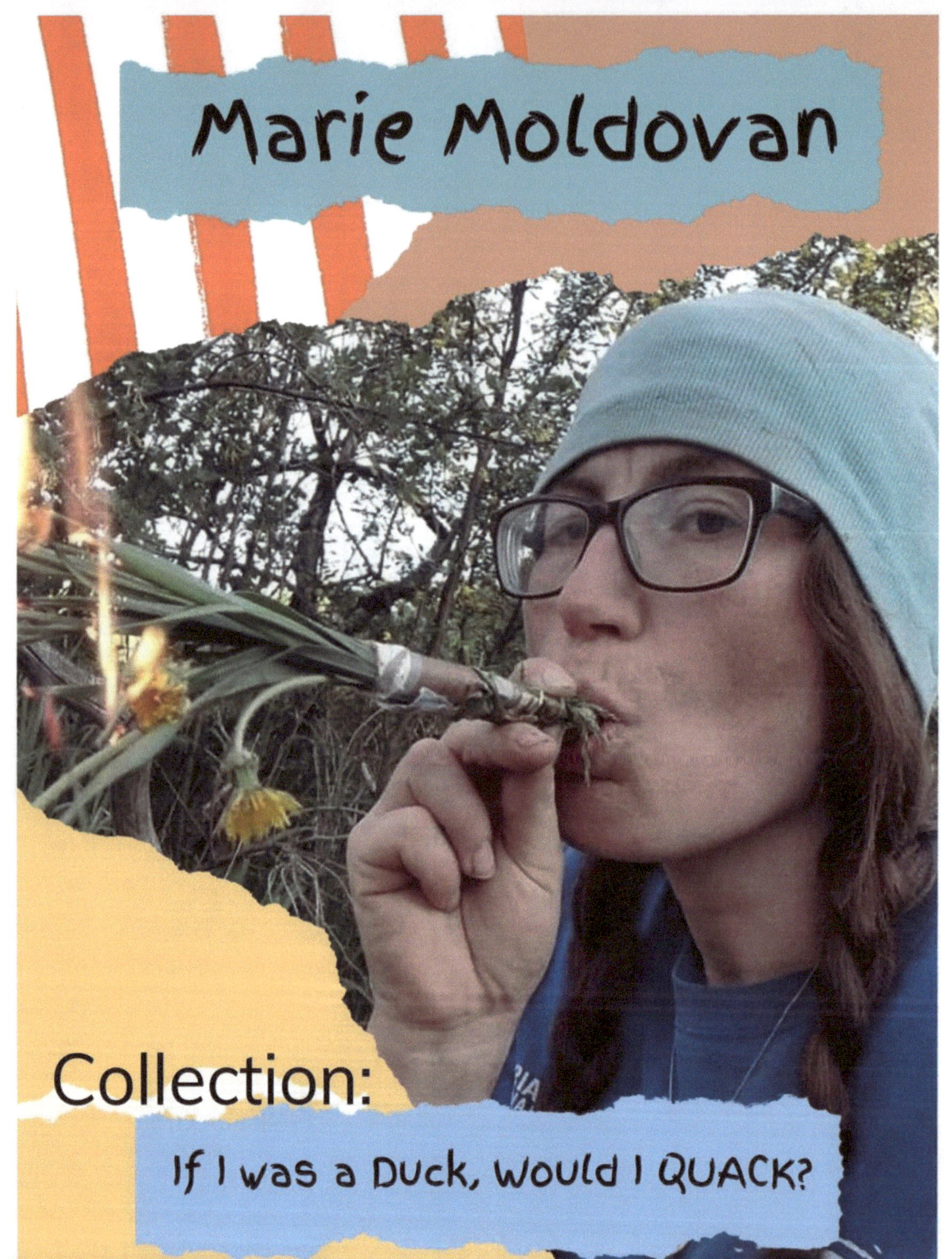
Marie Moldovan
Collection:
If I was a Duck, Would I QUACK?

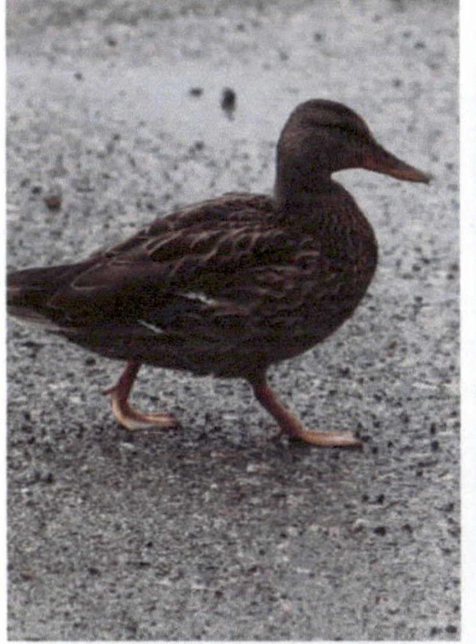

About the Collection

This collection is a photographic ode to the majestic mallard. An exceedingly adaptable species of 'flat billed' duck known for their males radiantly iridescent head and white collar.

I've always had a fascination with the mallard. It's presence is powerful and brings forth in me a sense of hope.

After the passing of my husband in 2018, I found myself wandering the wilderness of Canada like a nomad in search of peace. For me the images in this collection represent my journey through grief.

~ Marie Moldovan

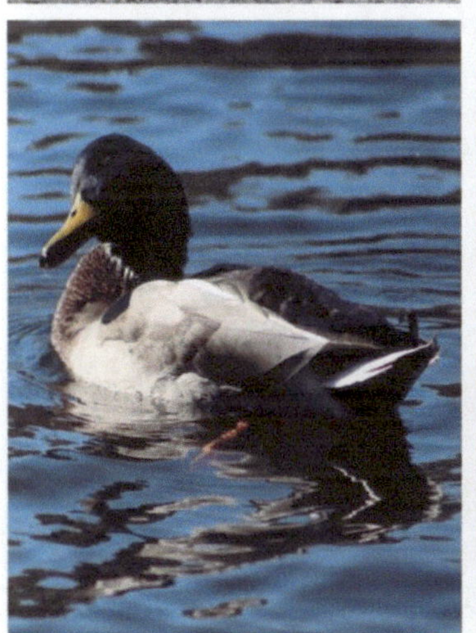

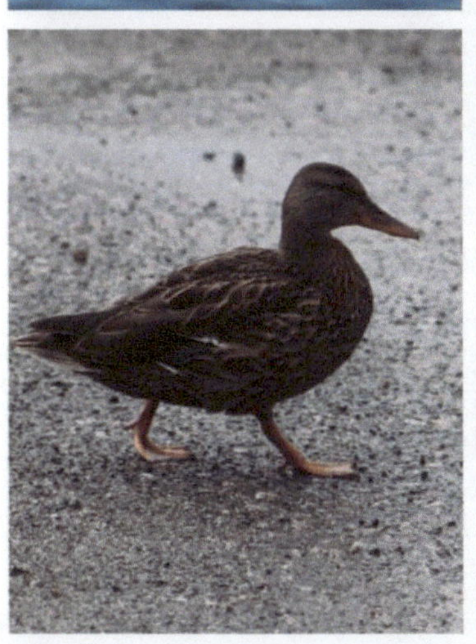

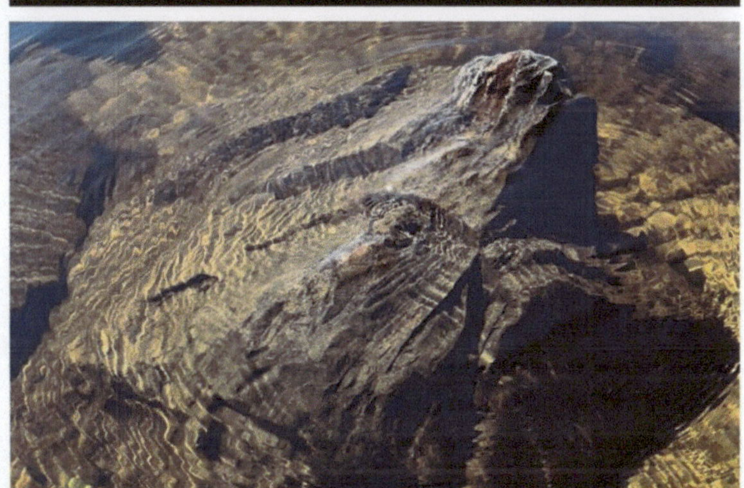

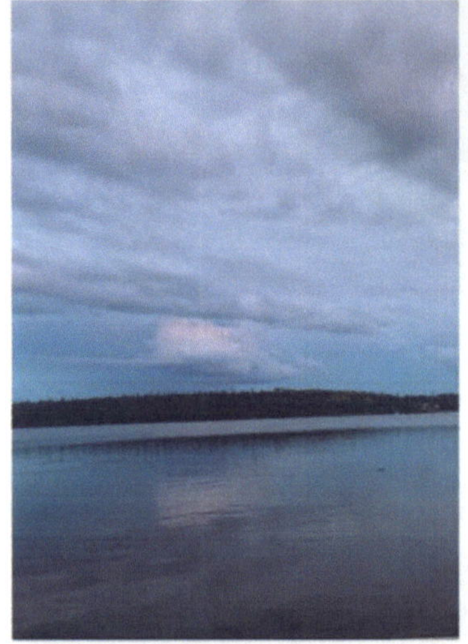

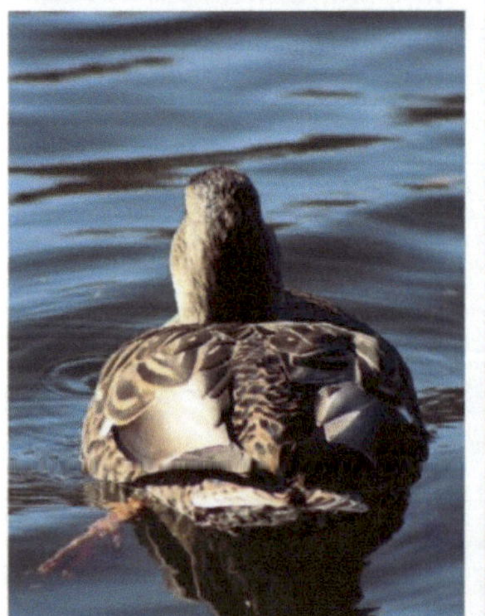

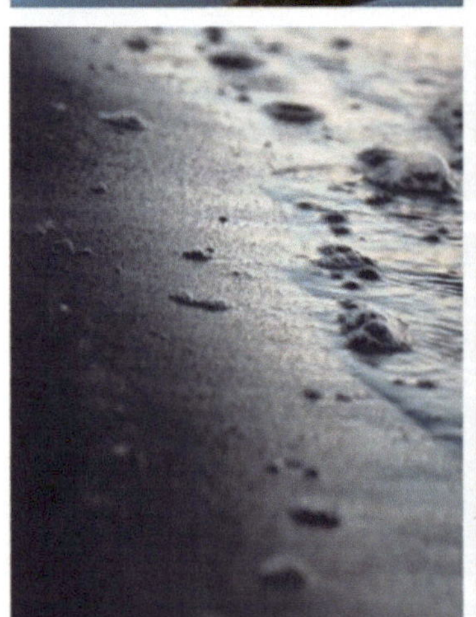

About the Artist

Marie Moldovan is a writer, artist, Canadian Forces veteran, jack-of-all-trades, and independent publisher at I Ain't Your Marionette. Shortly after her diagnosis with service-related PTSD and the passing of her husband in 2018, she began writing poetry to free her tormented mind. She is the author of 20 Years of Winter.

For more of Marie's work check out:

HTTPS : RUSTYSDIGITALART . COM

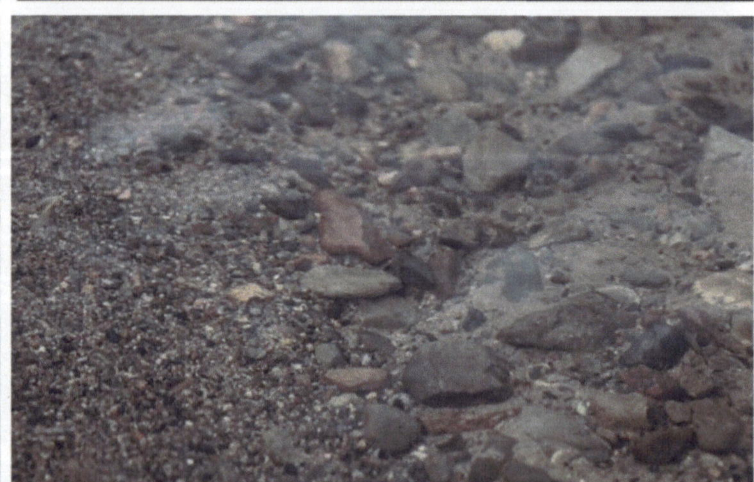

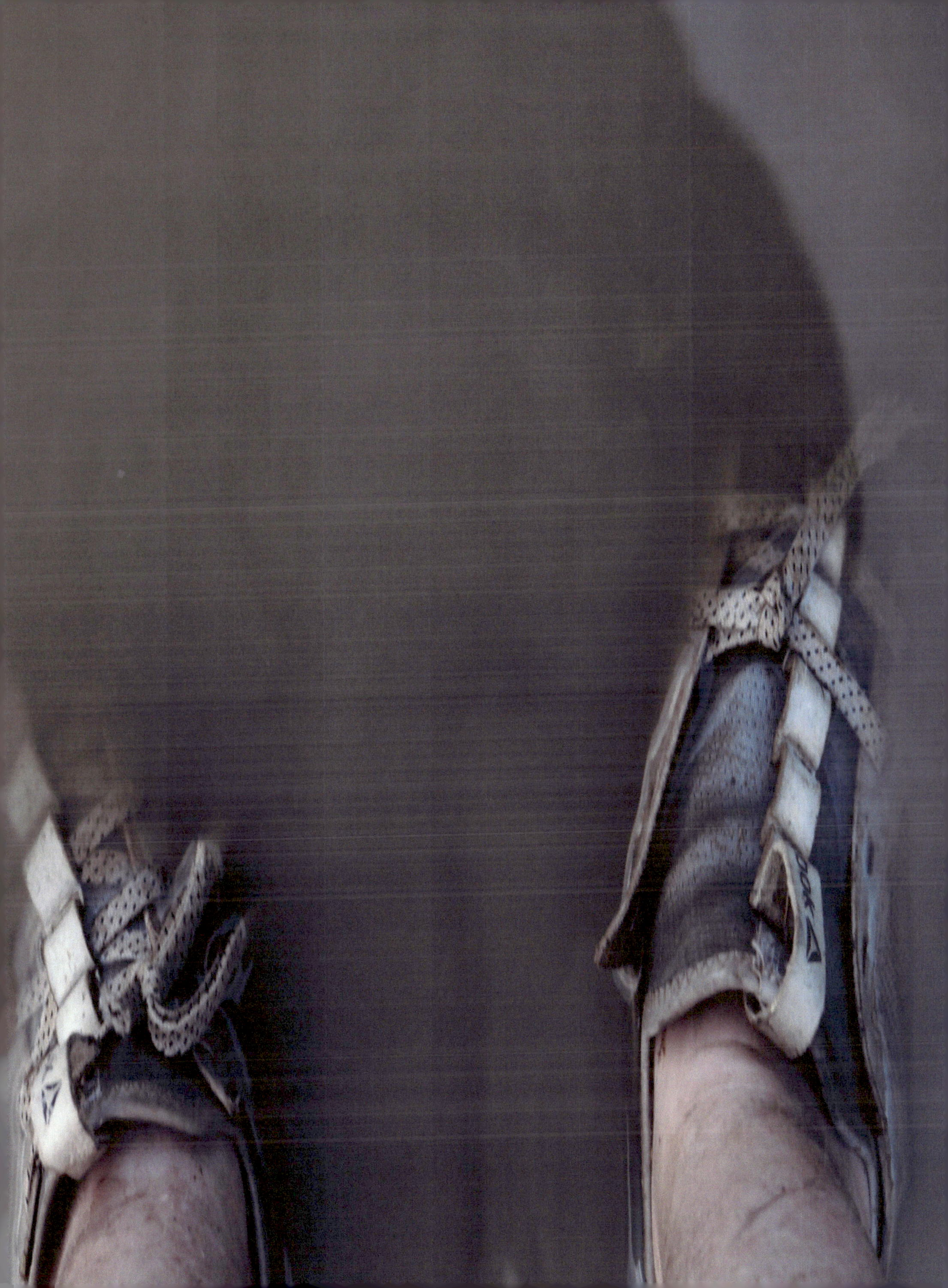

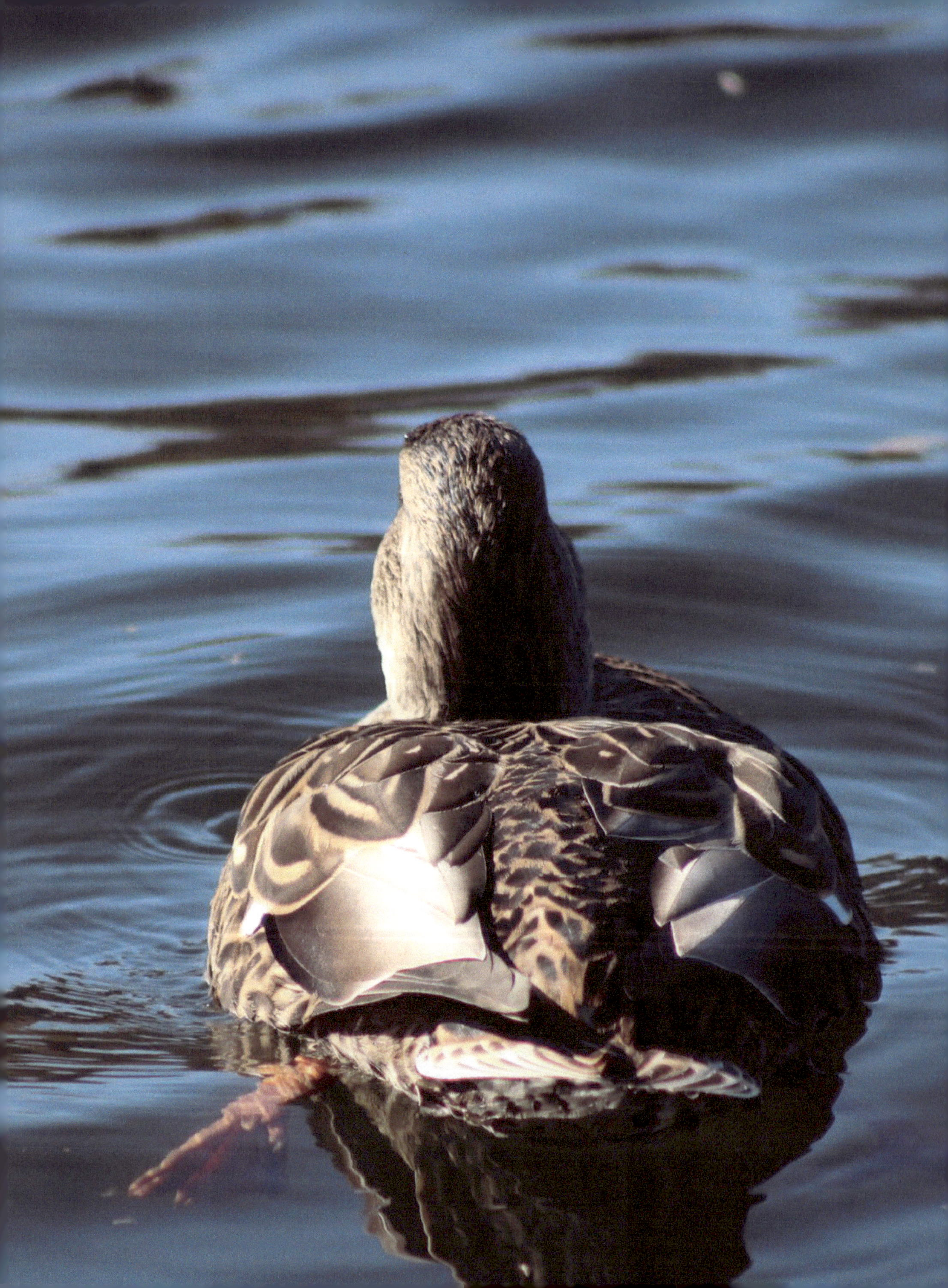

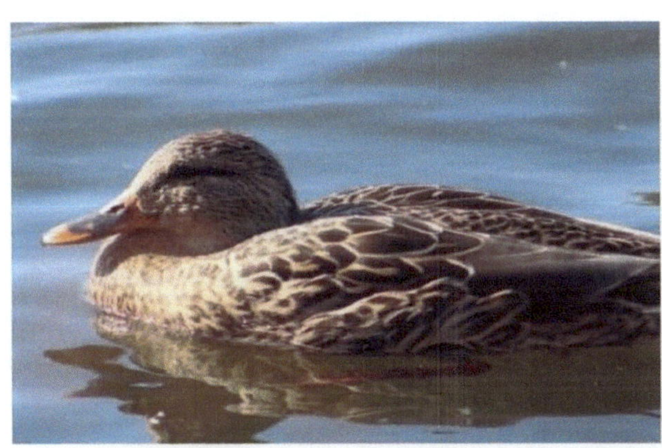

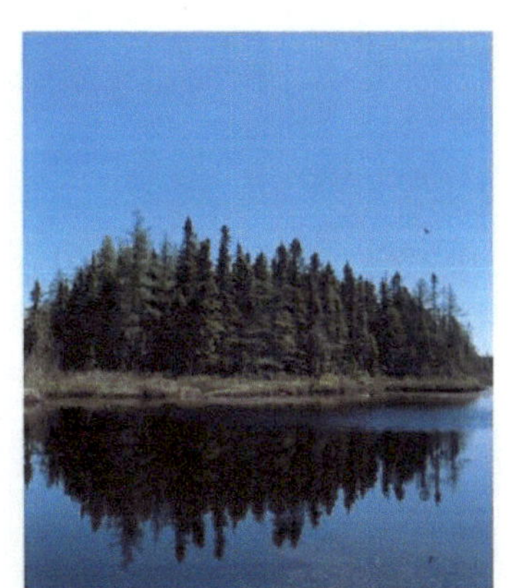

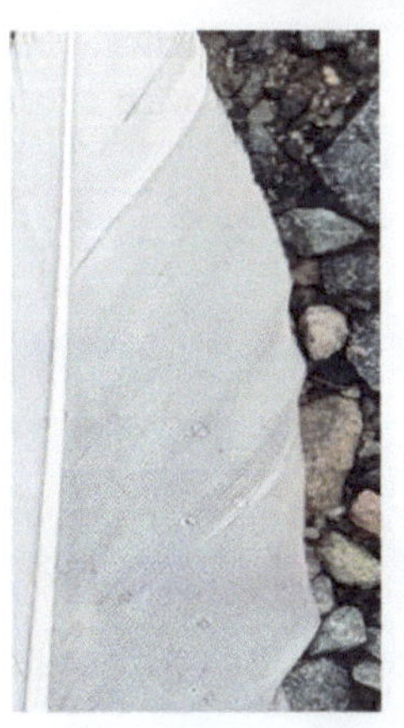

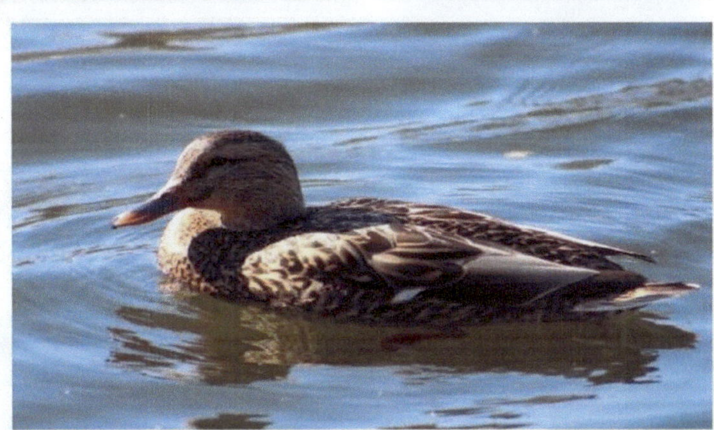

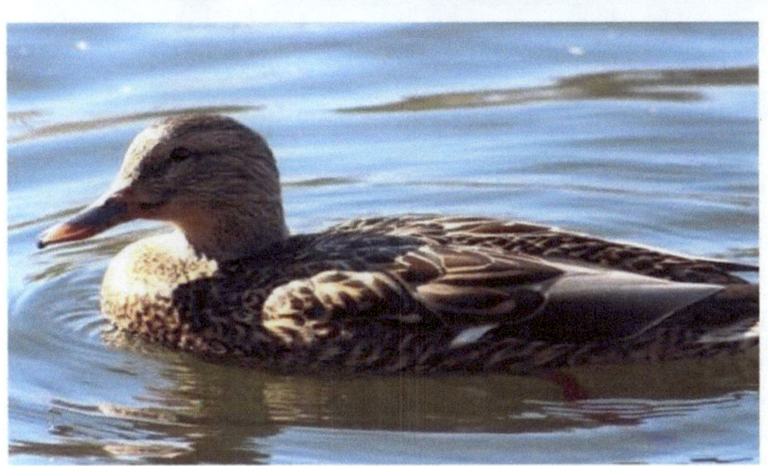

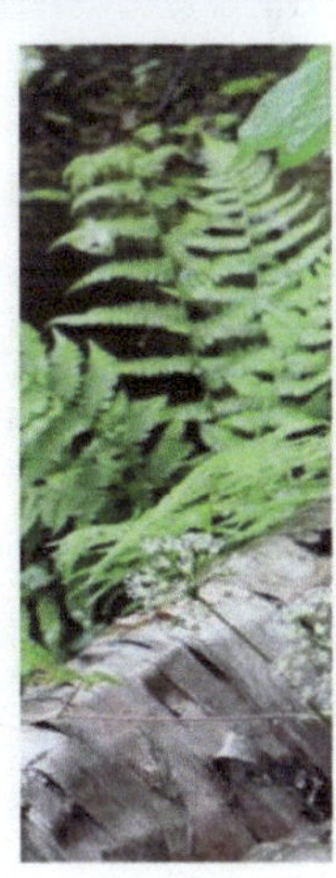

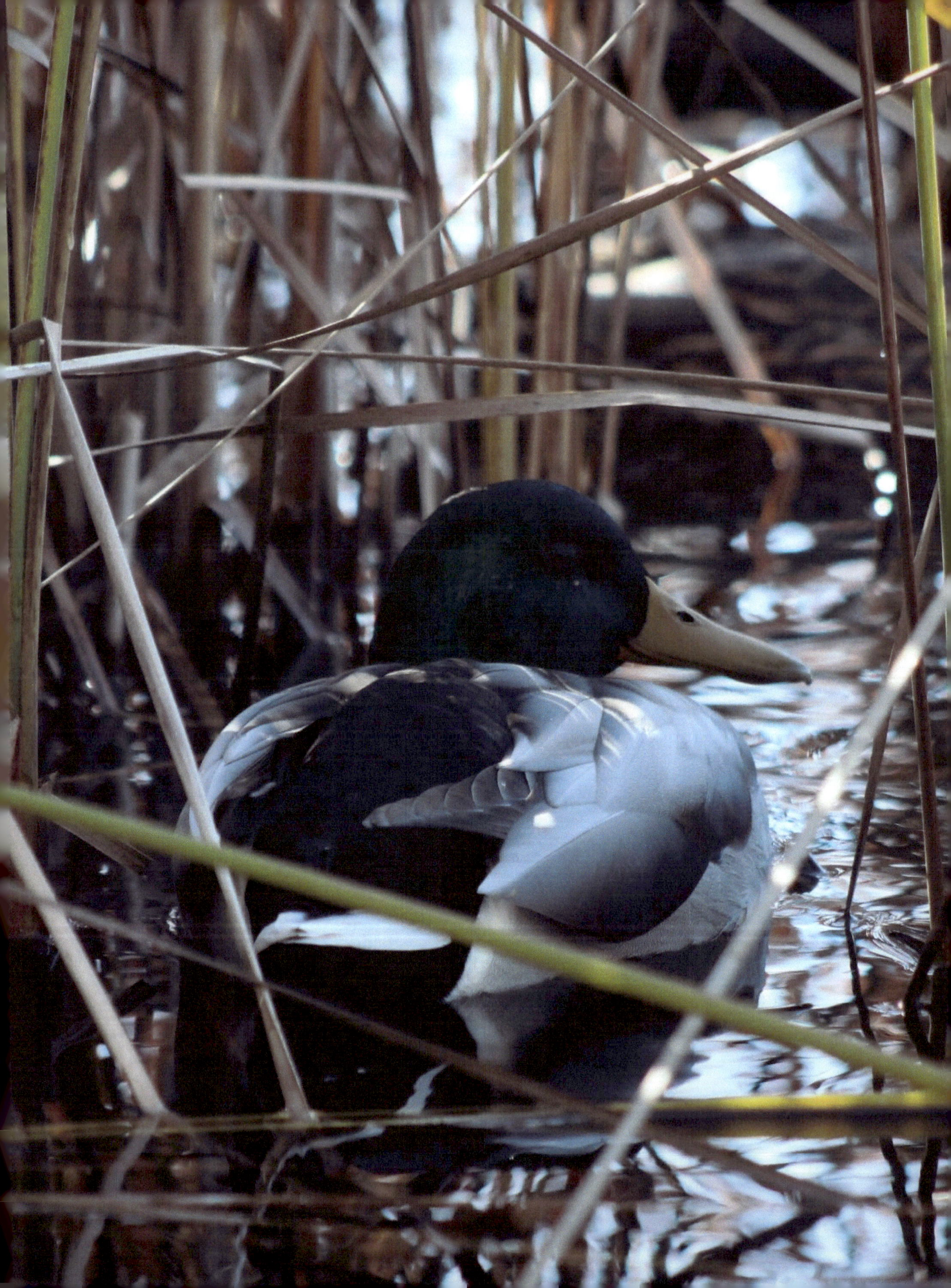

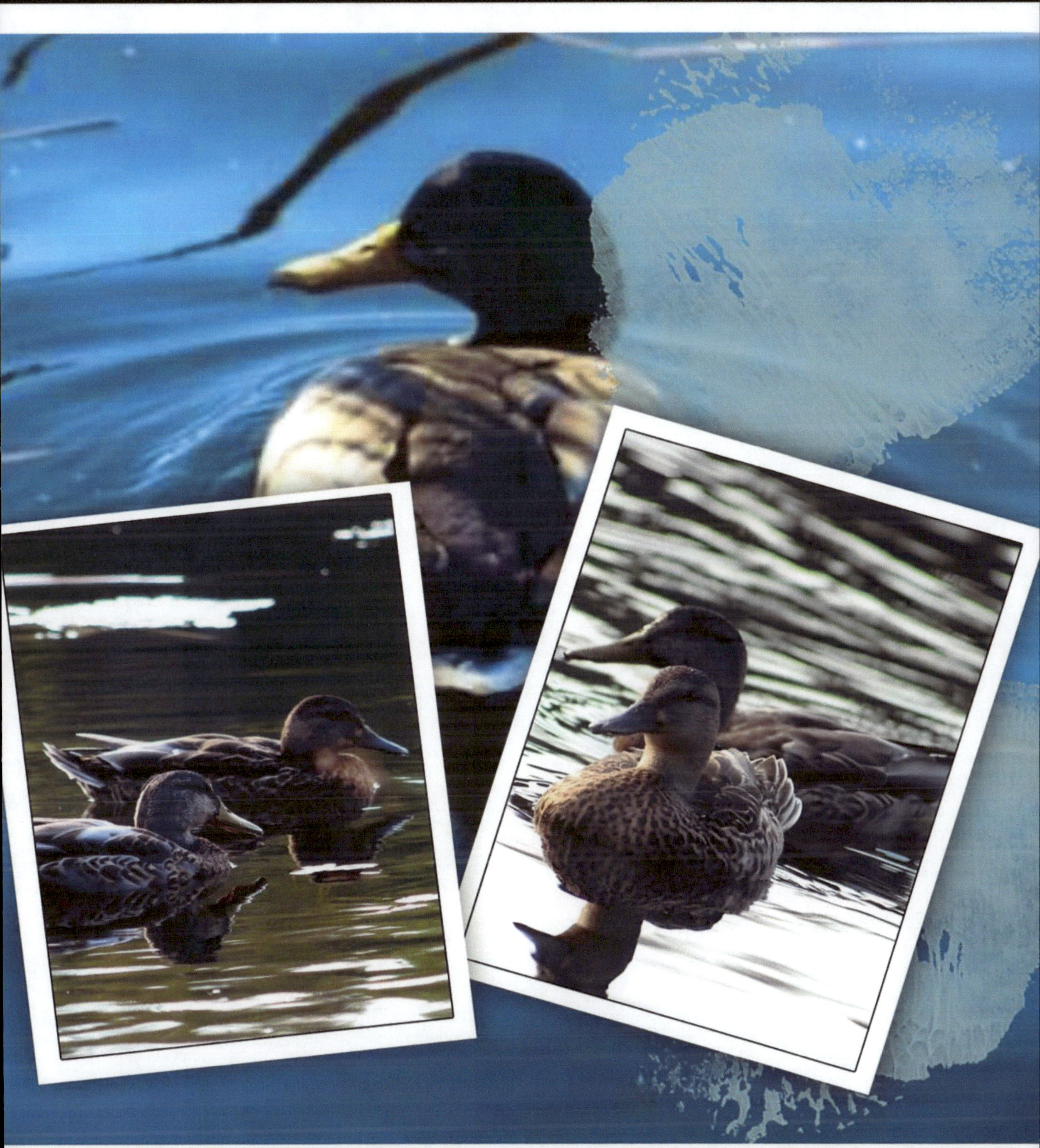

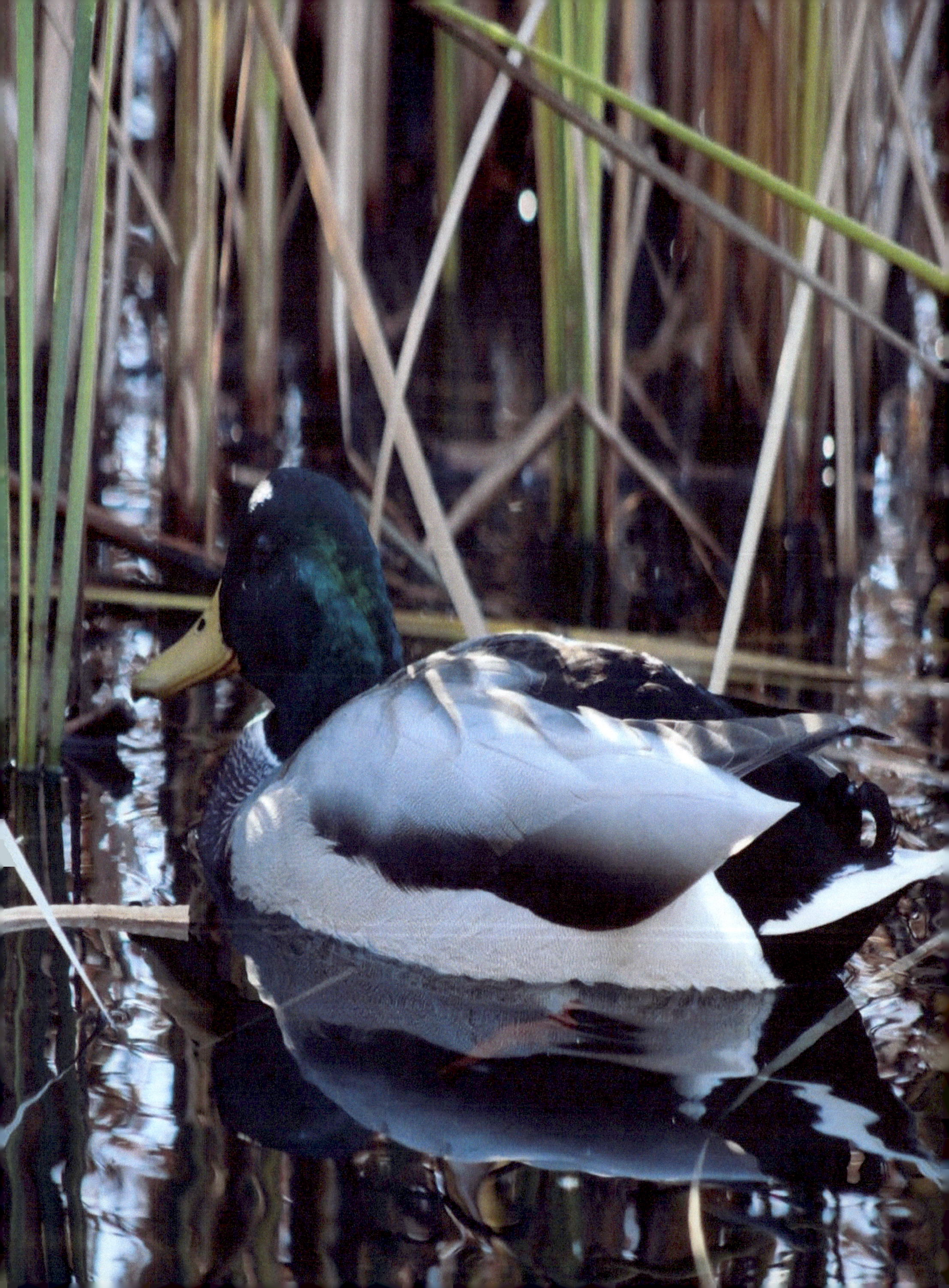

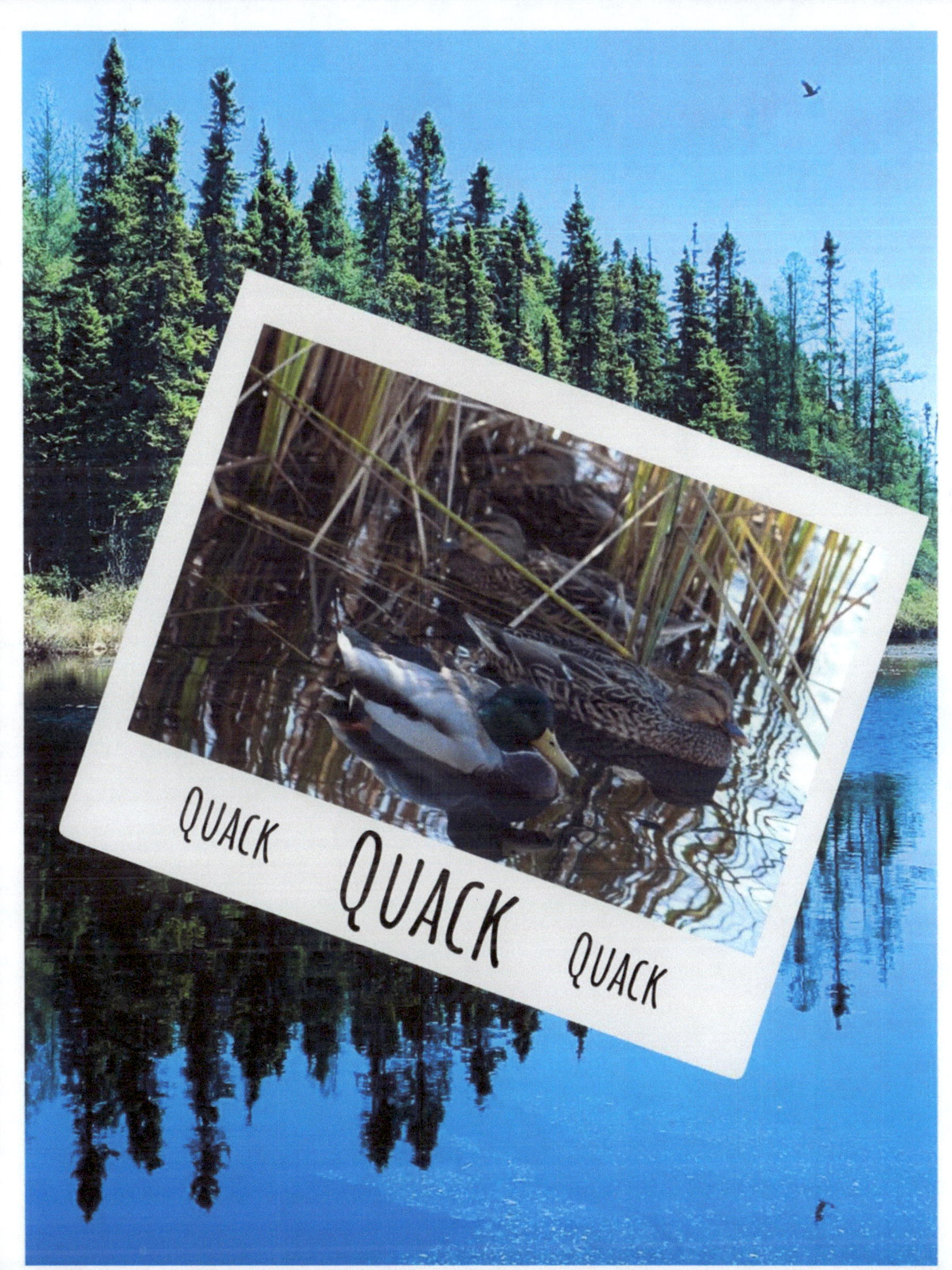
QUACK
QUACK
QUACK

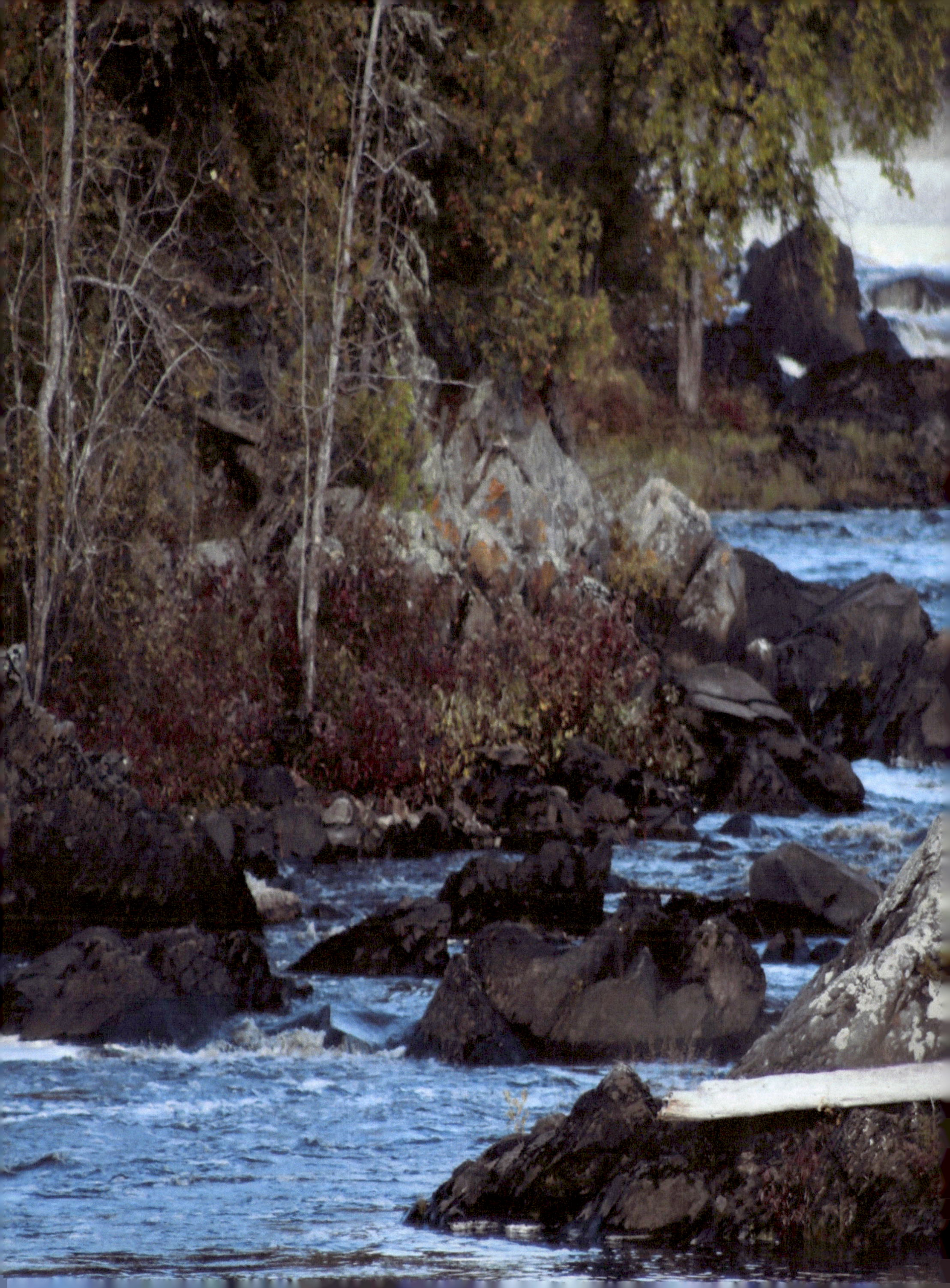

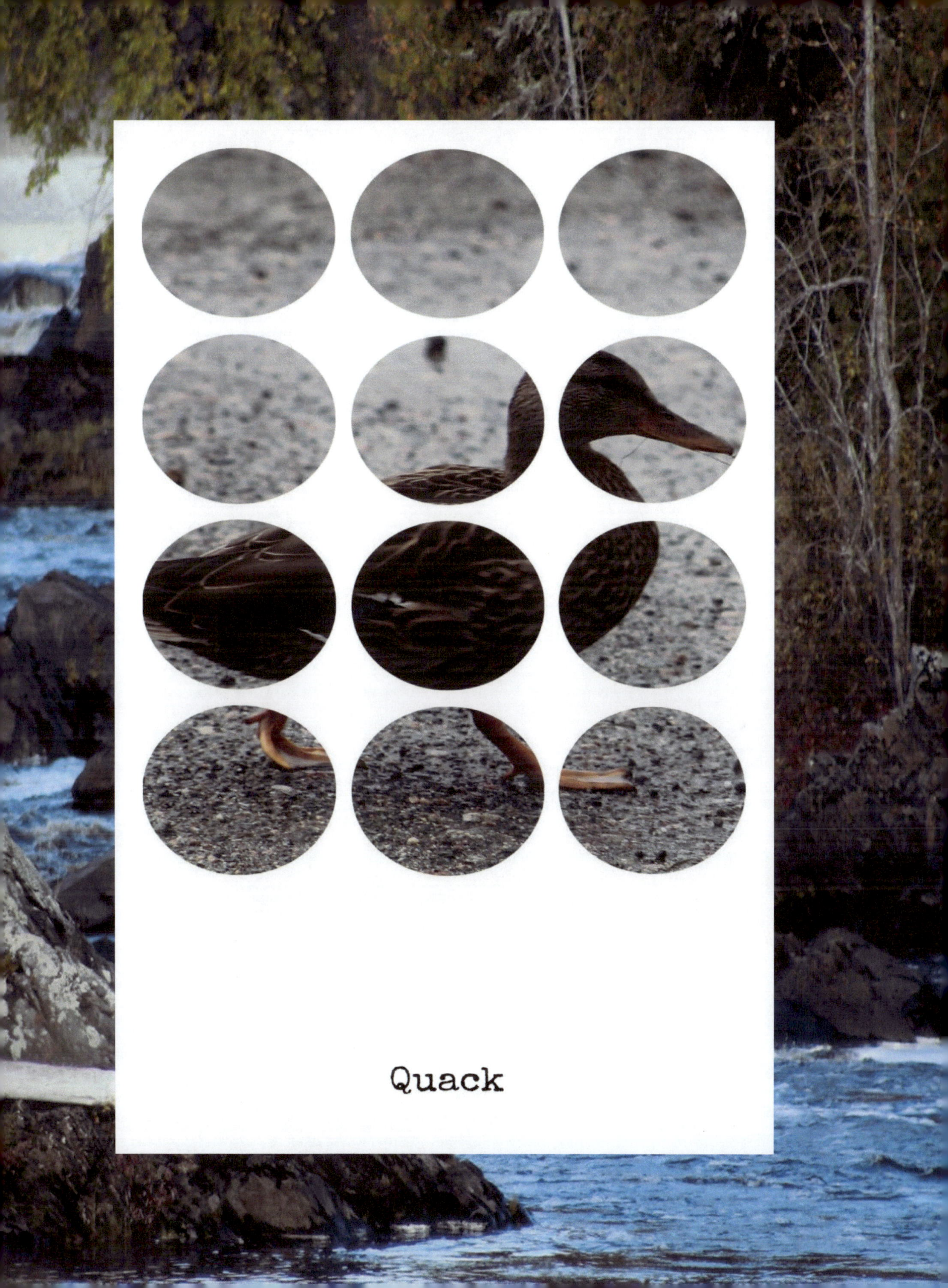

Quack

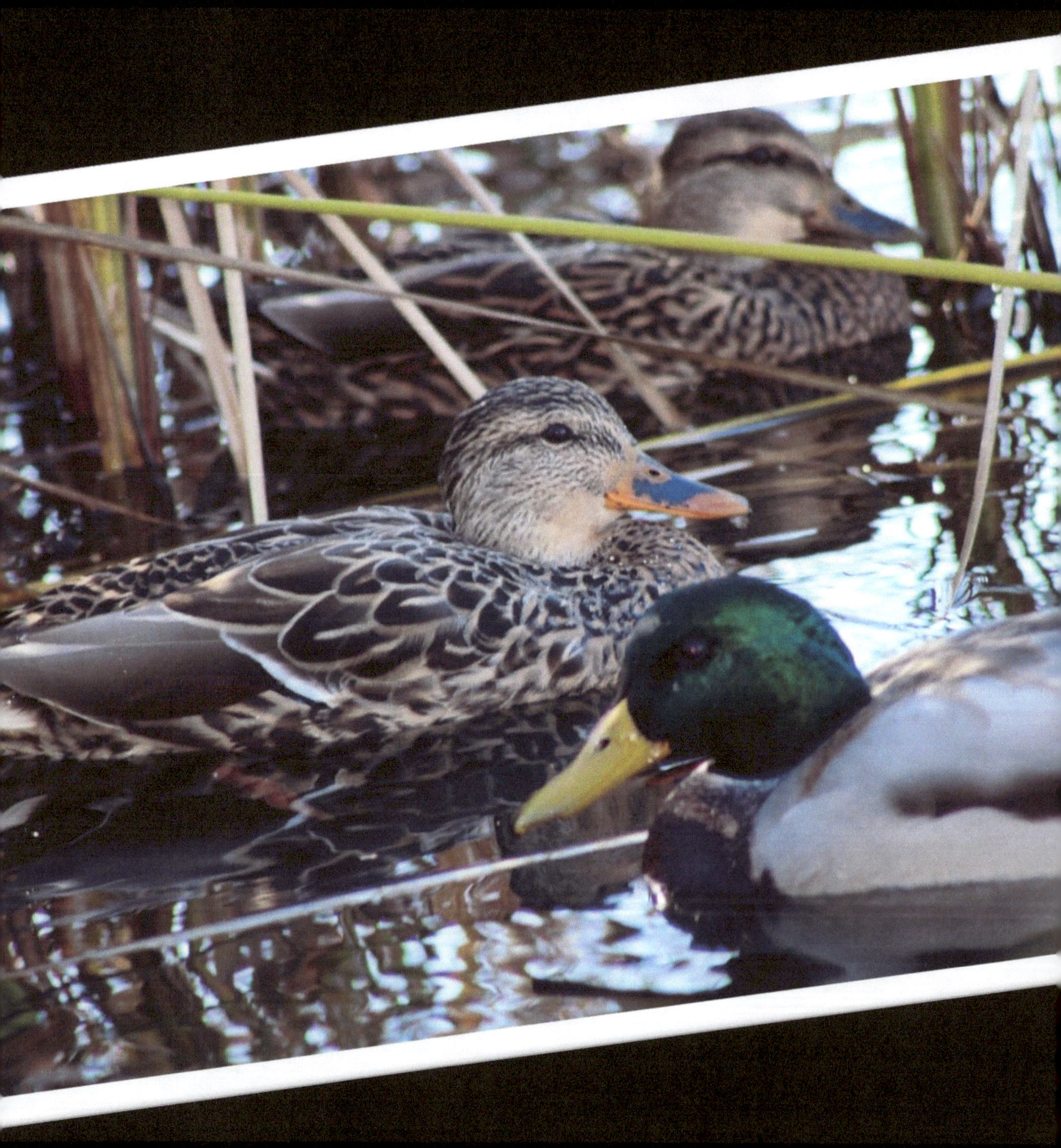

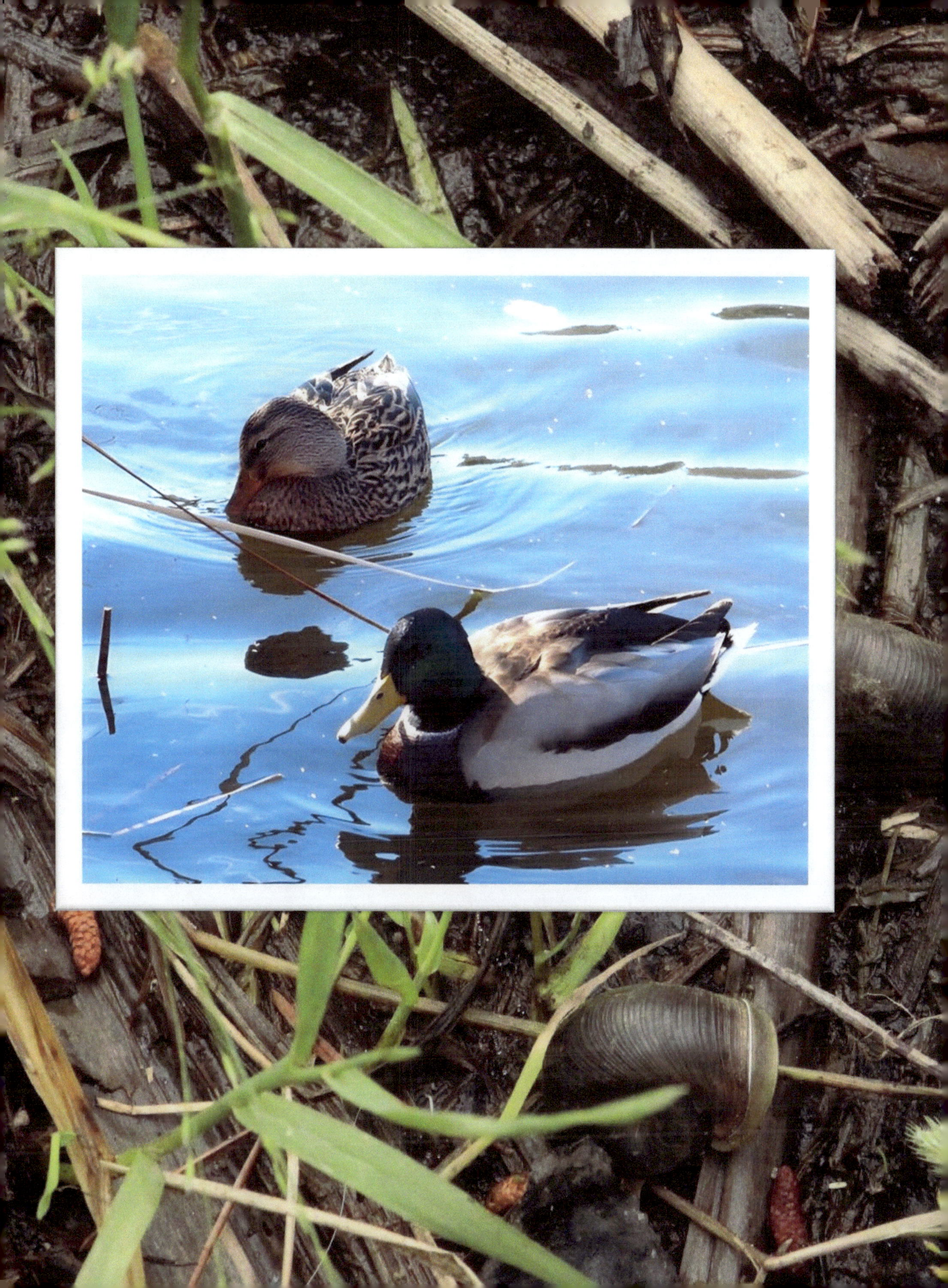

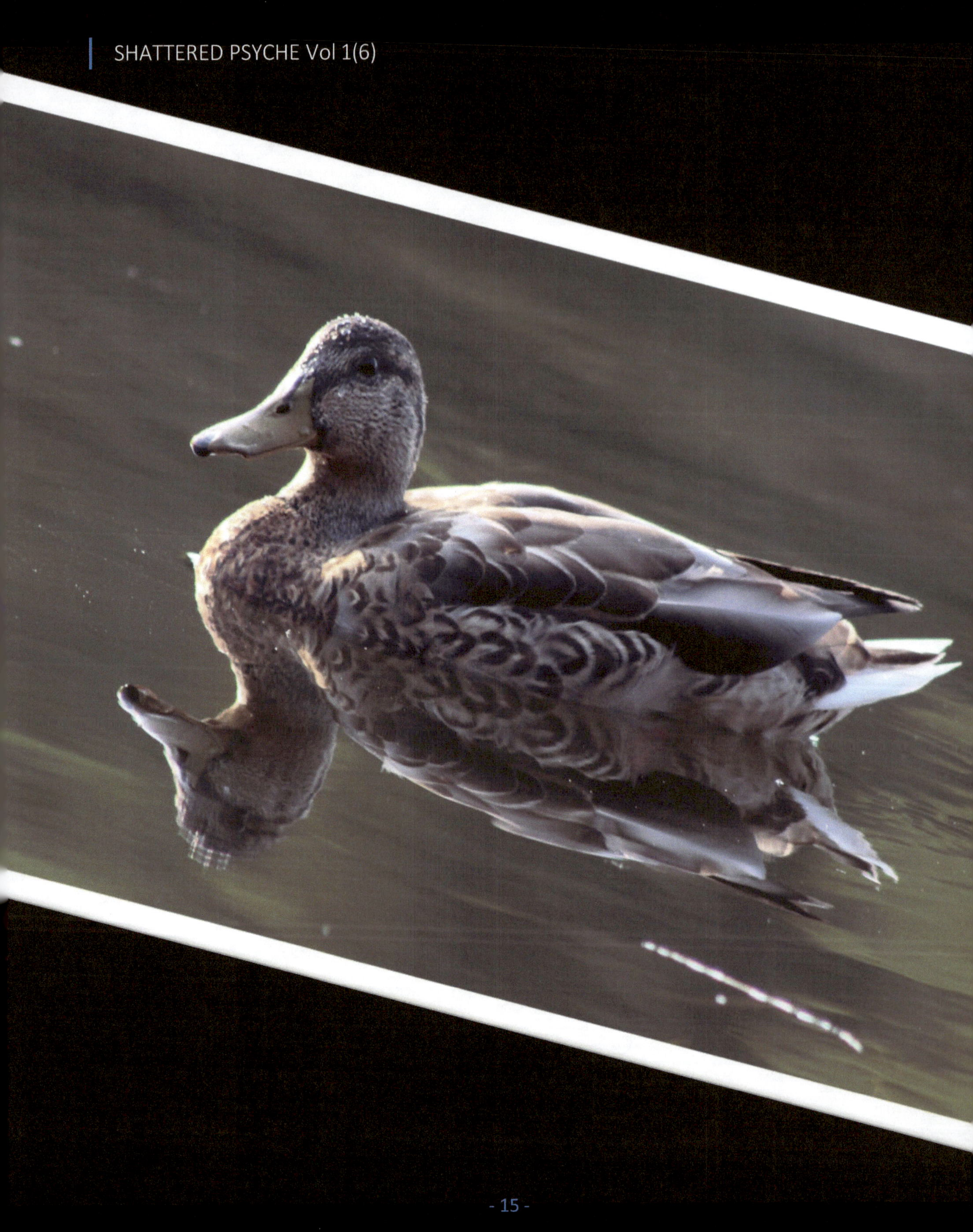

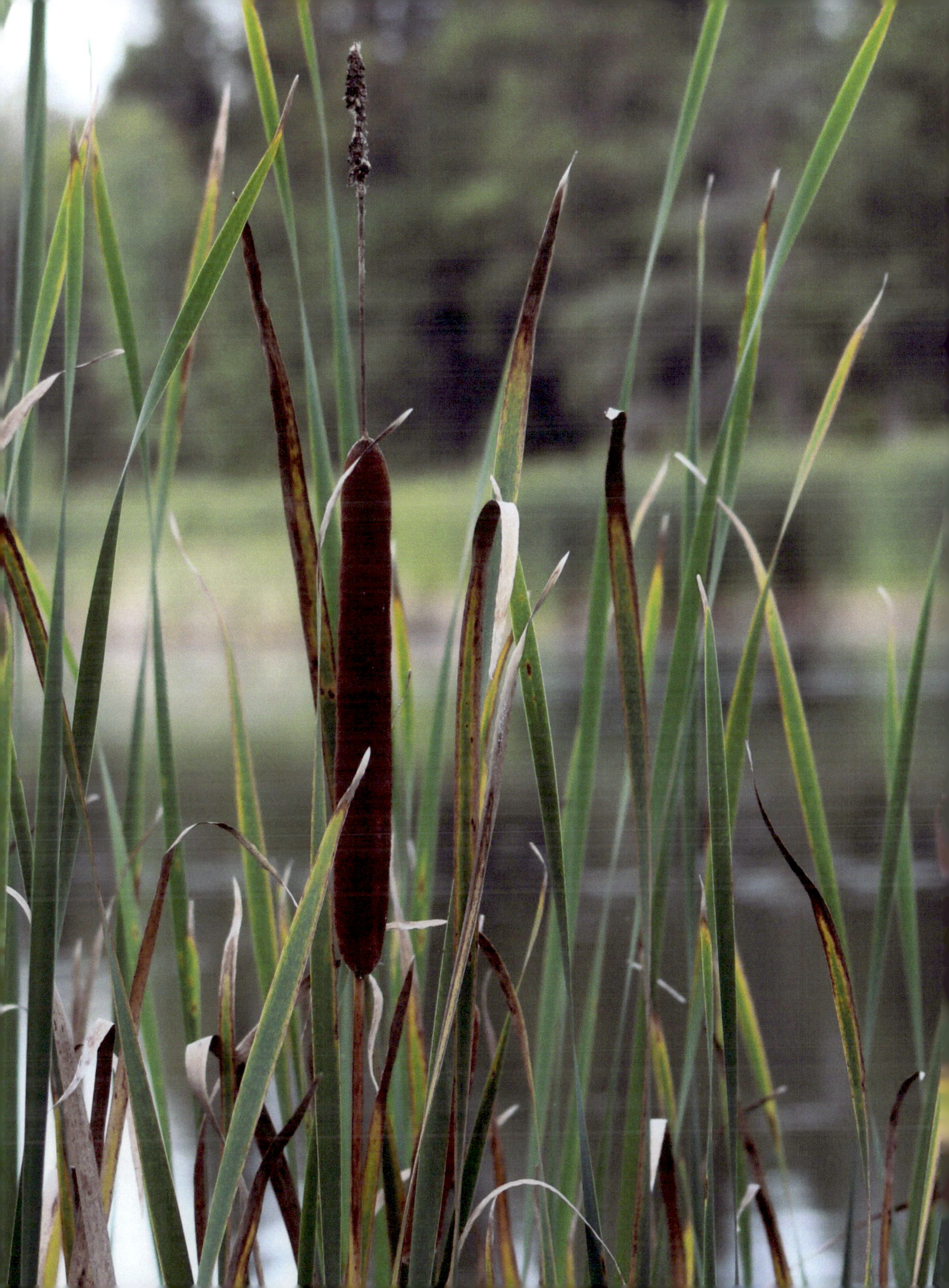

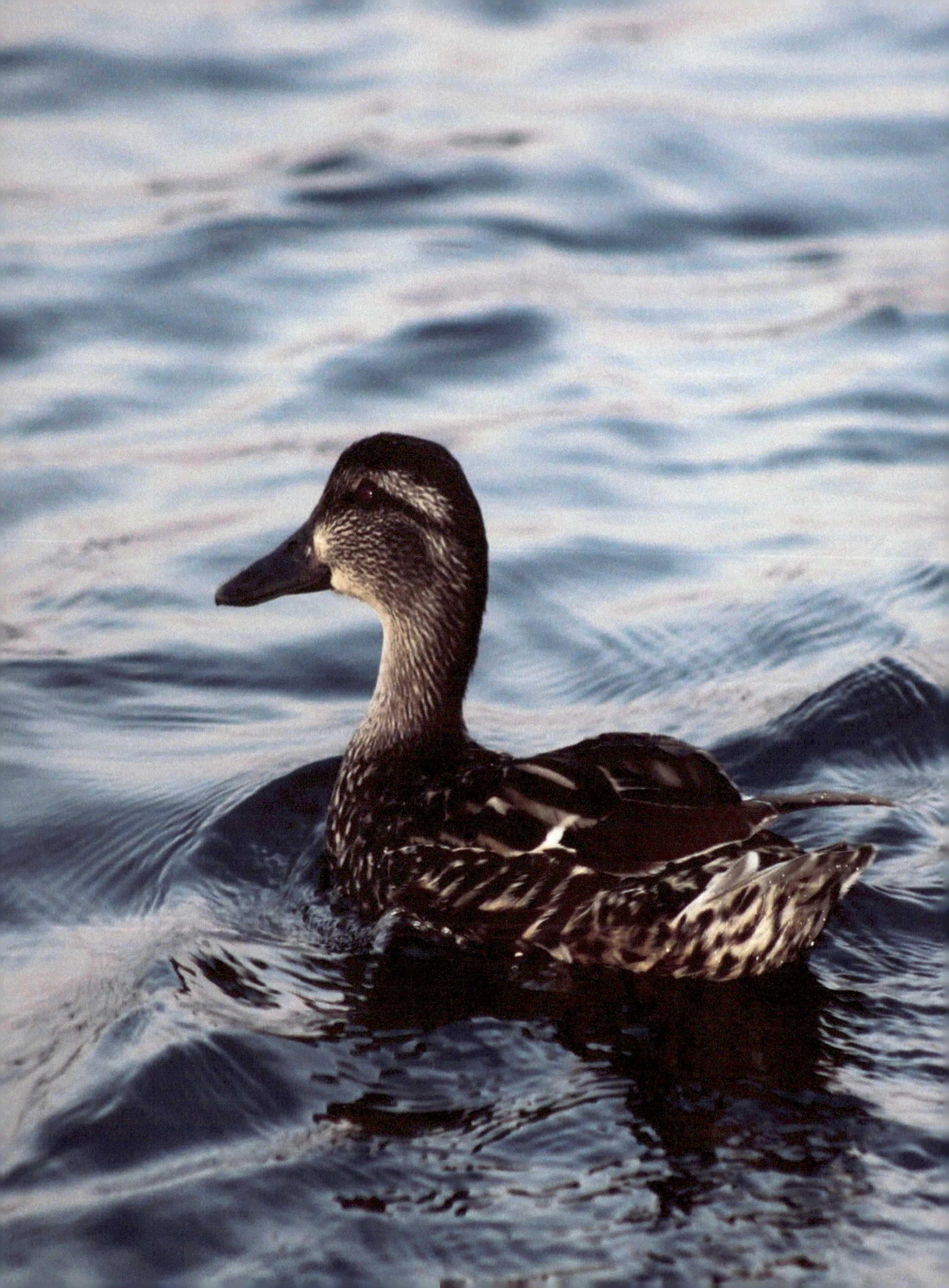

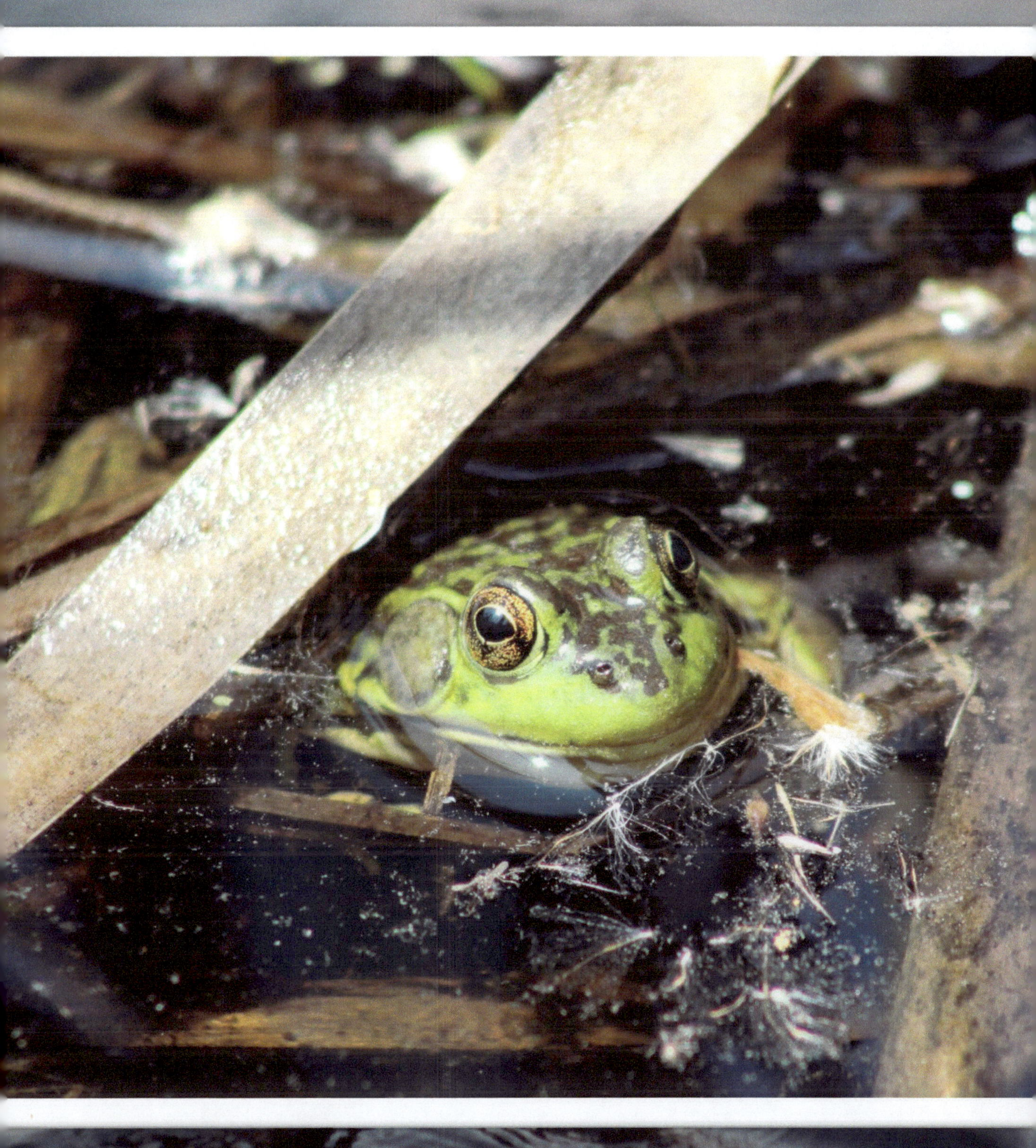

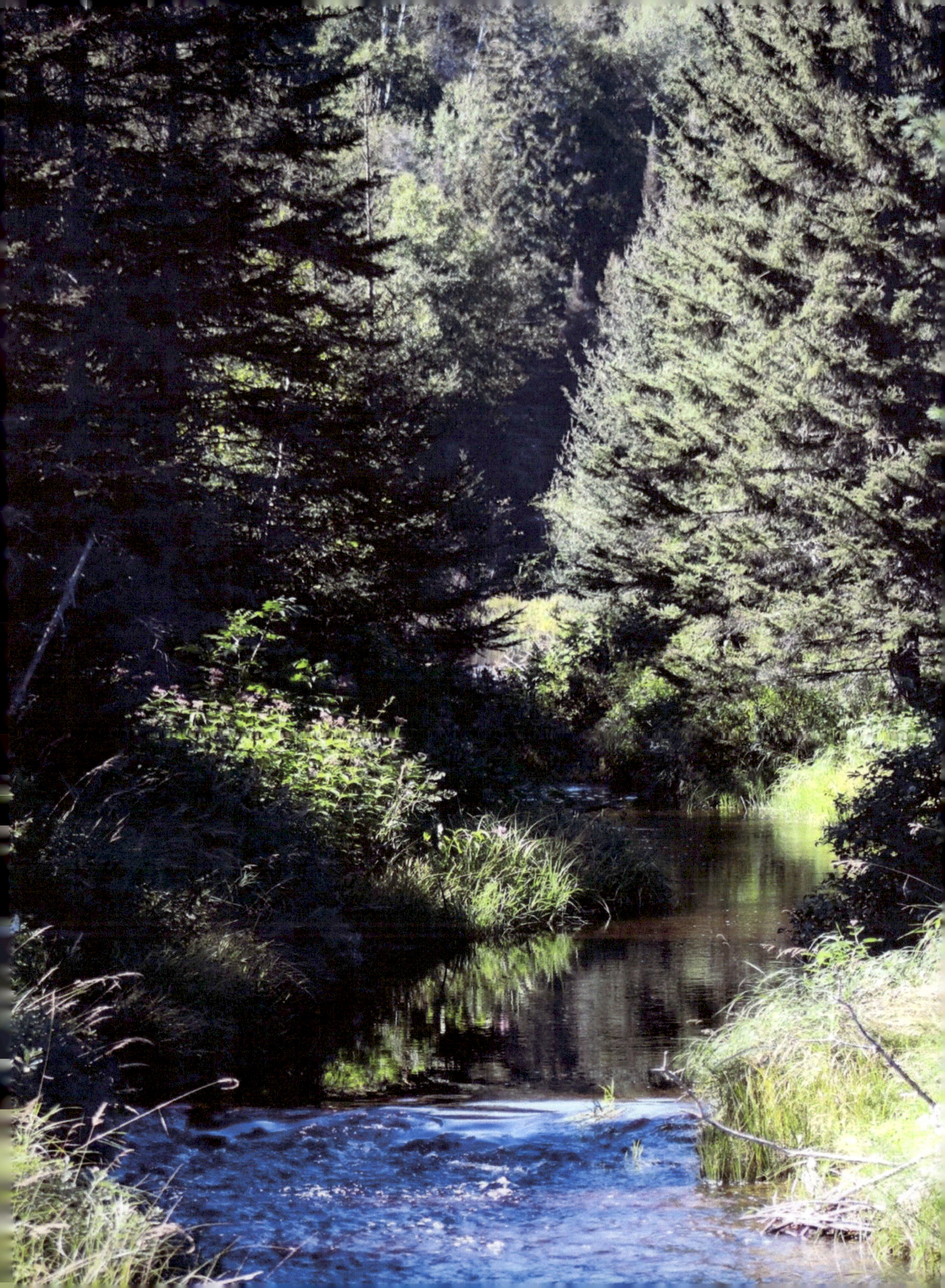

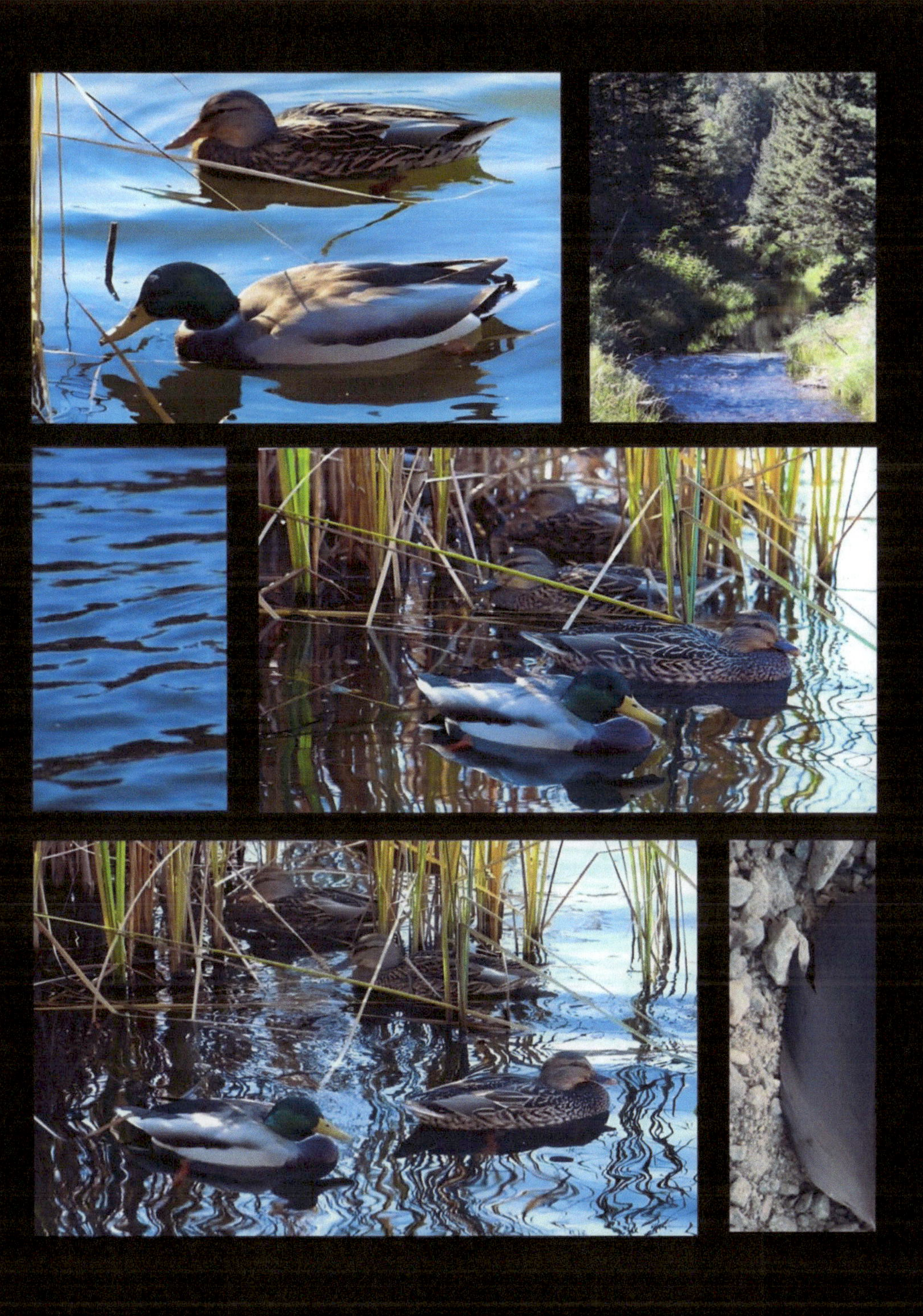

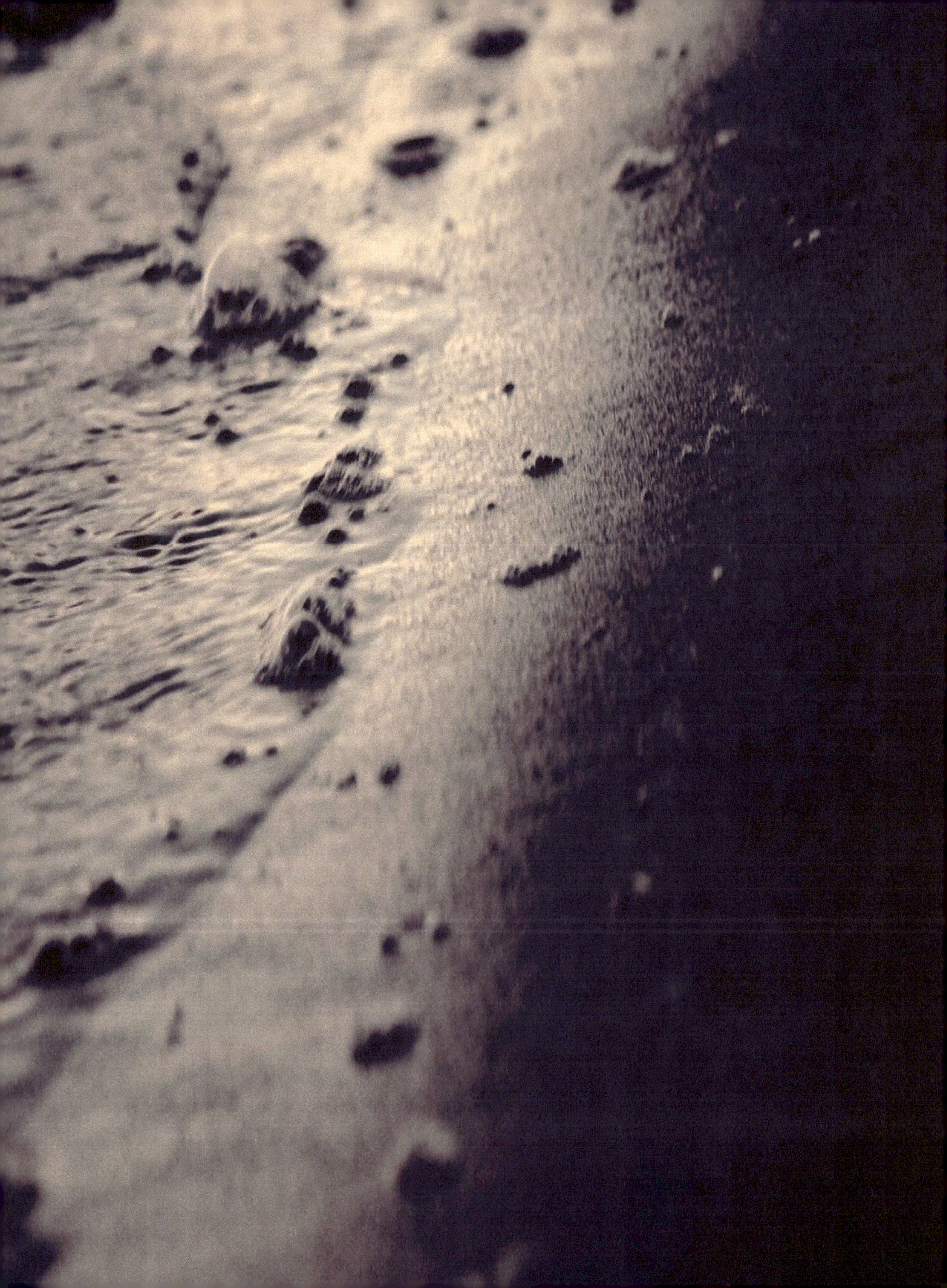

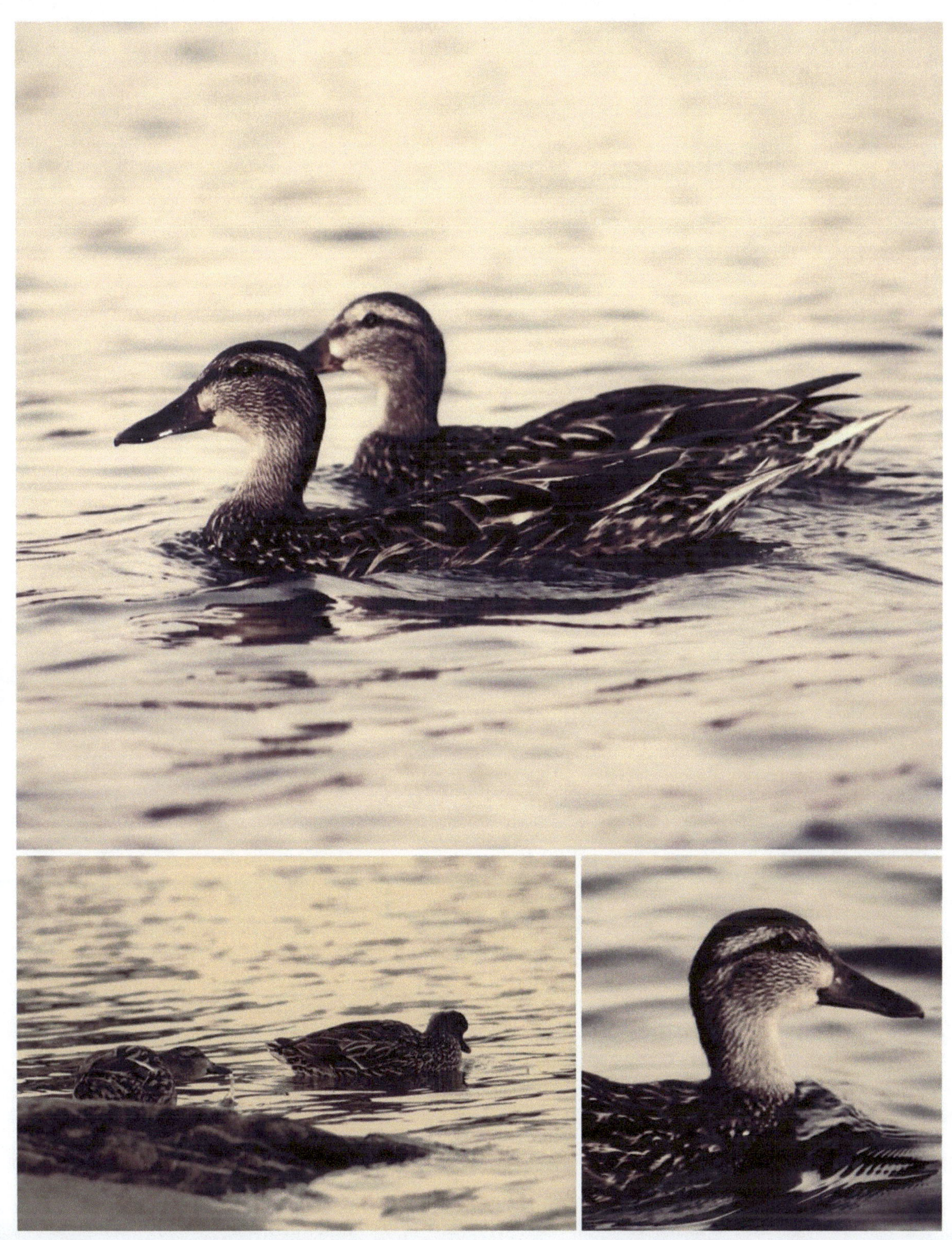

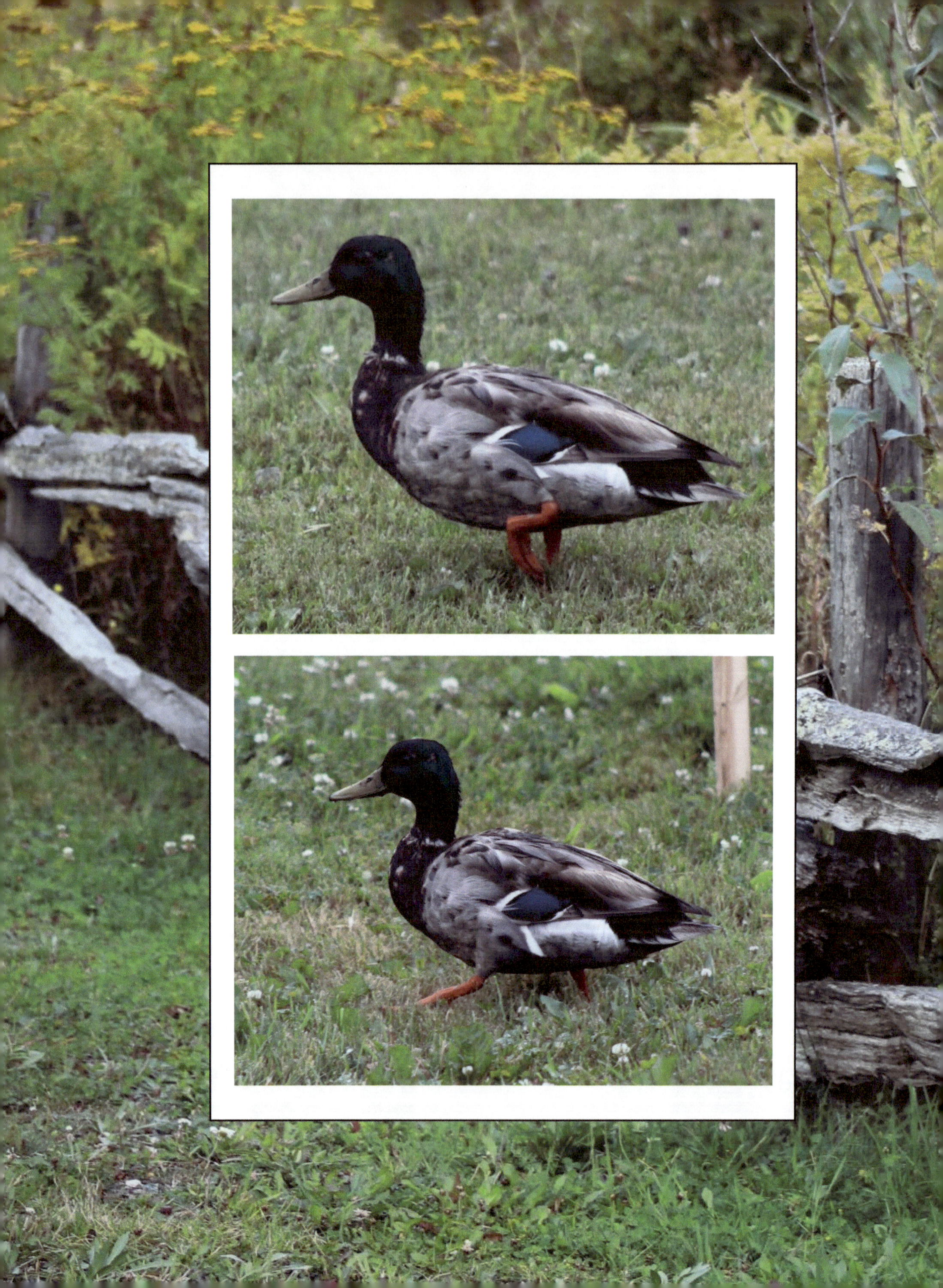

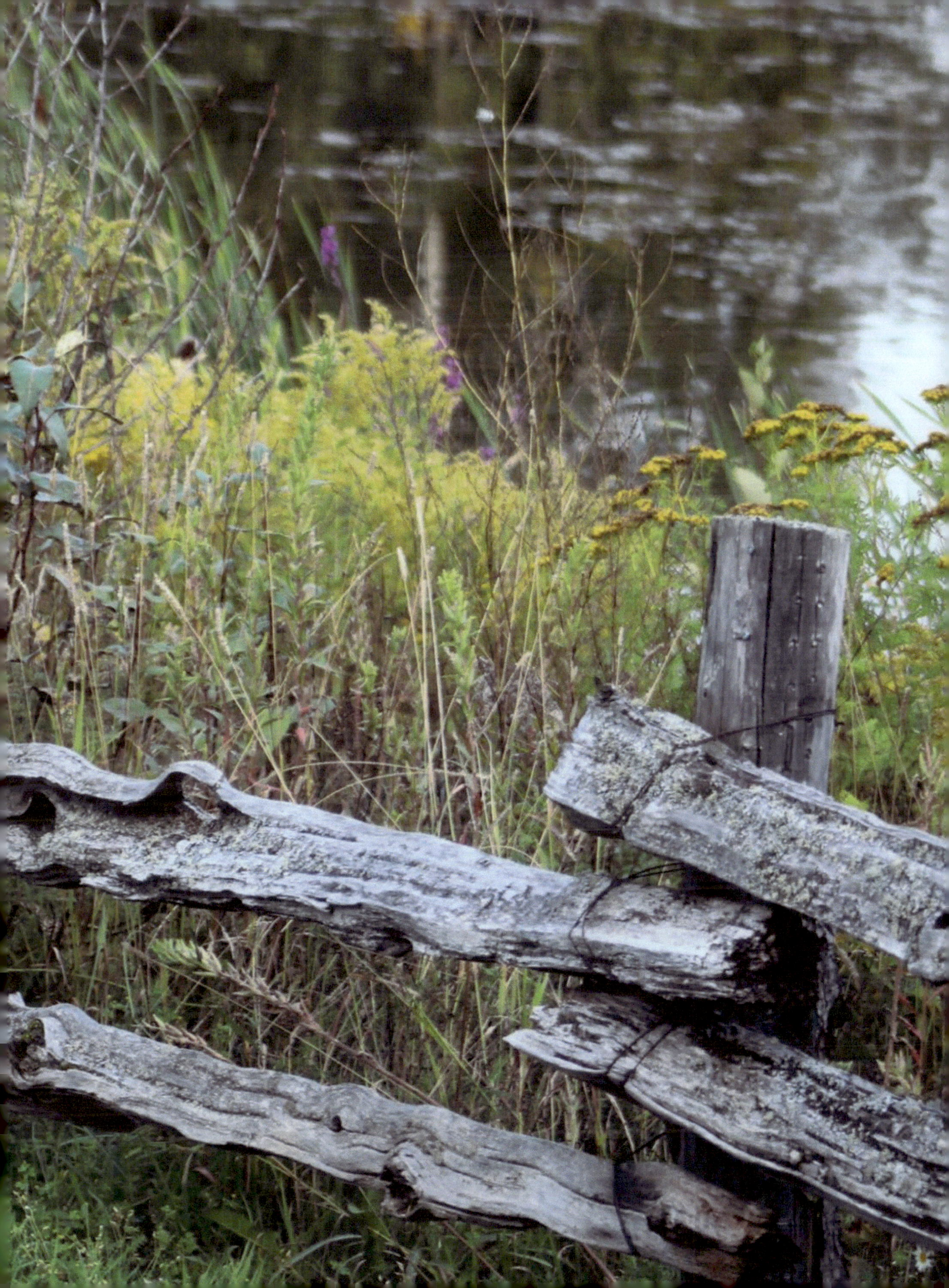

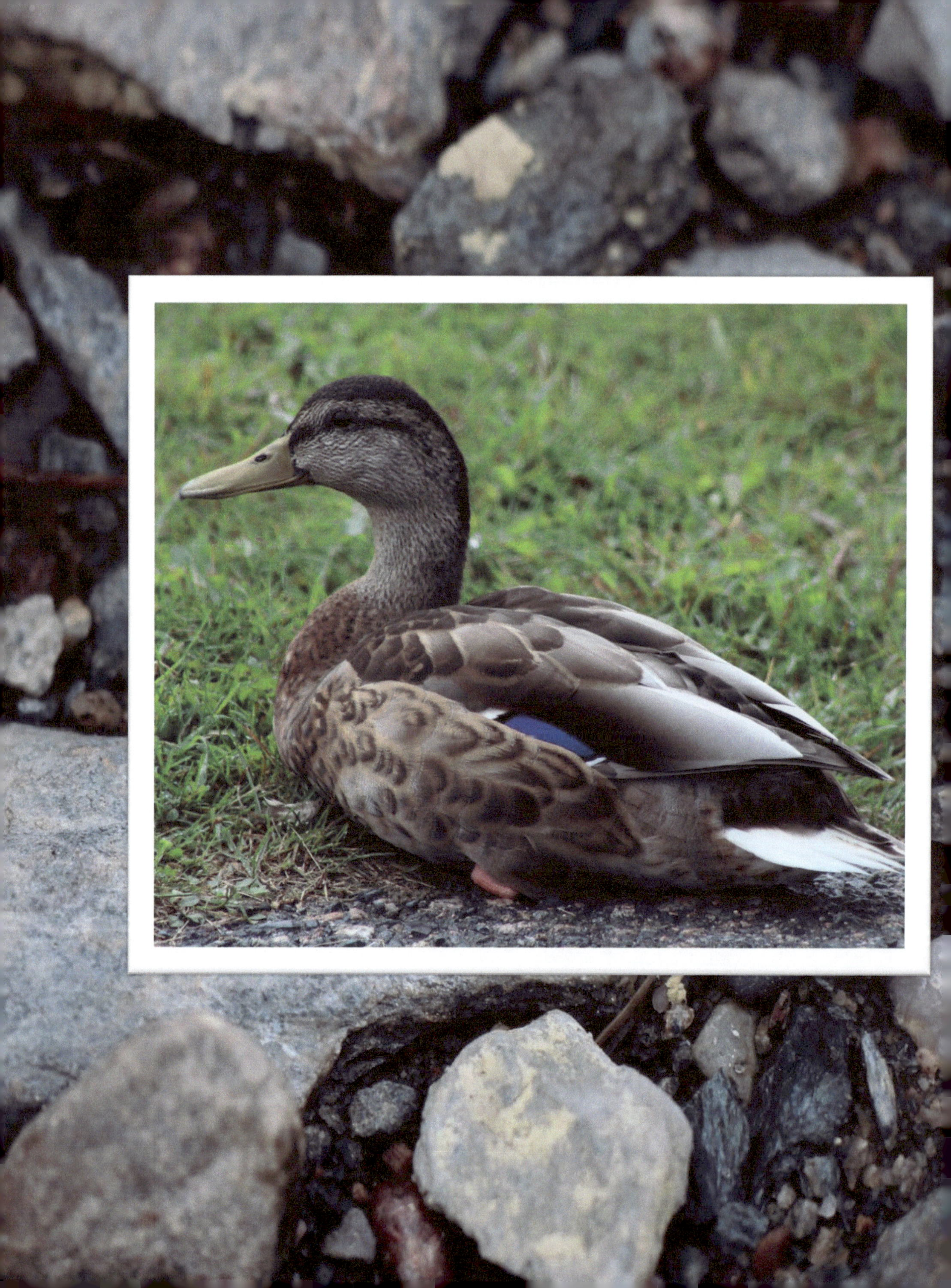

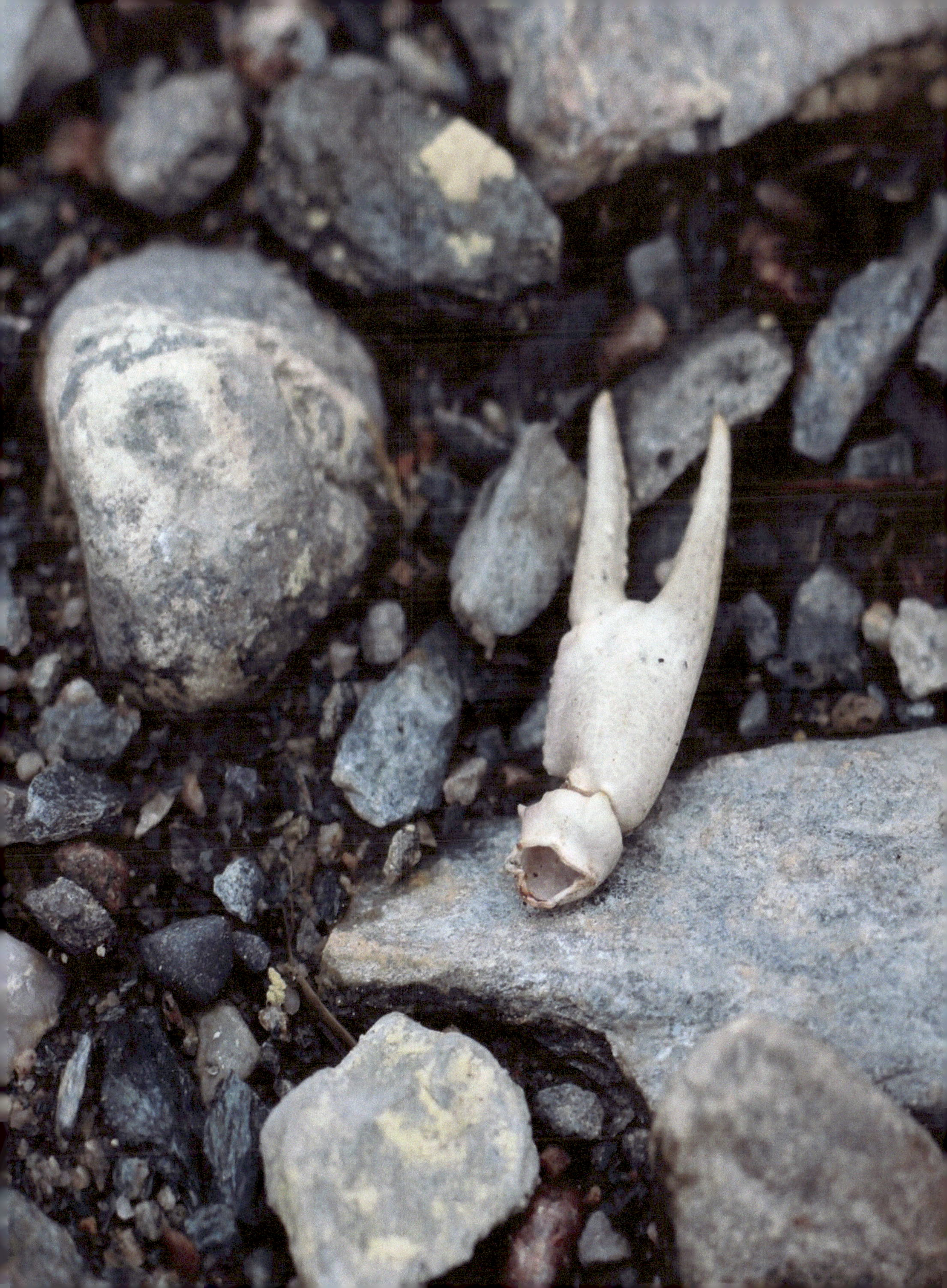

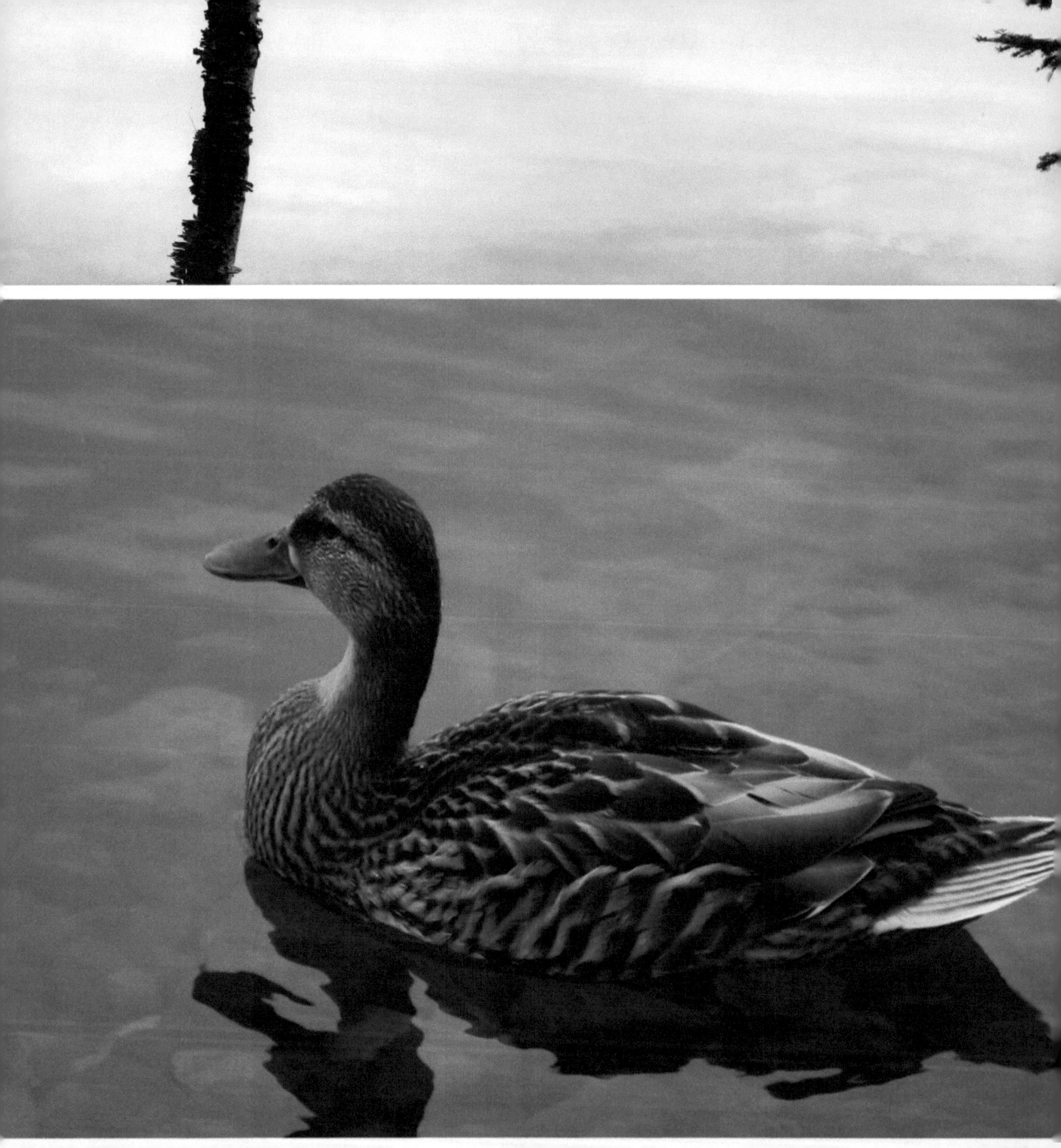

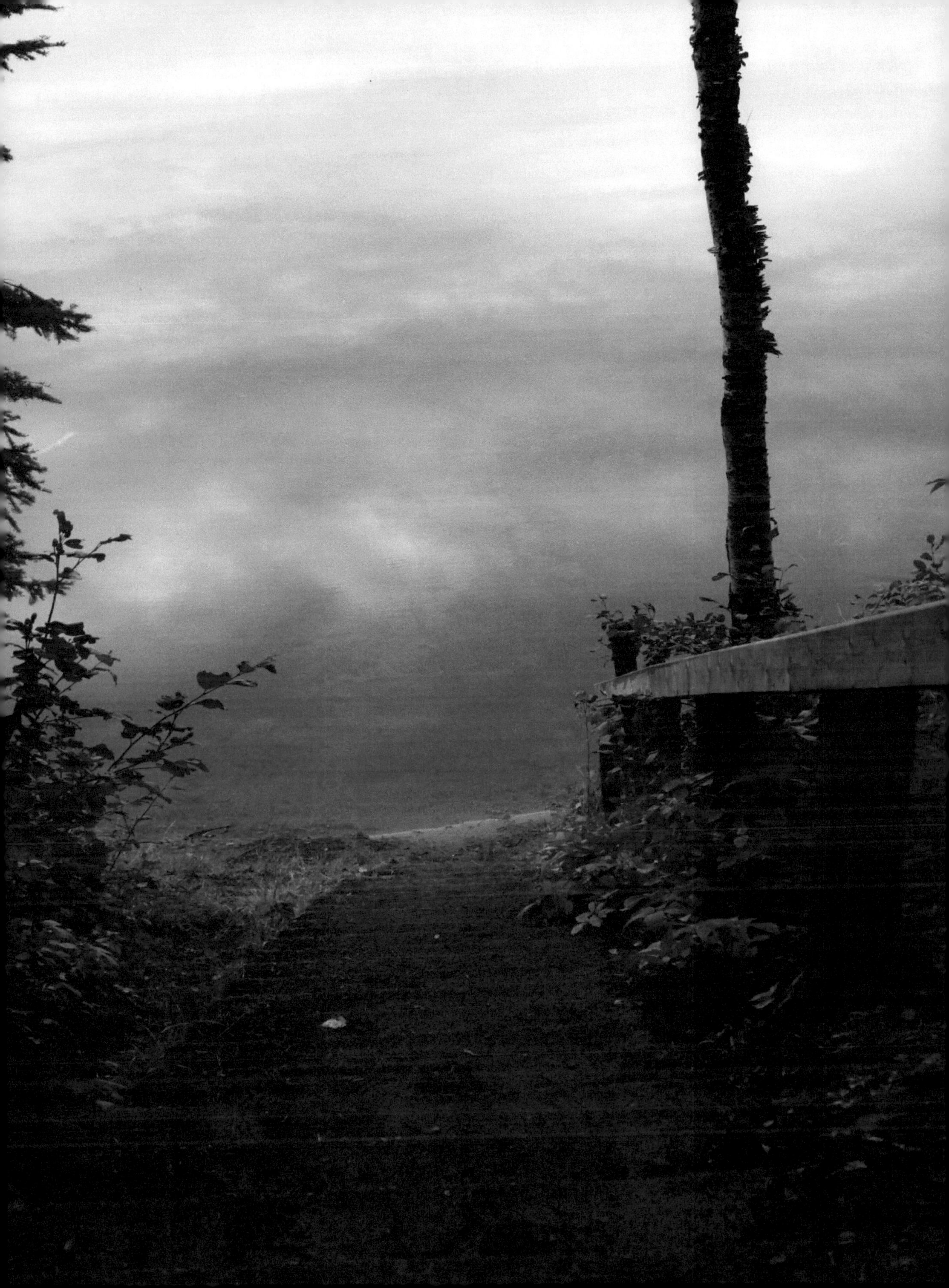

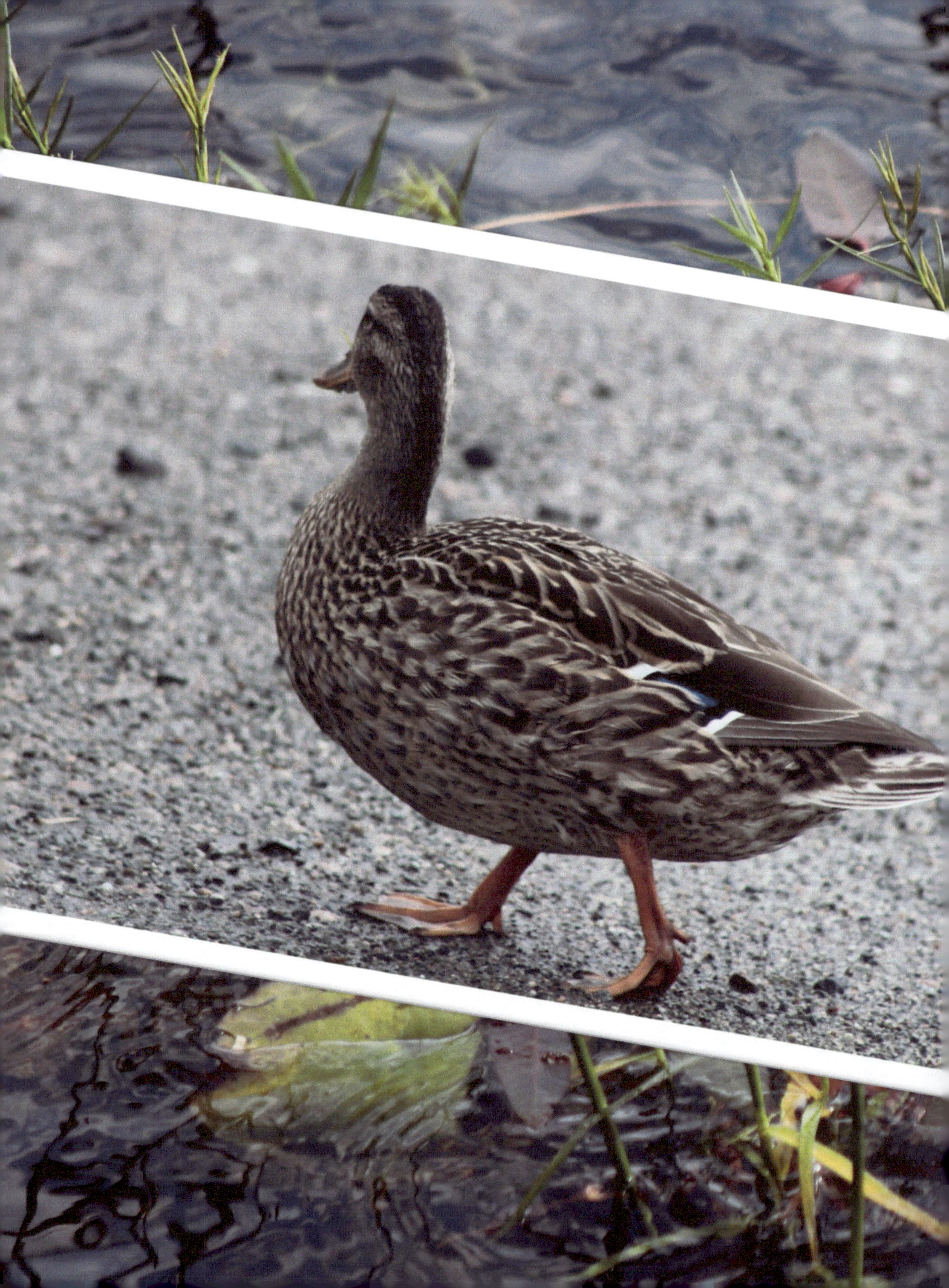

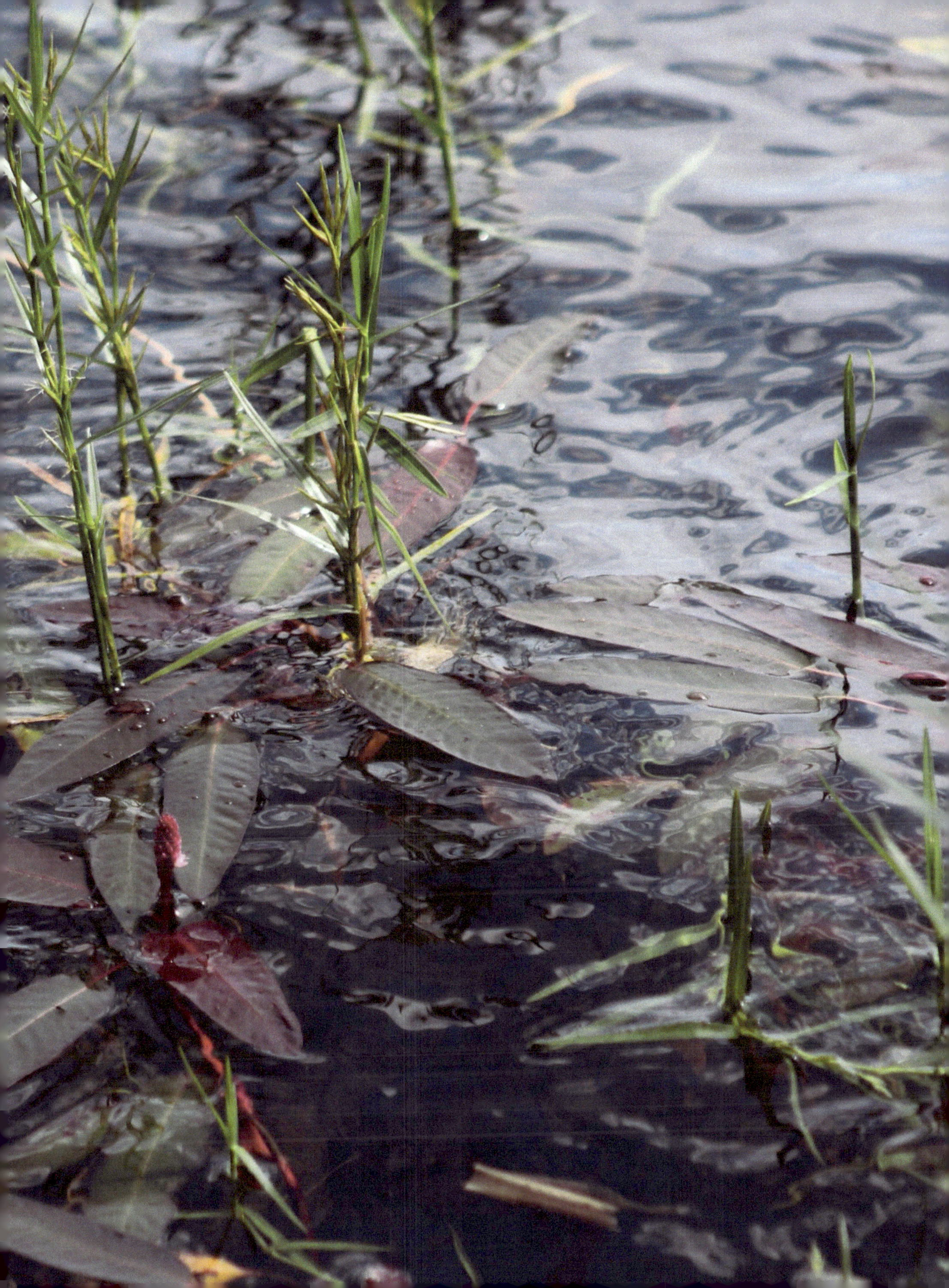

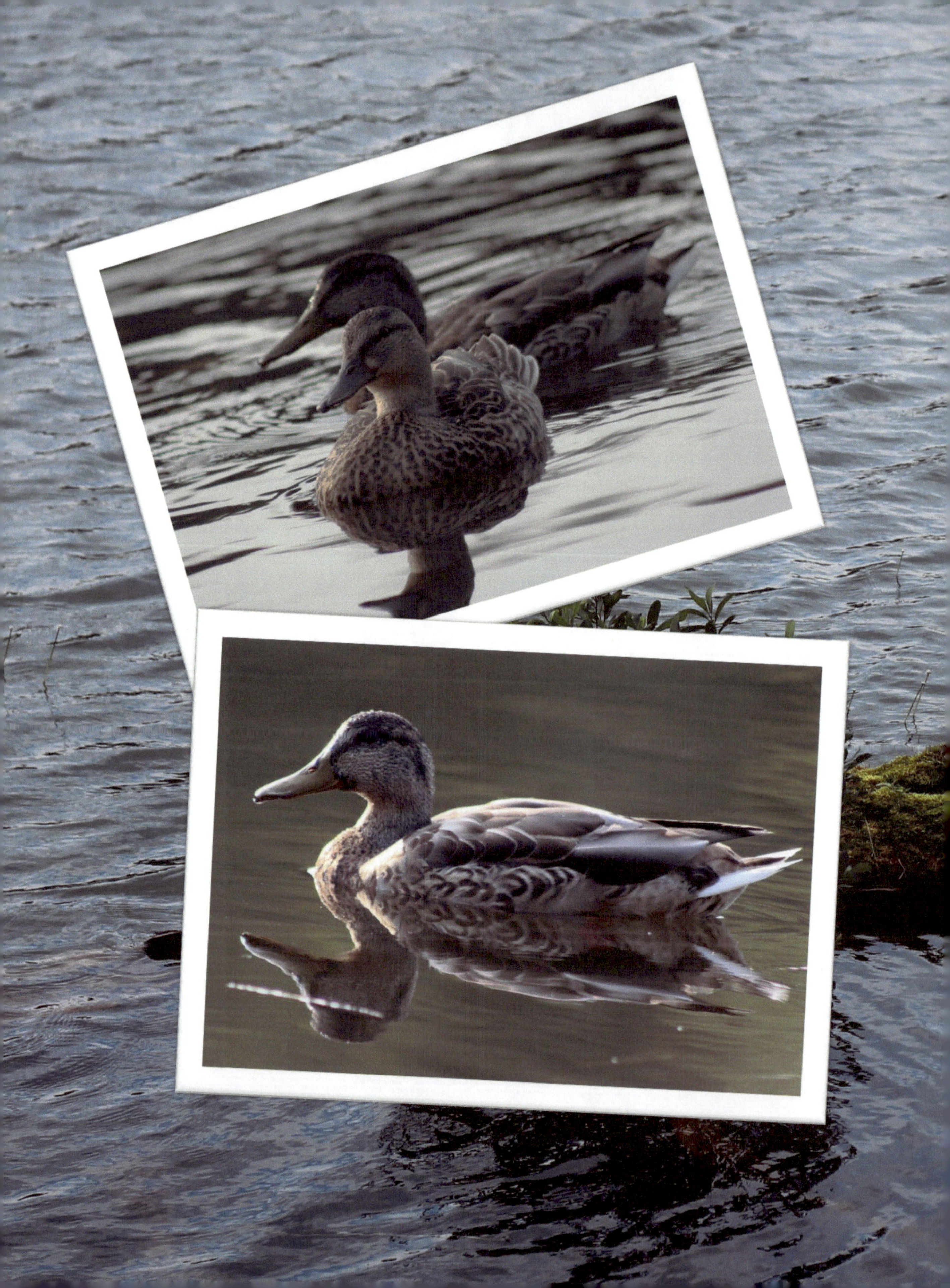

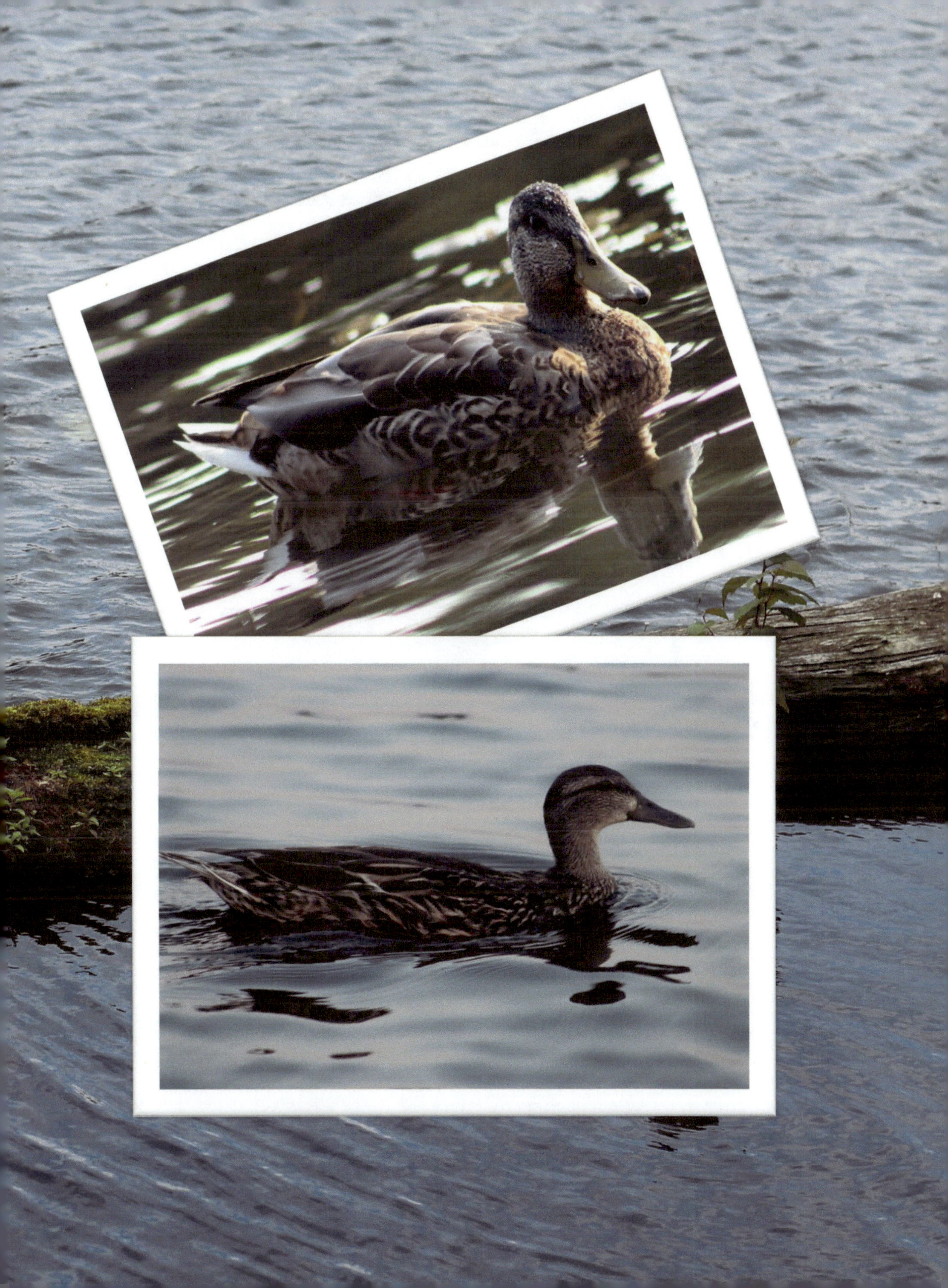

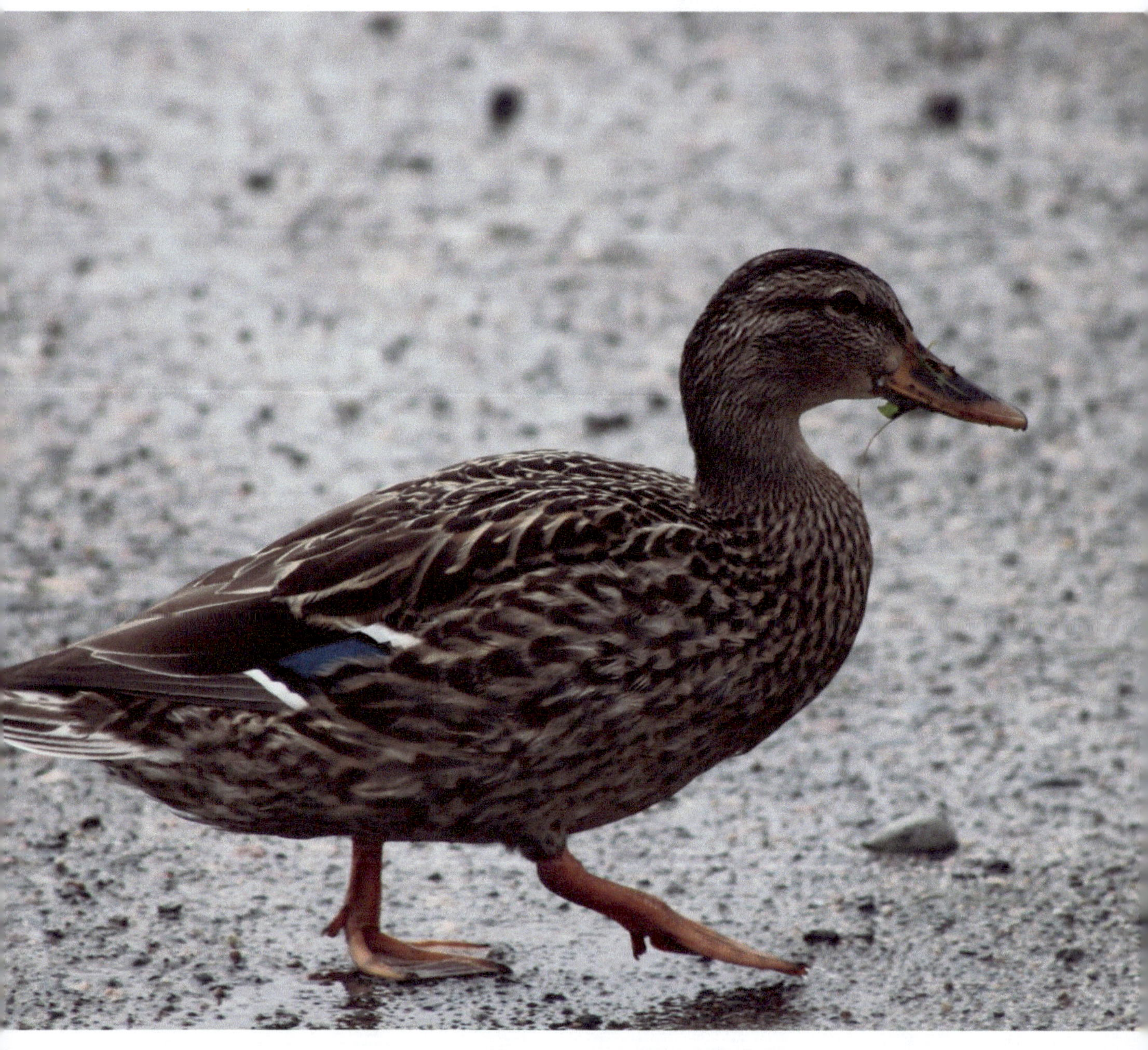

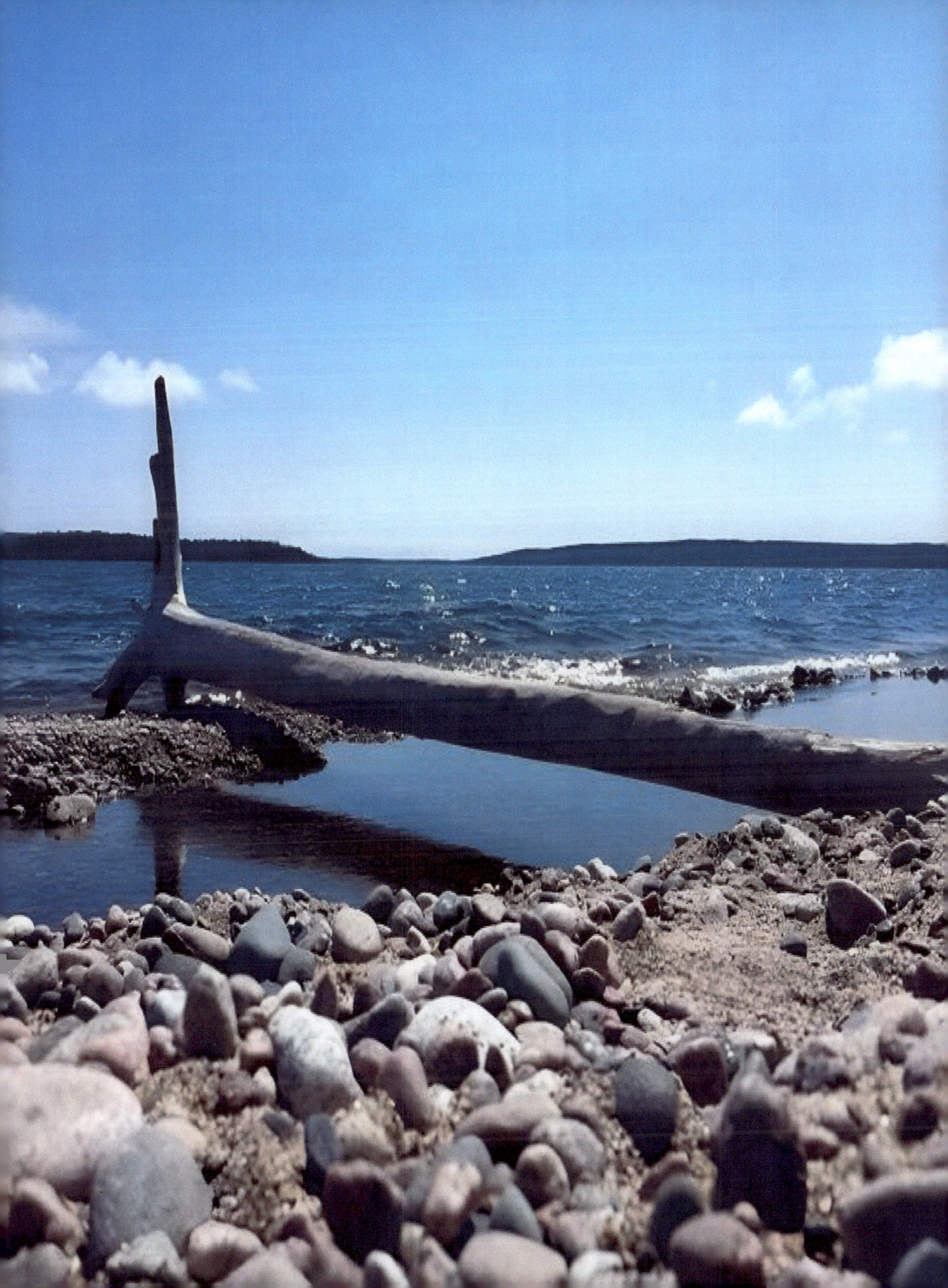

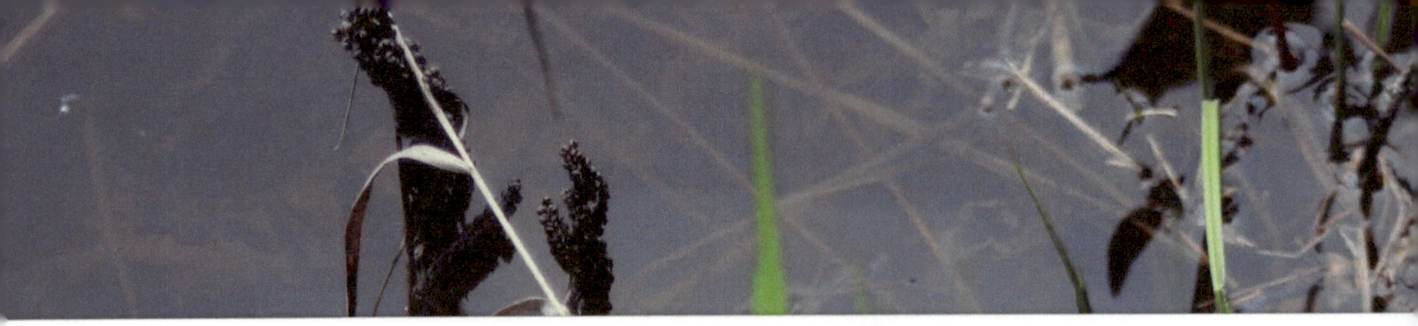

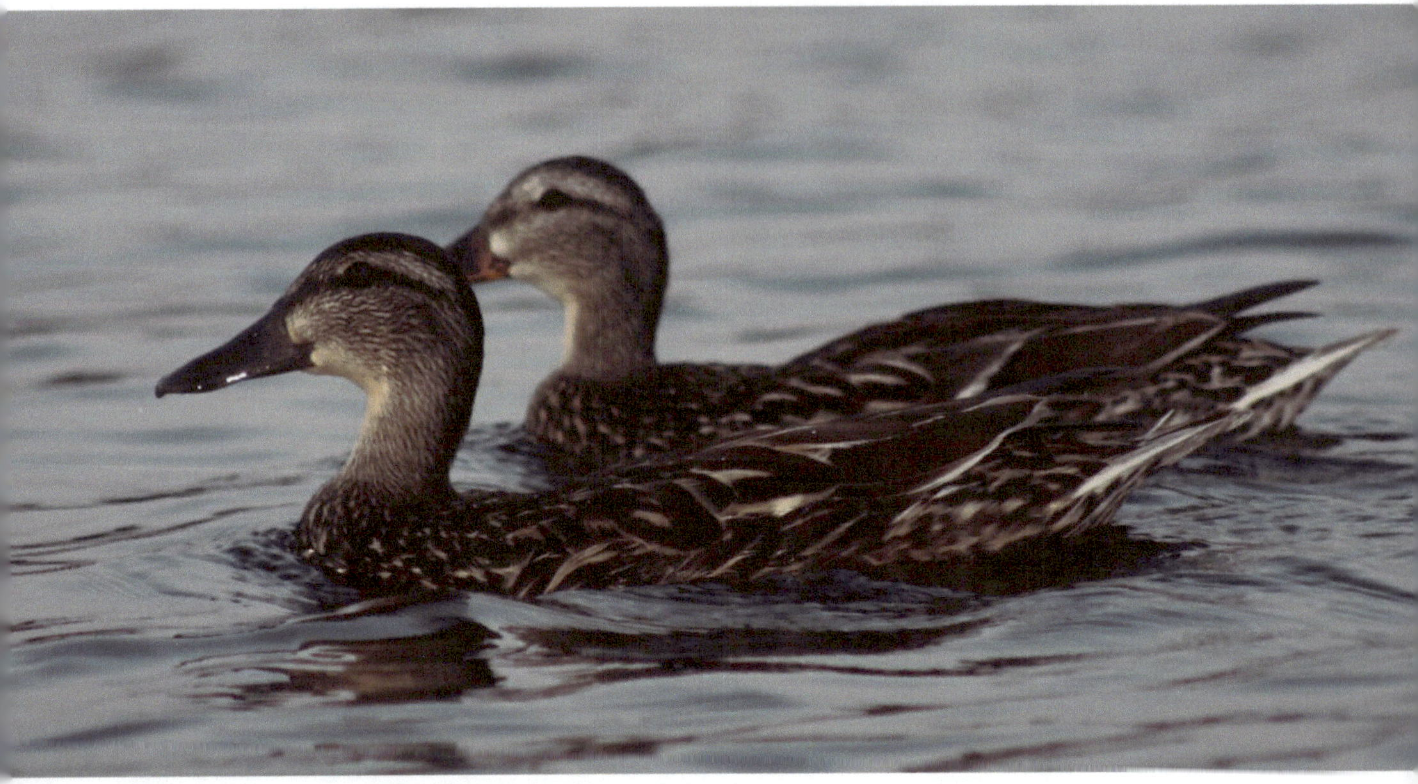

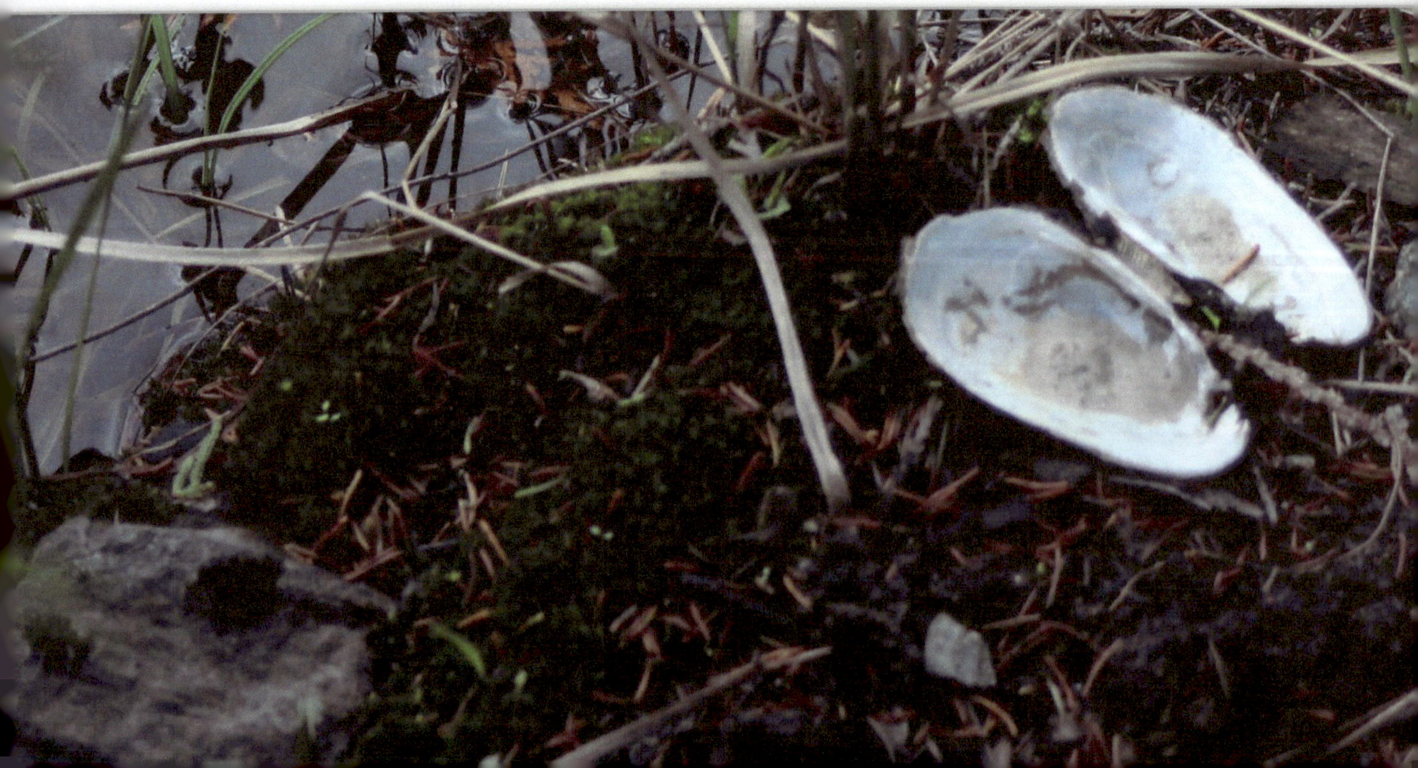

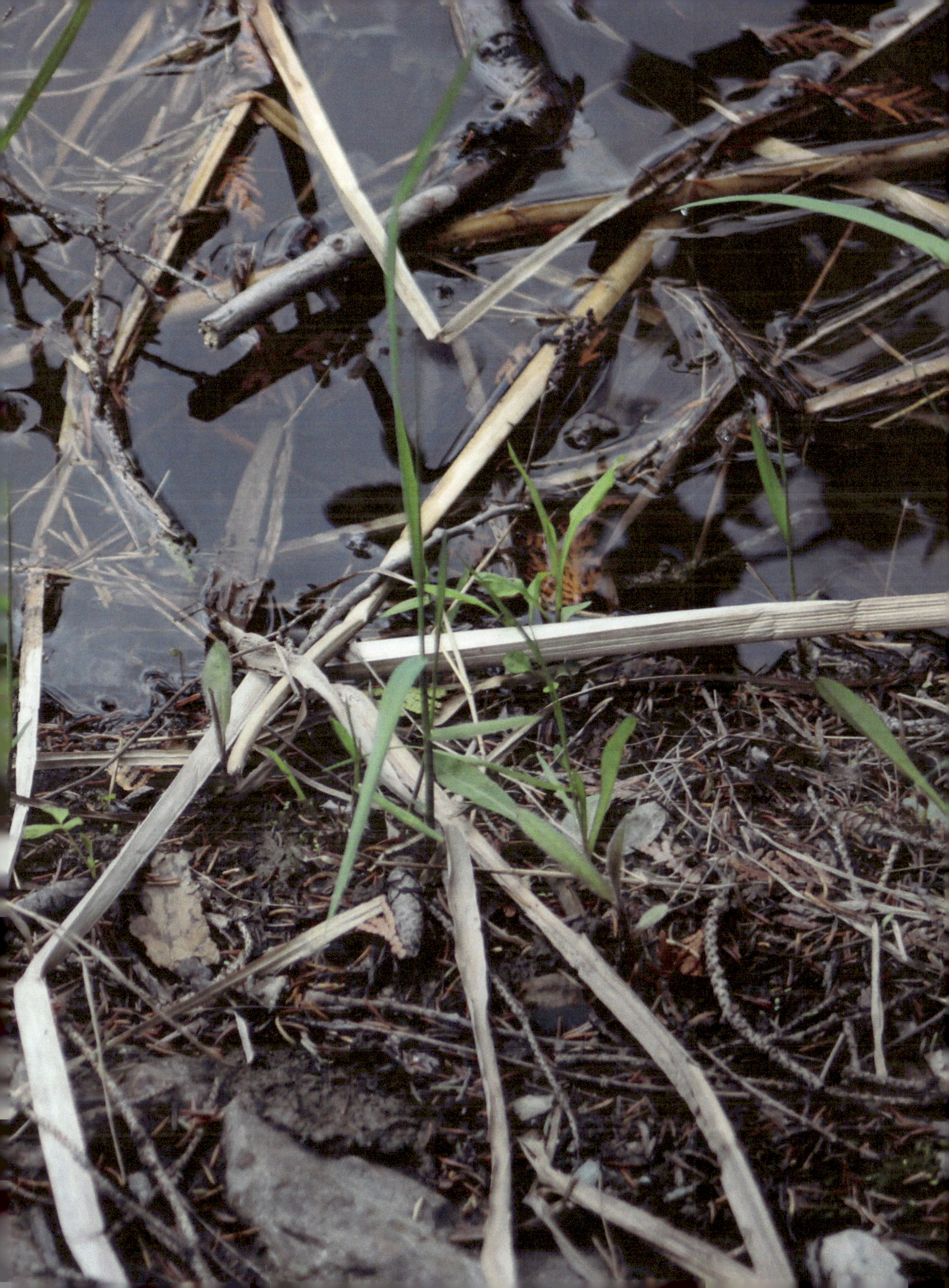

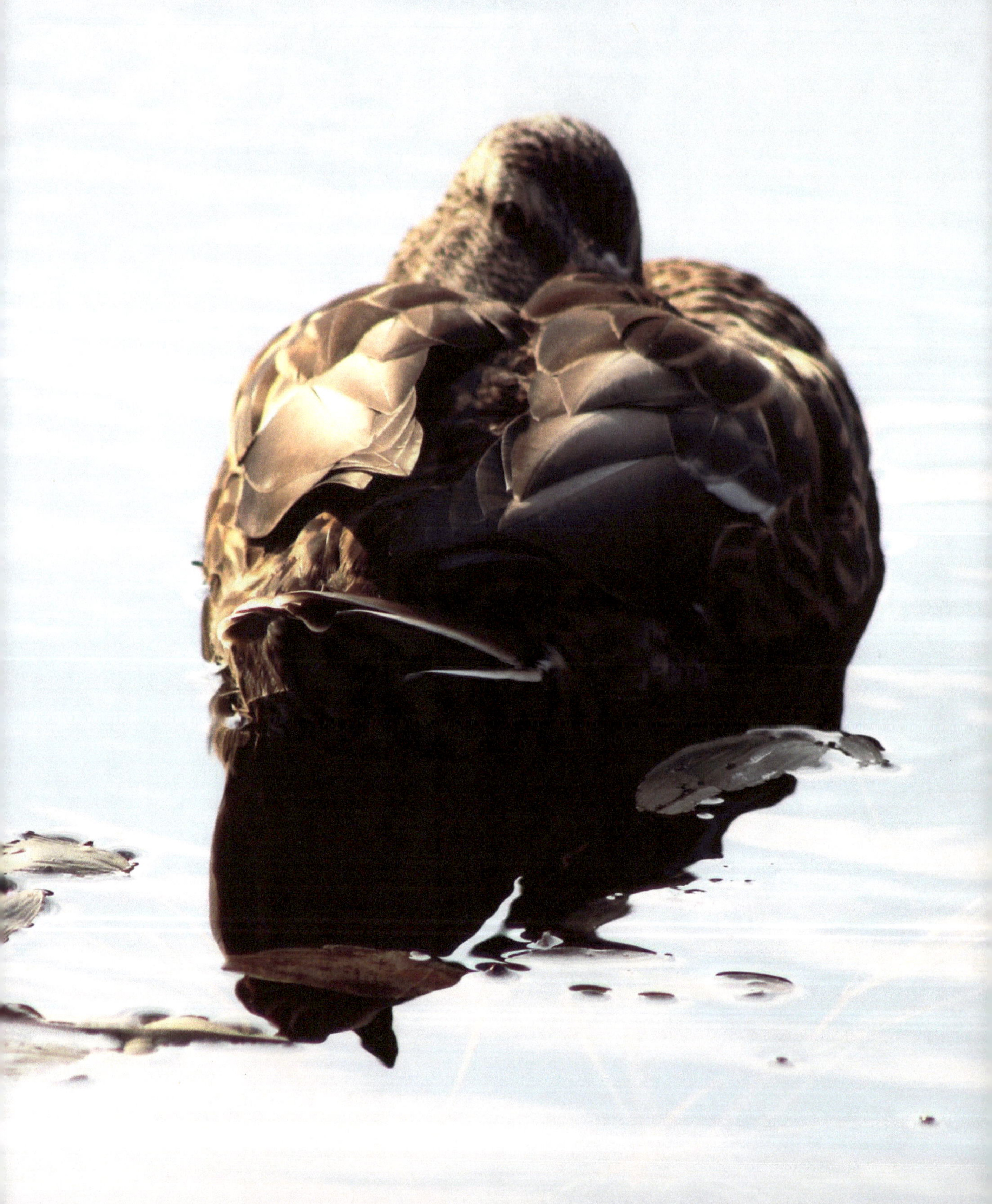

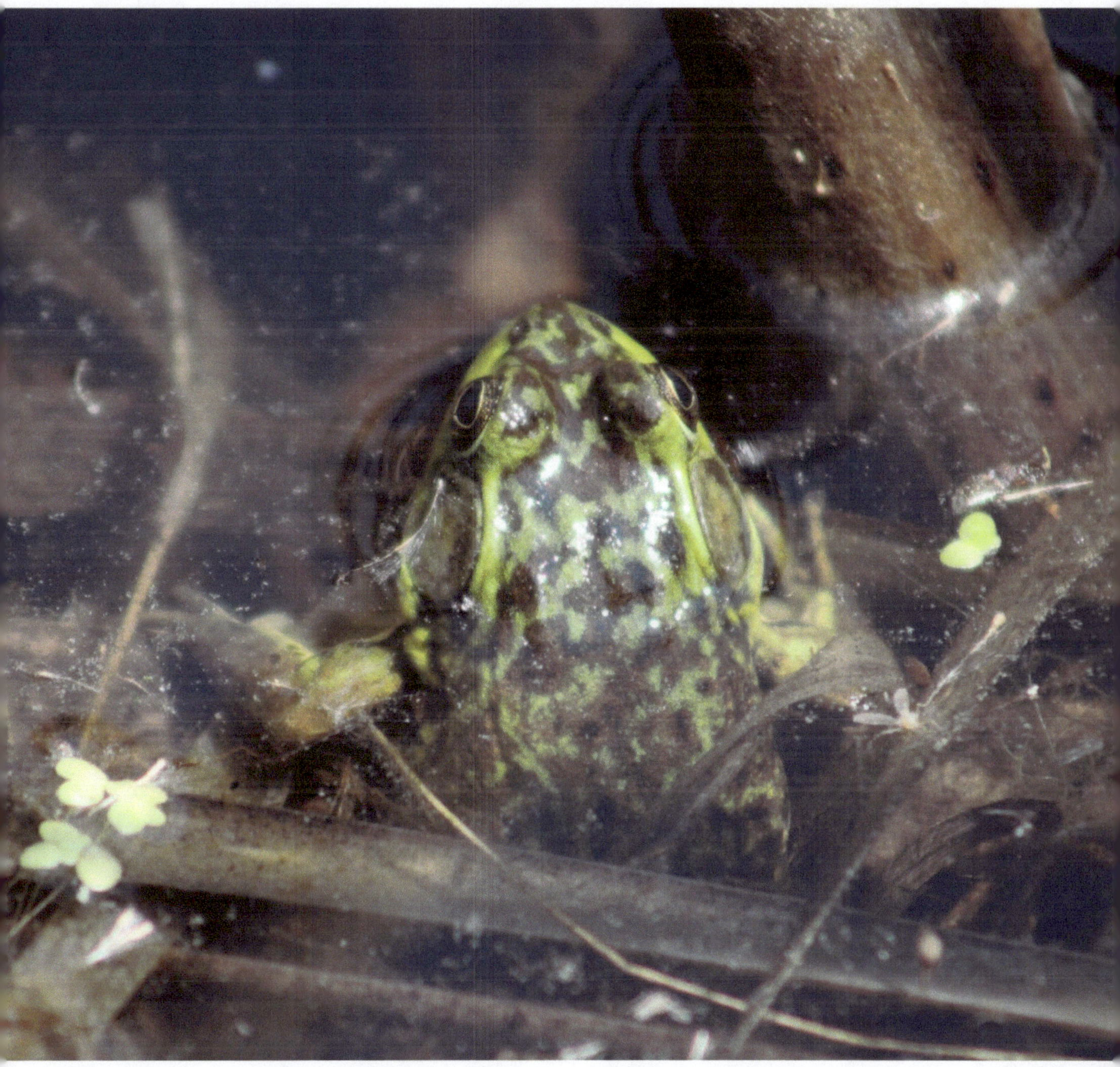

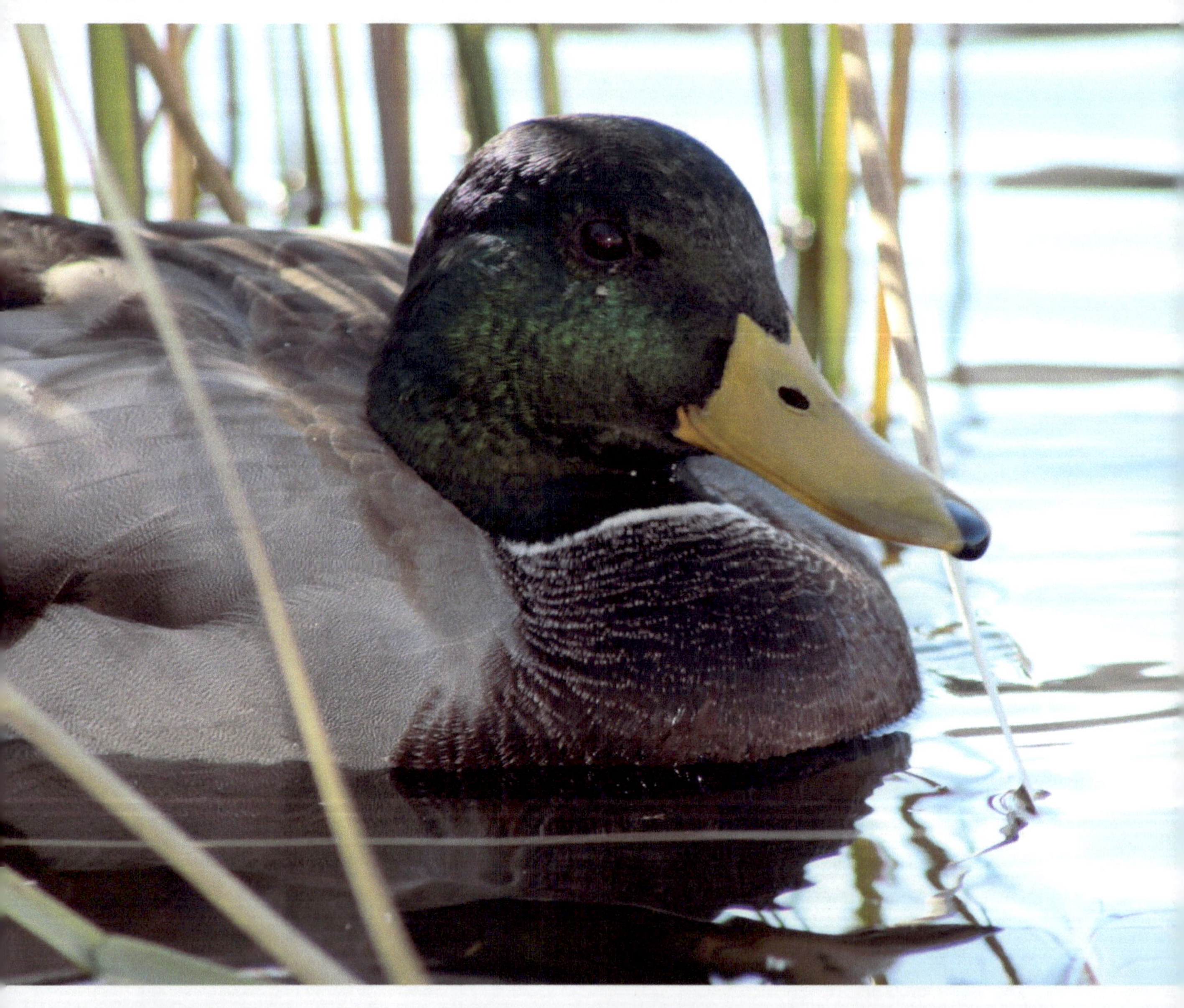

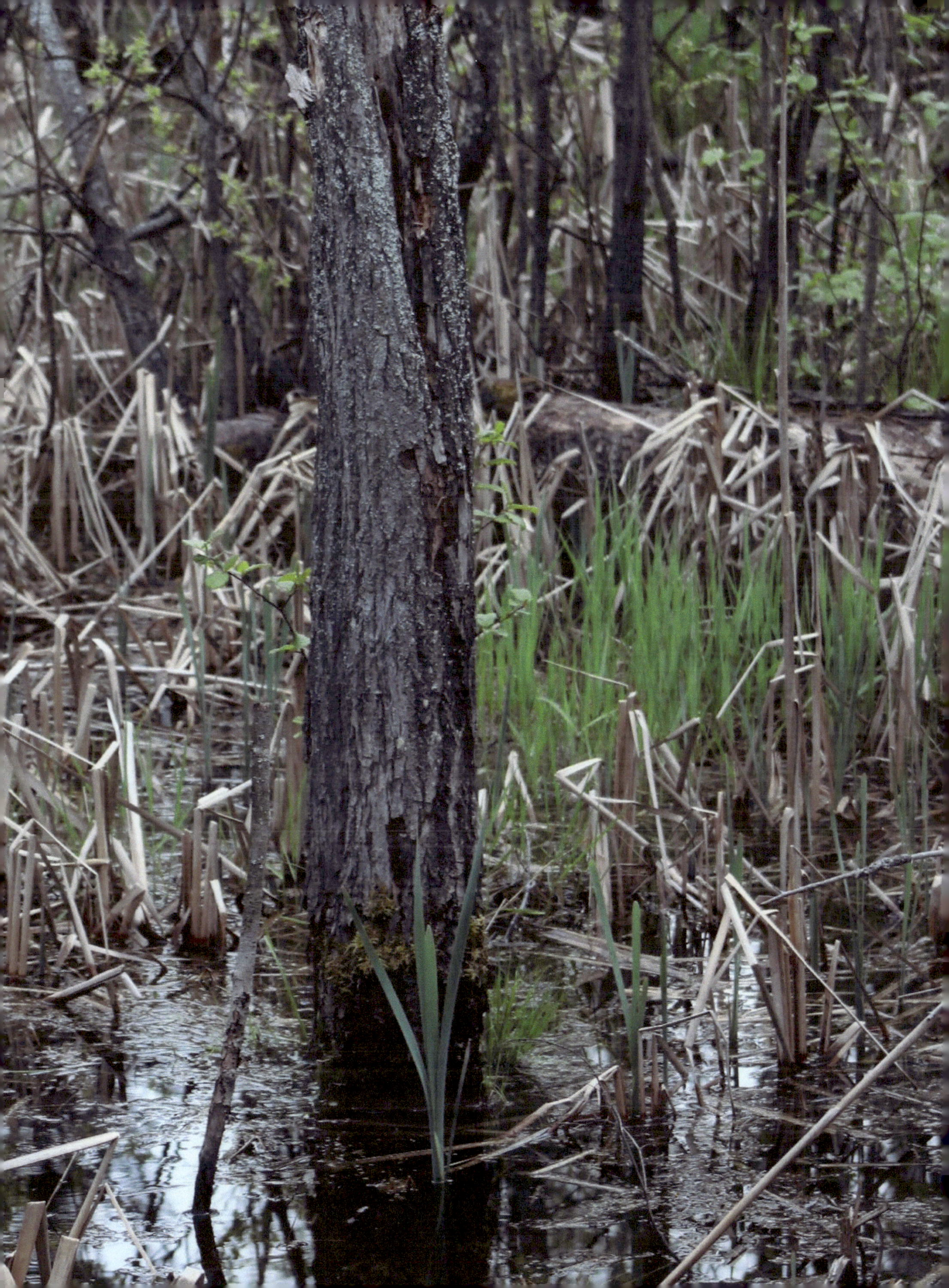

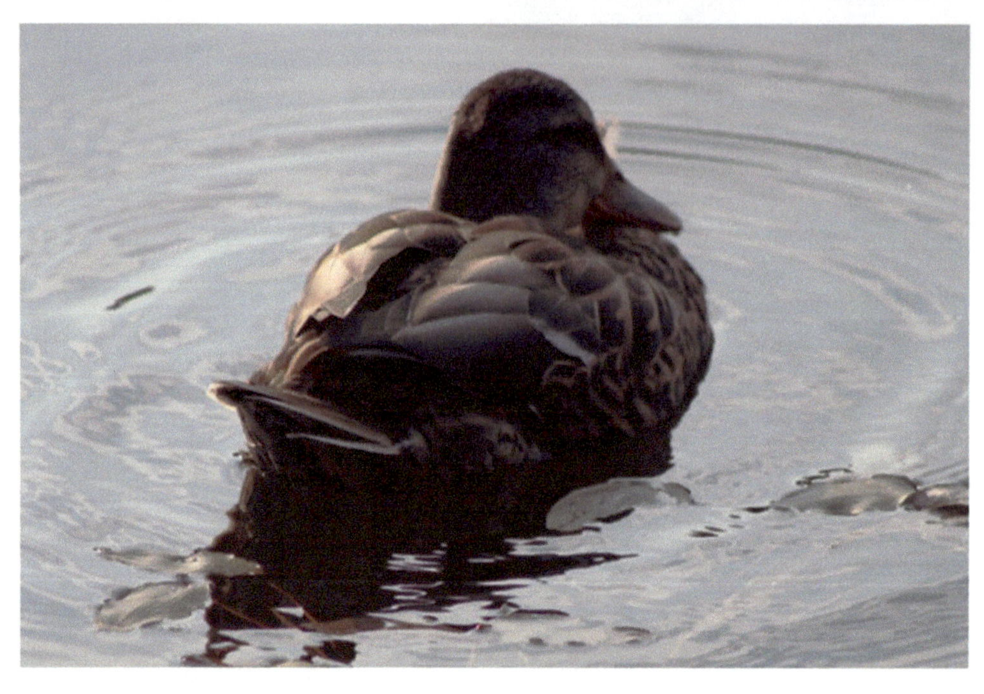

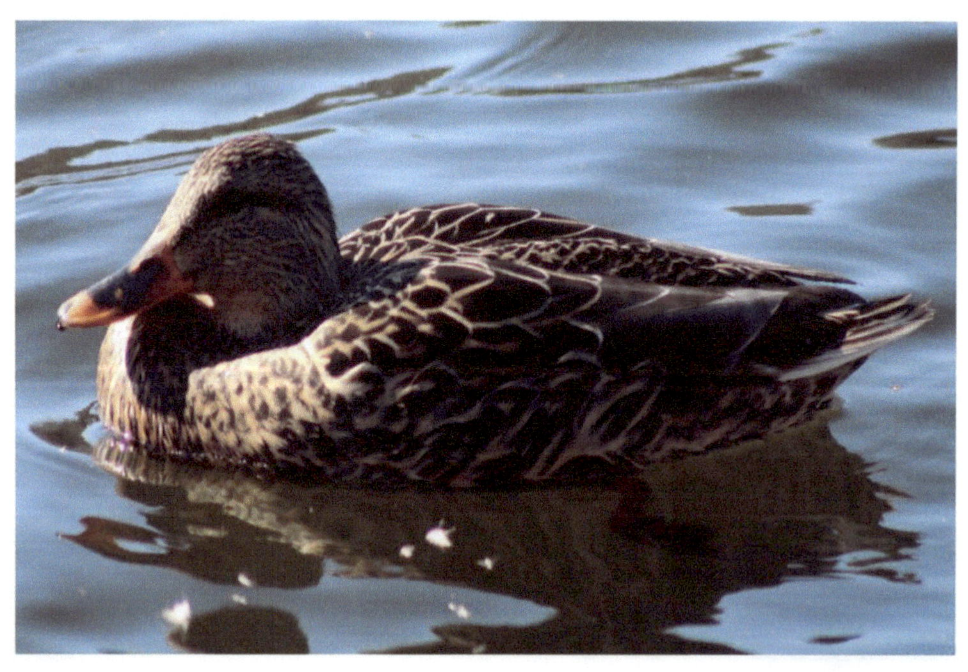

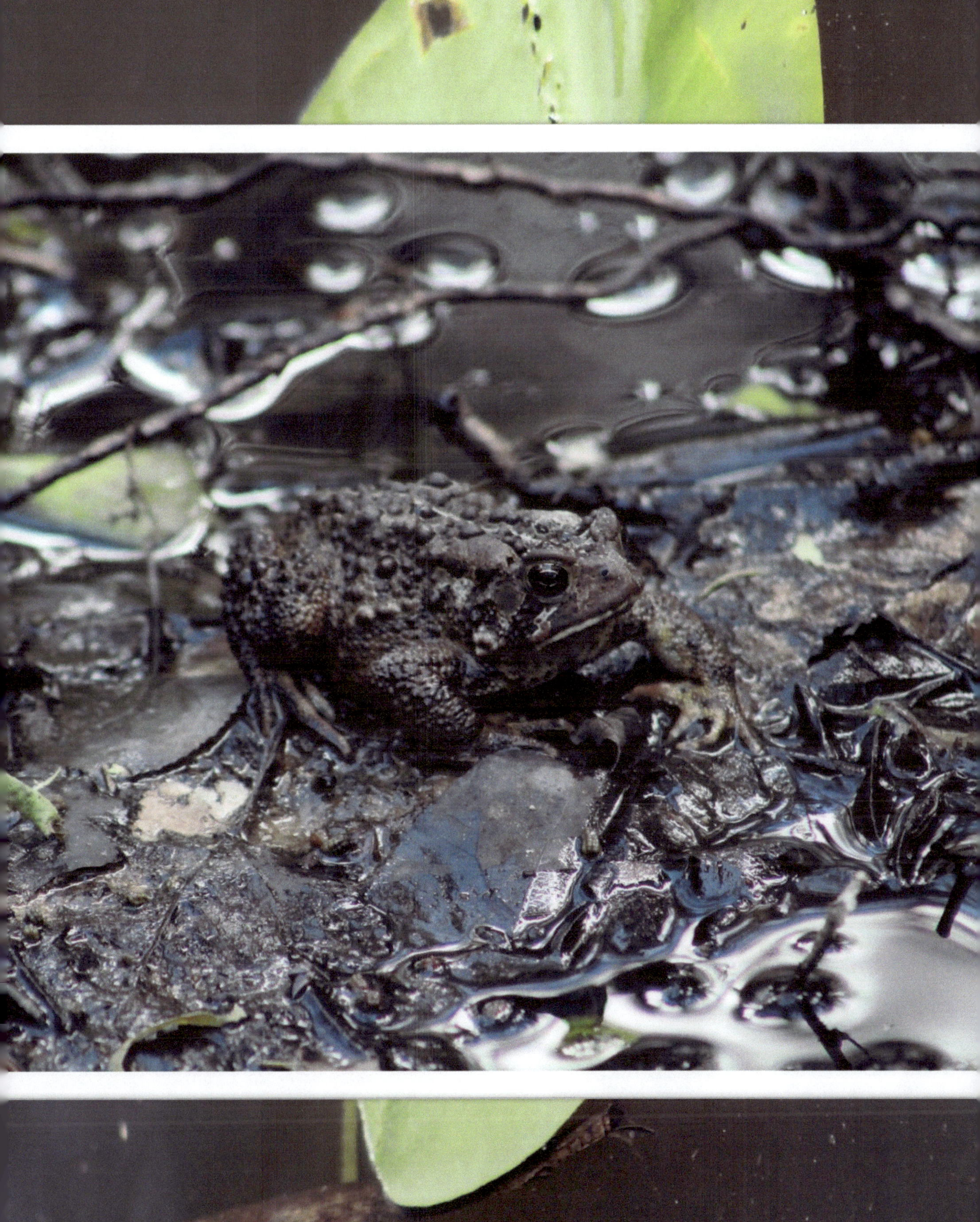

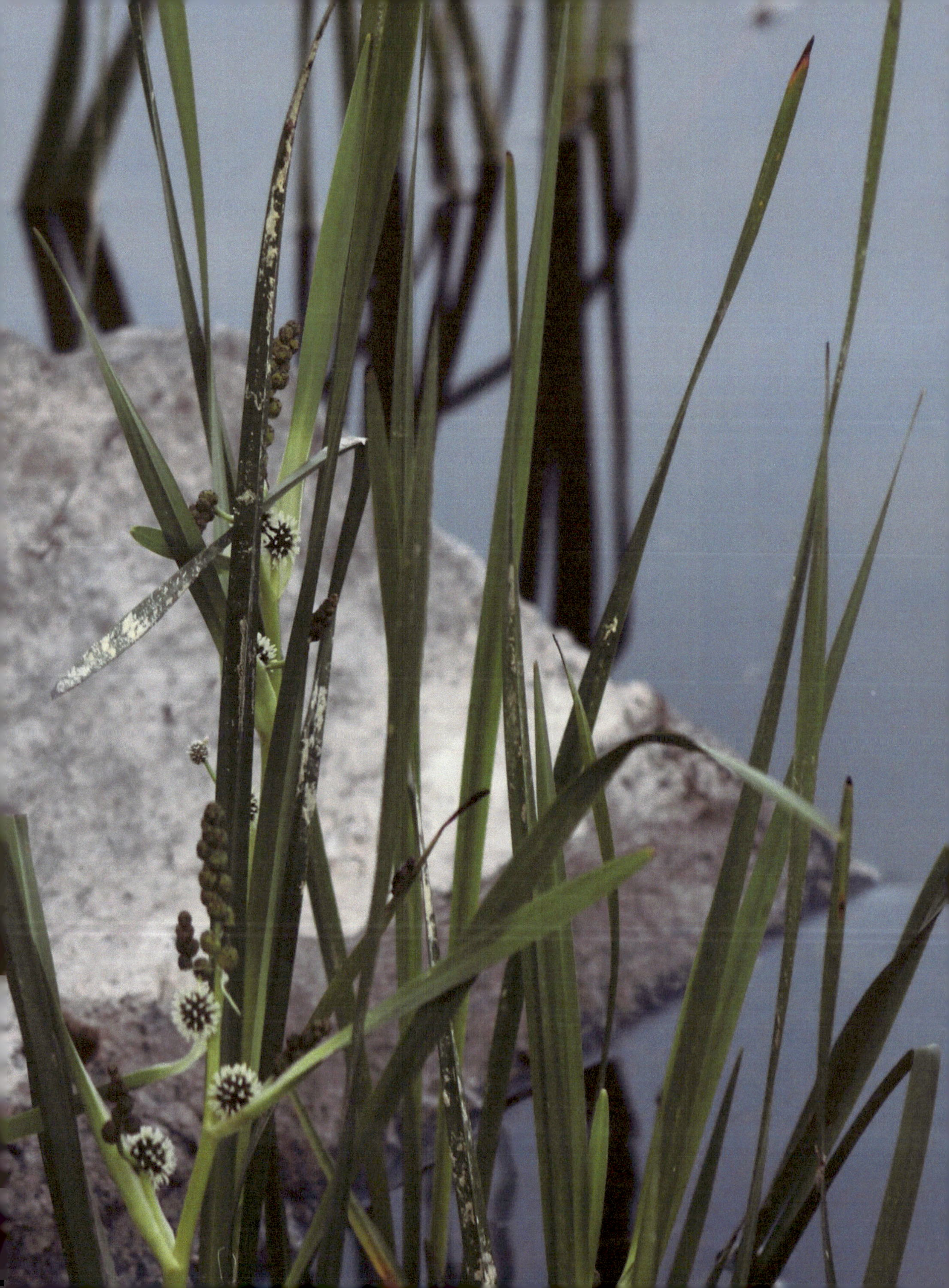

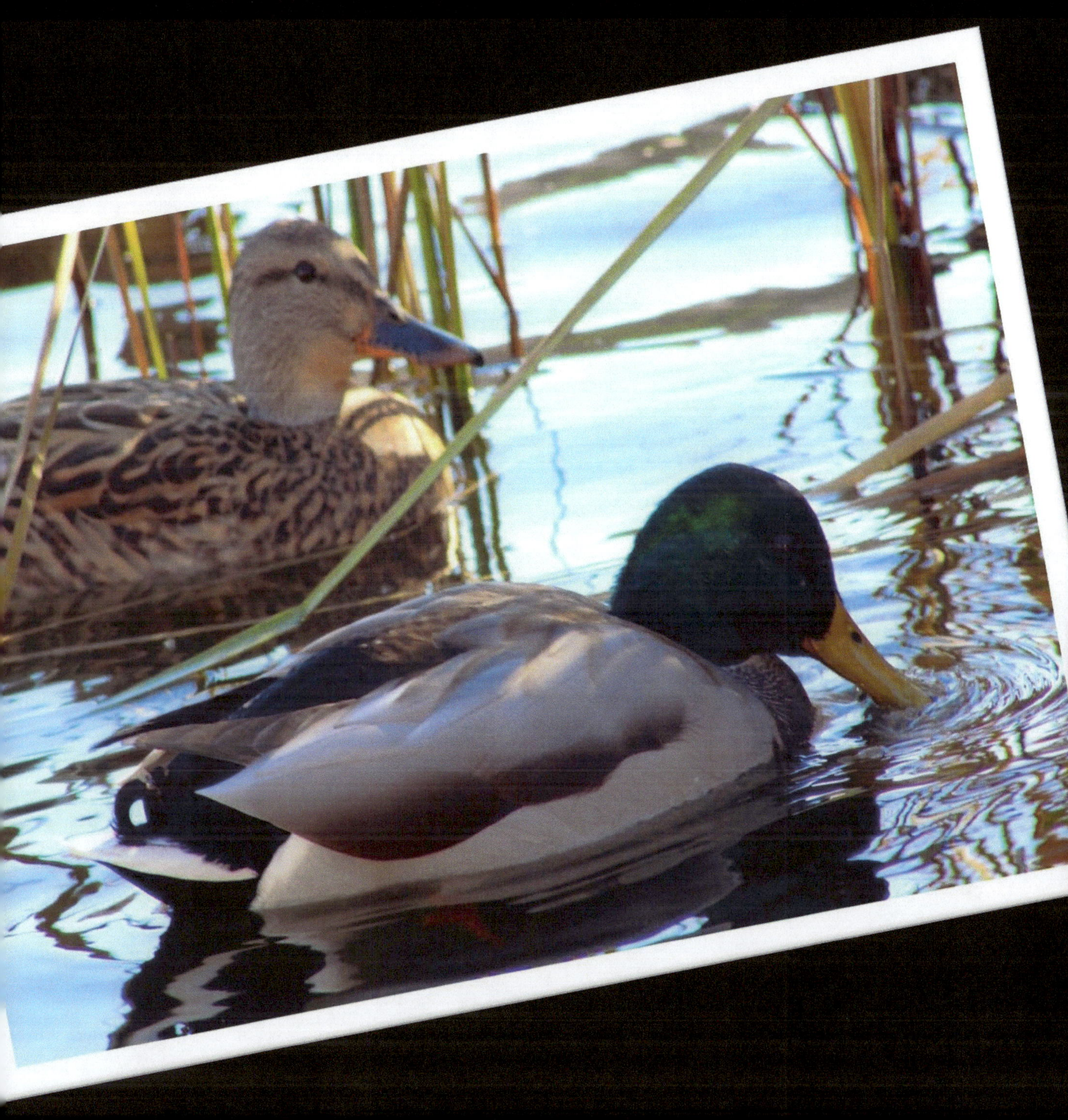

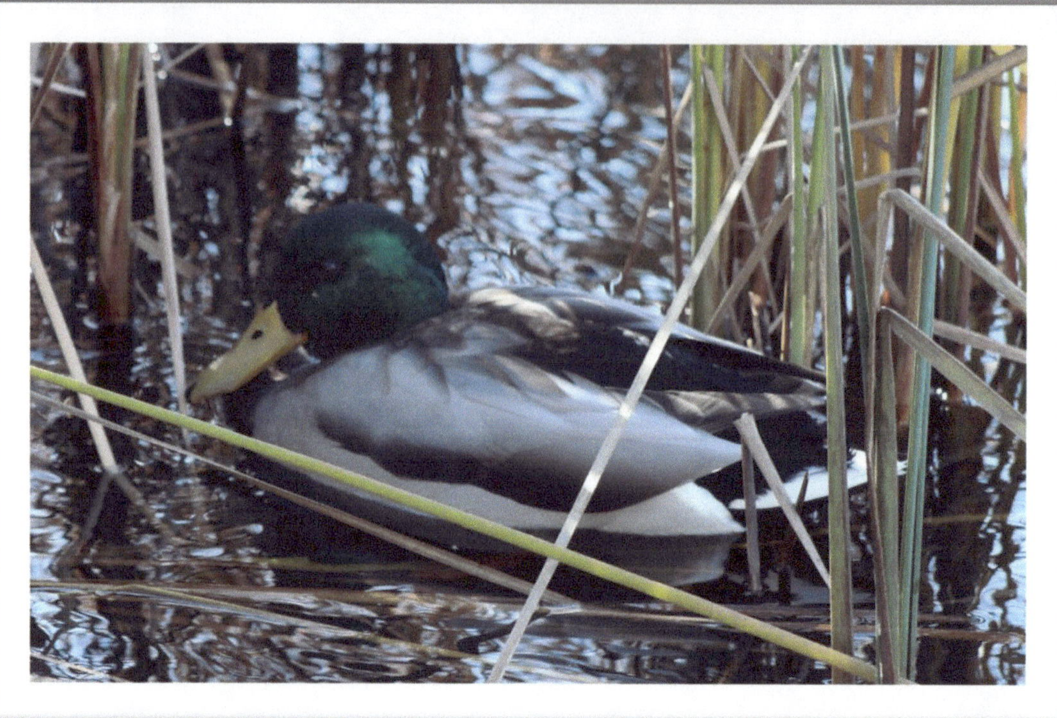

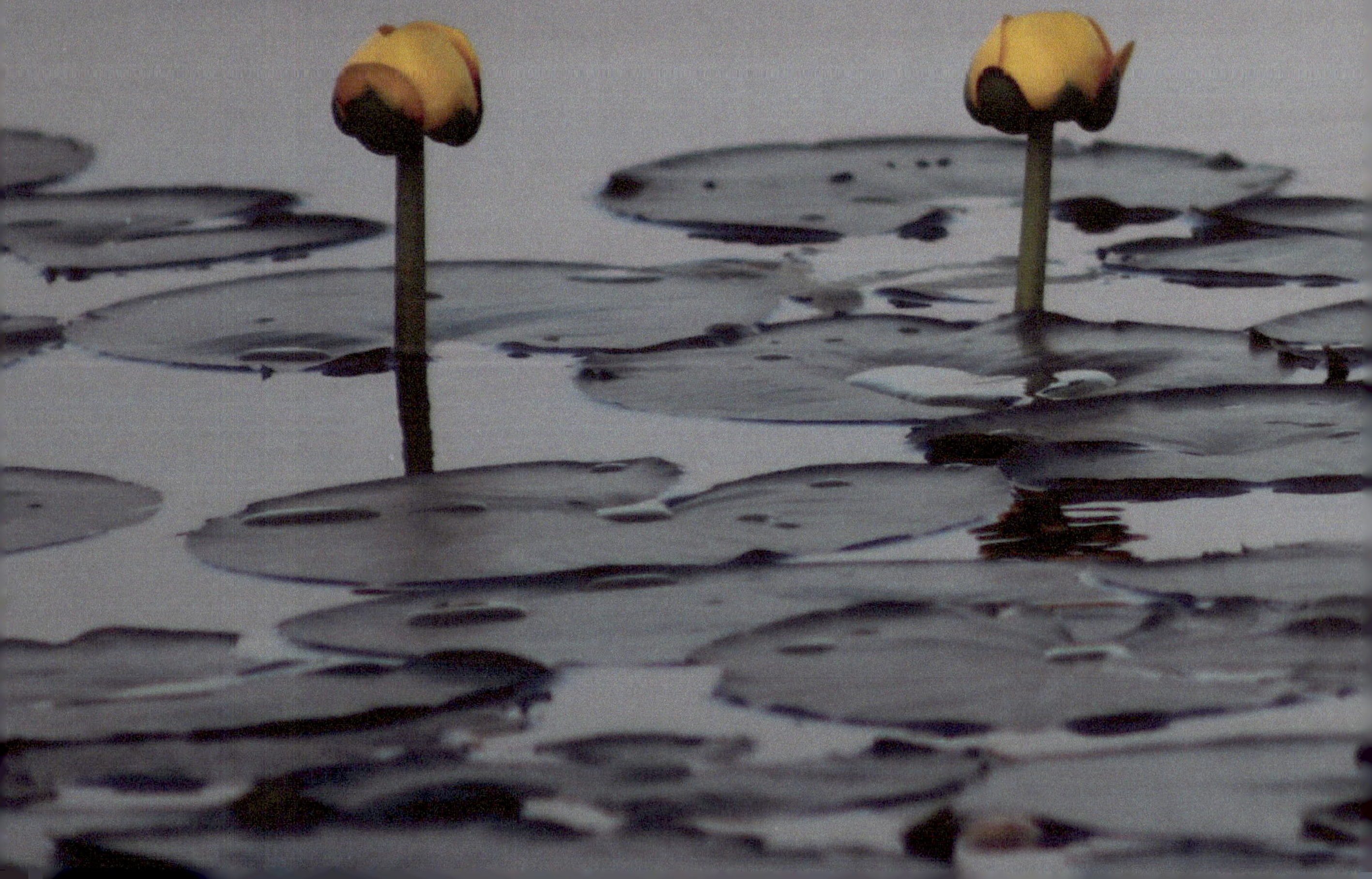

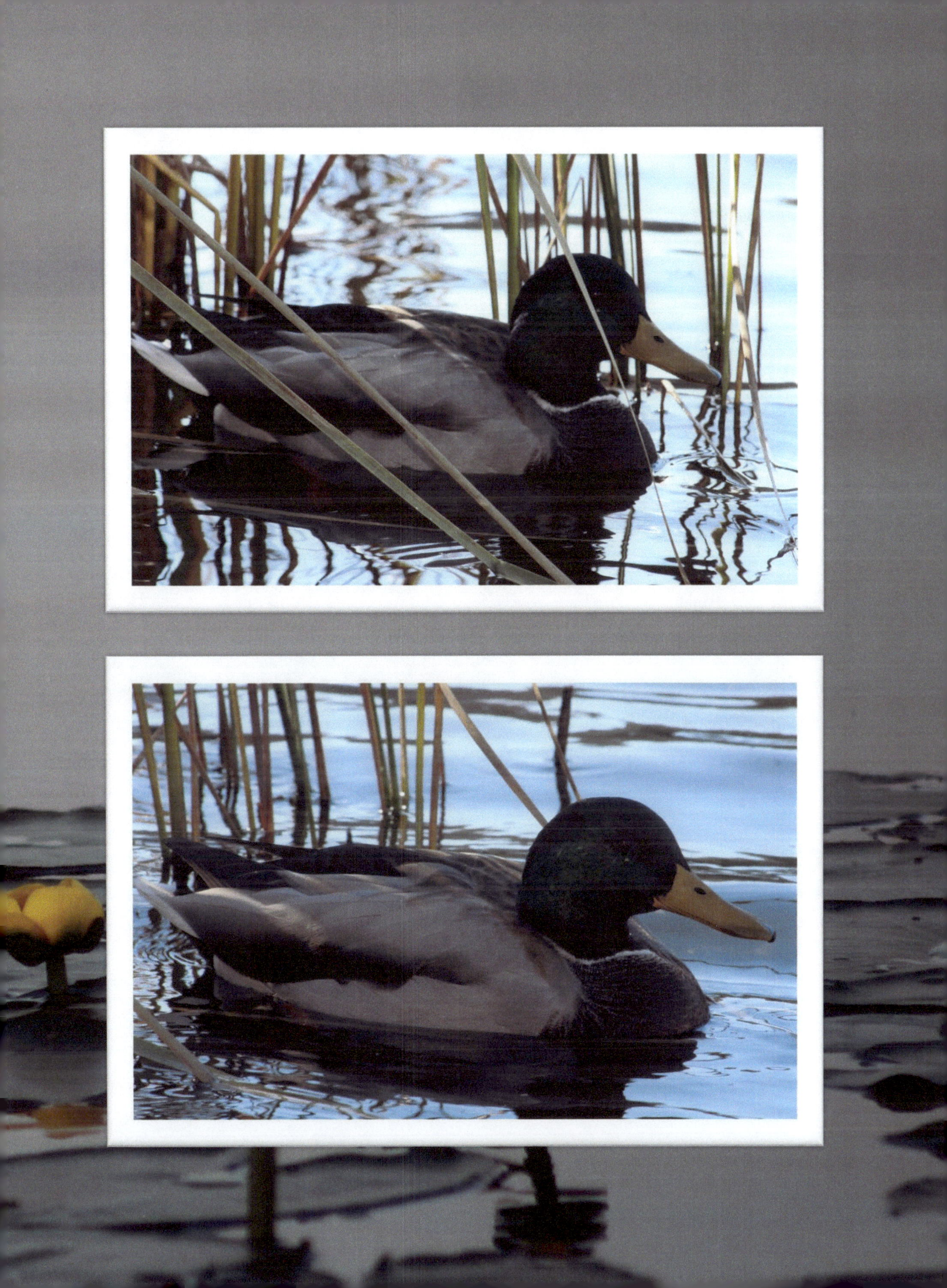

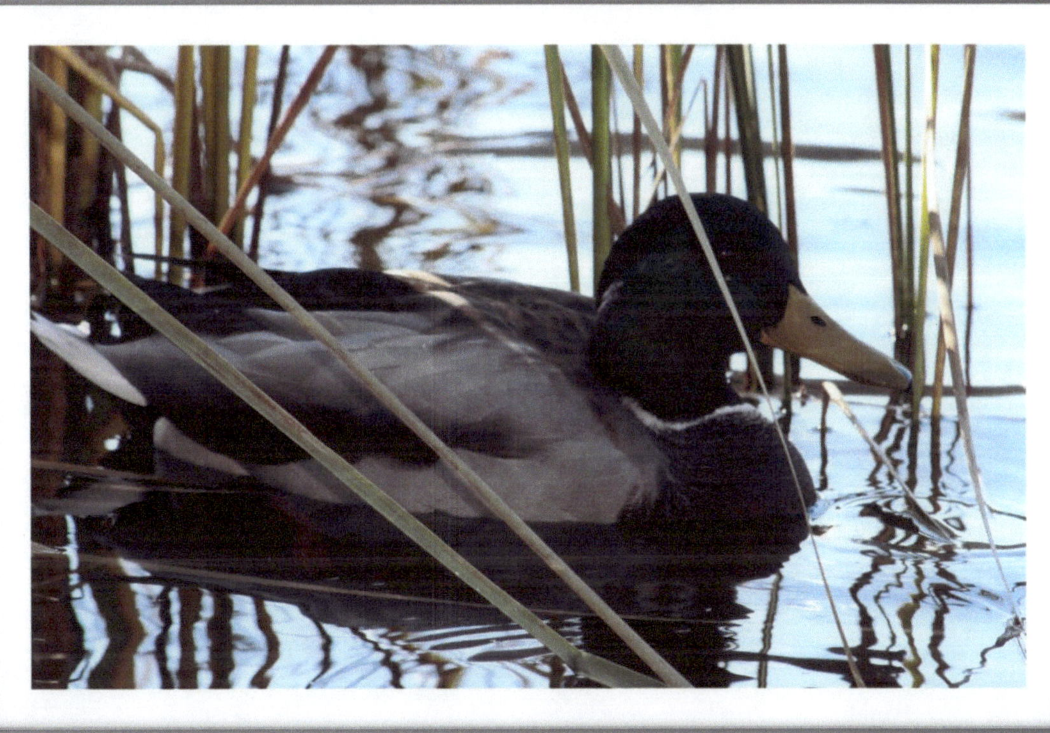

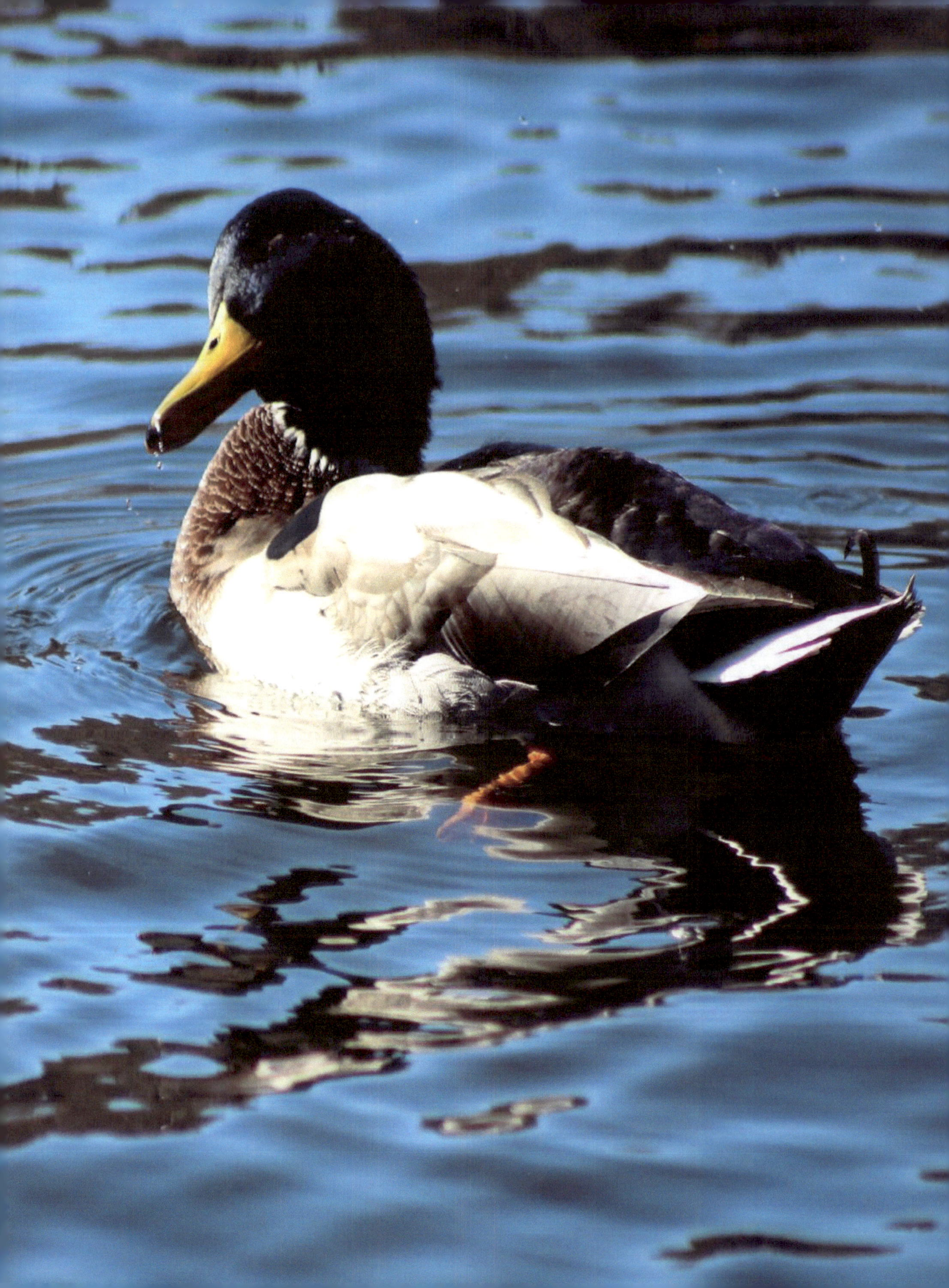

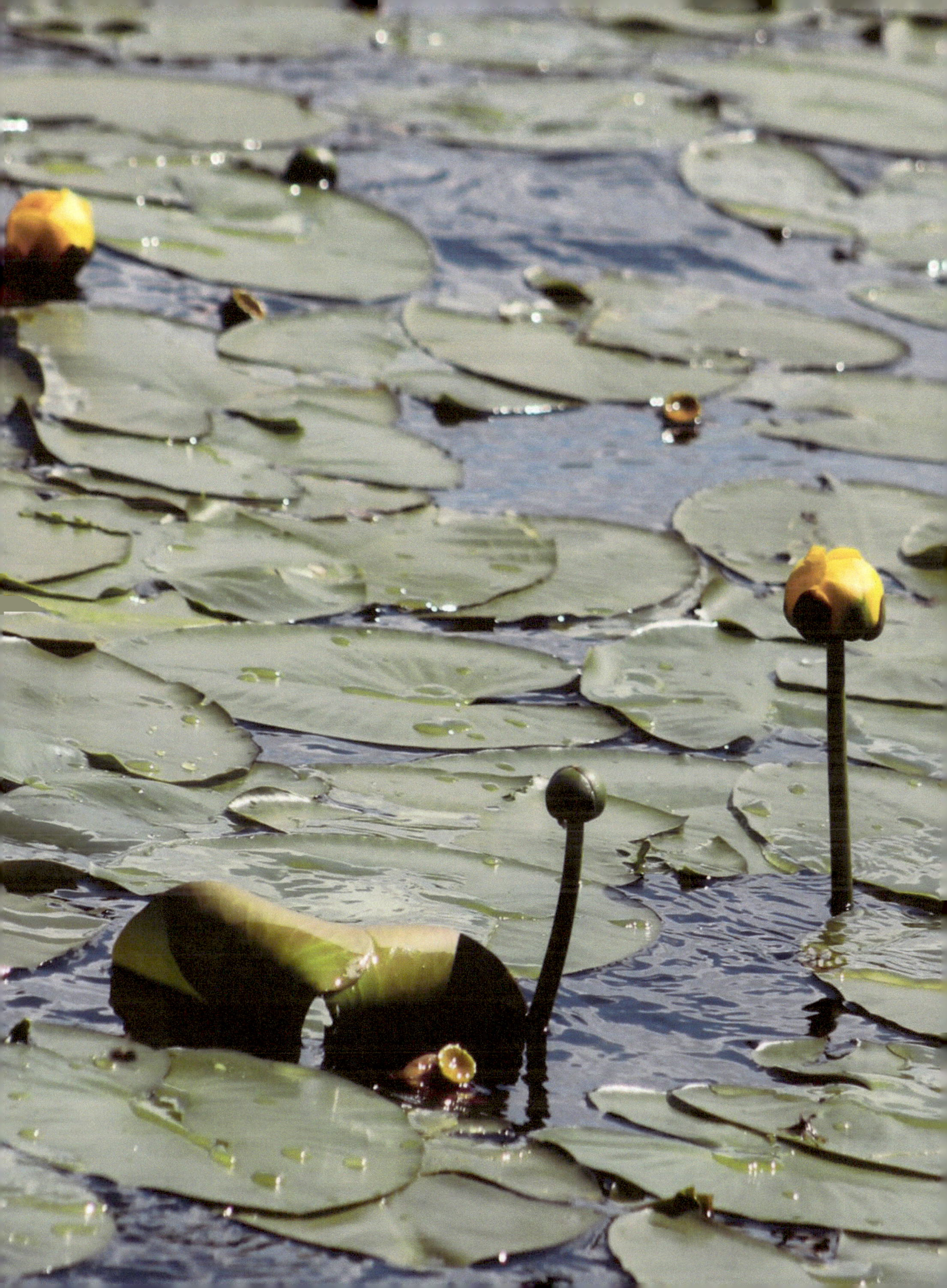

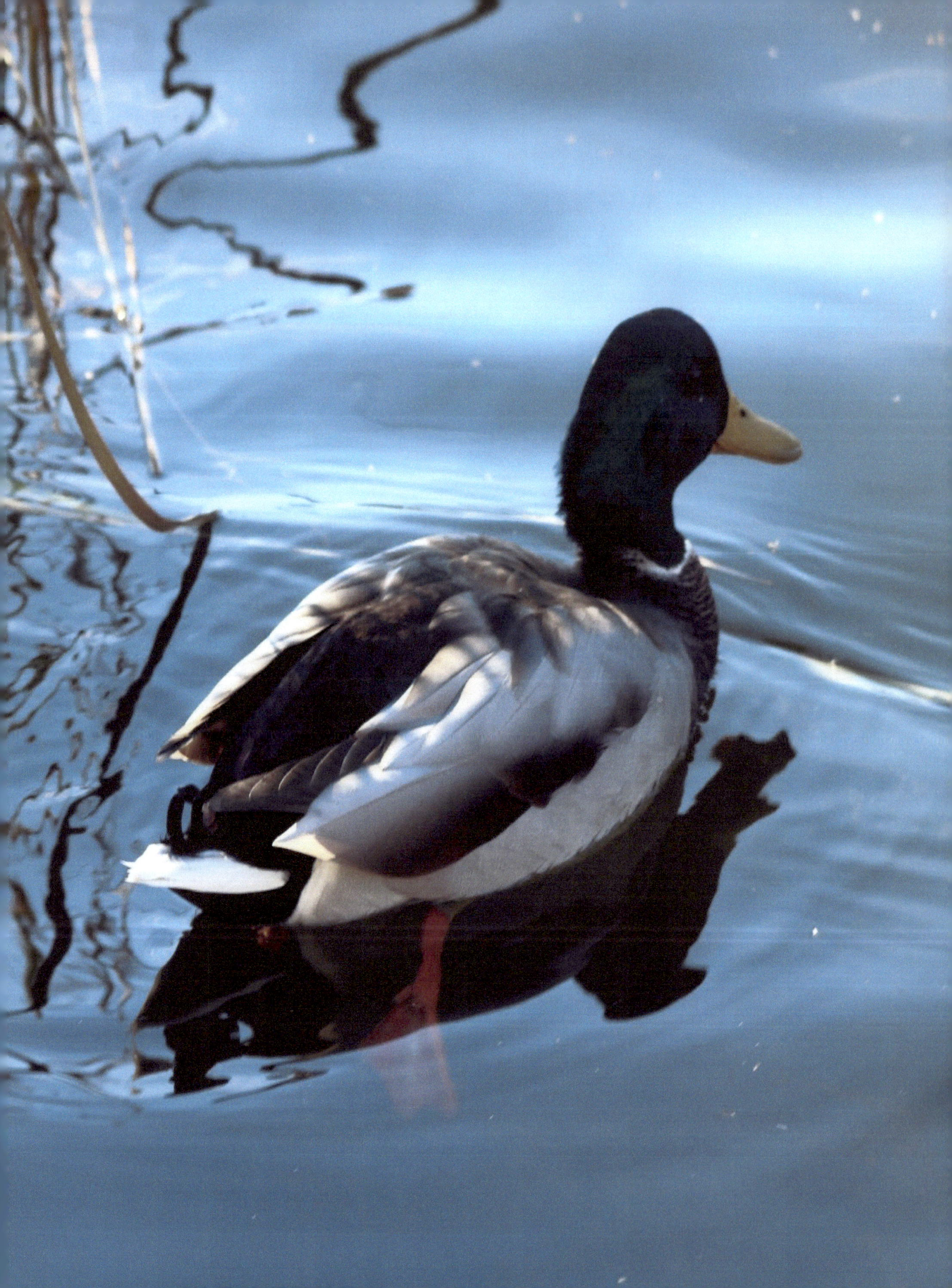

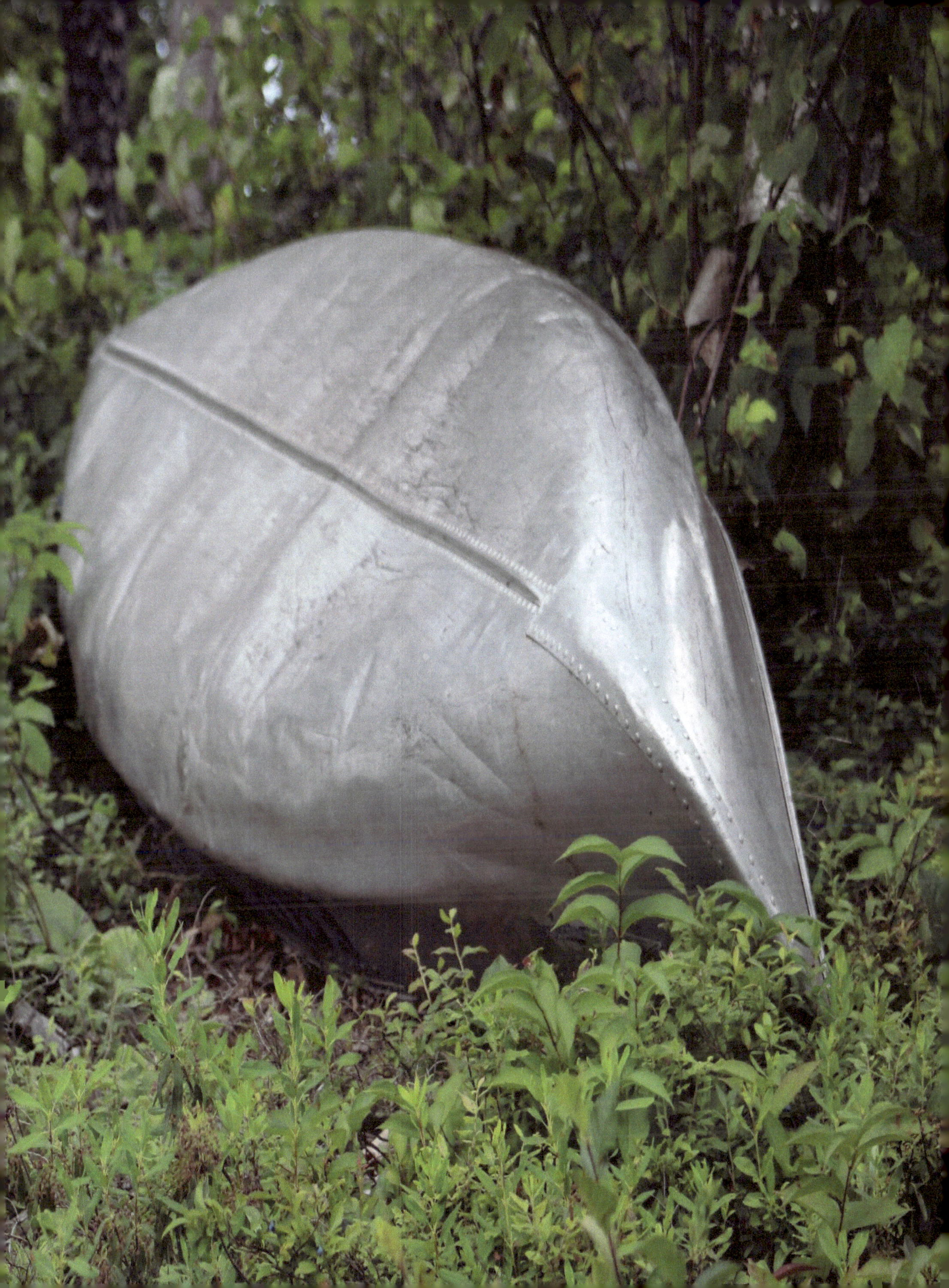

Esther Marcella Hoffmann

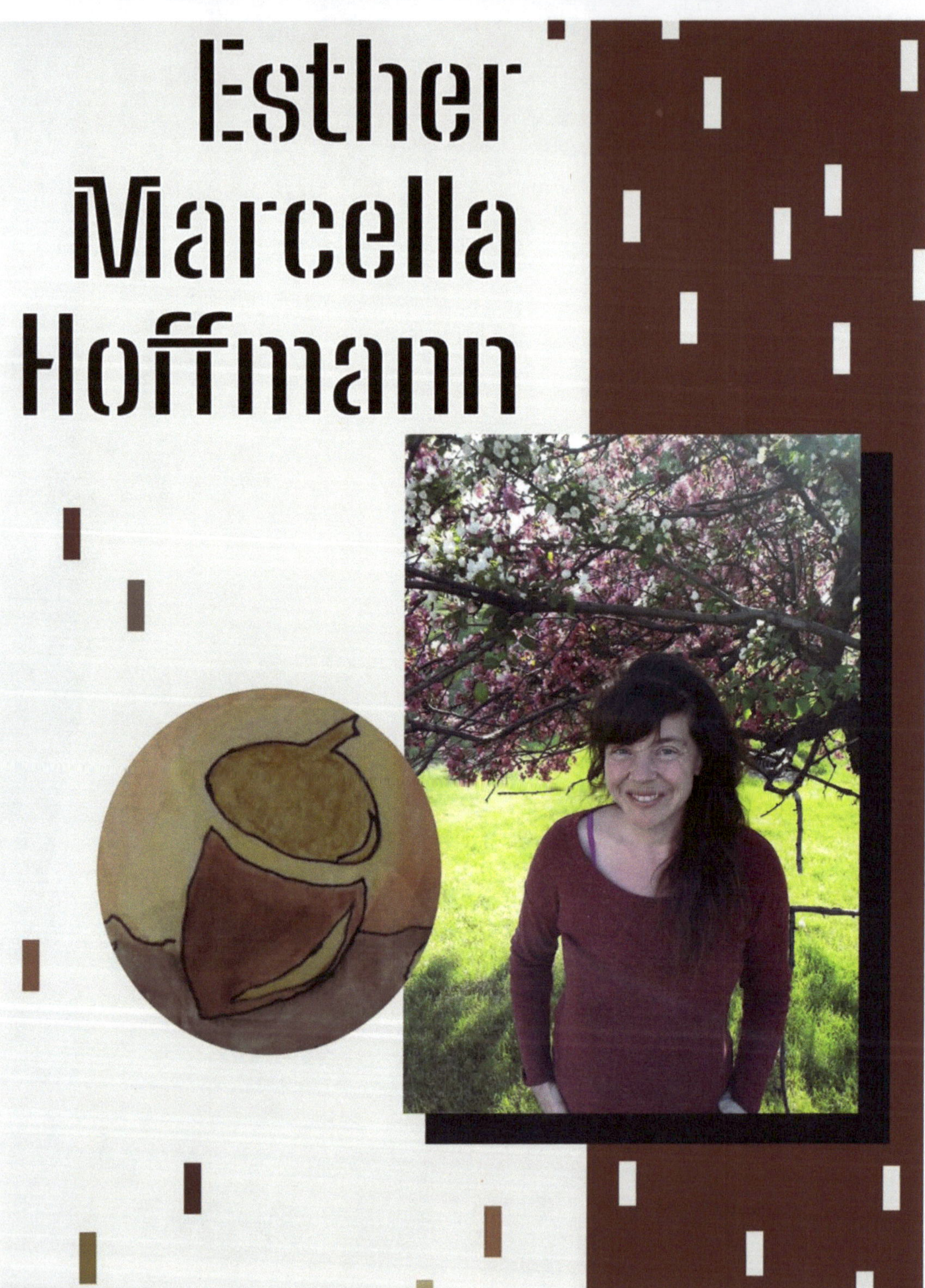

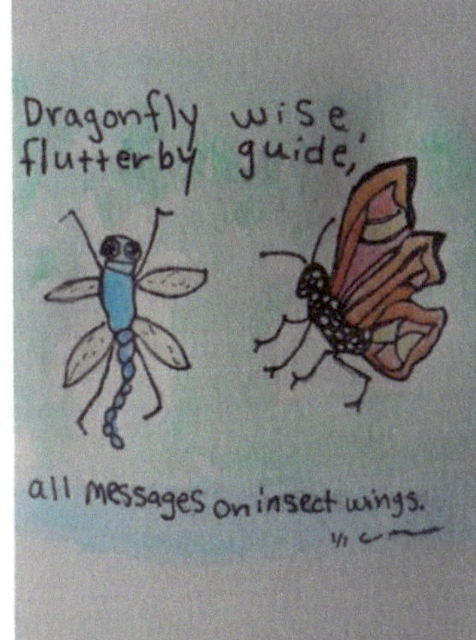

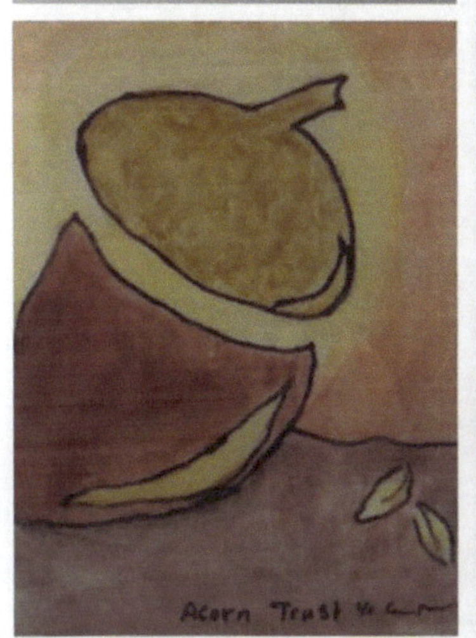

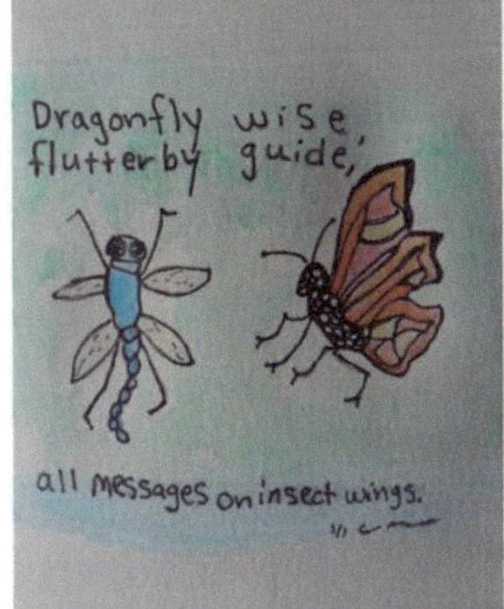

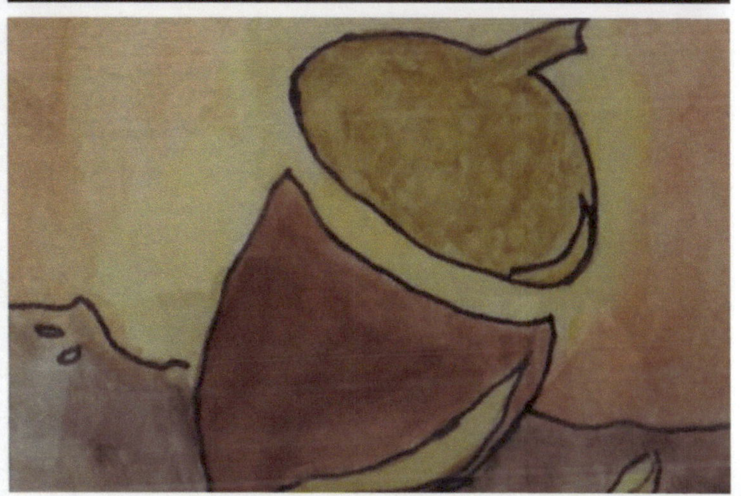

About the Artist

Esther Marcella Hoffmann is the creator of ARTrageous Mankato Studio, who didn't consider herself a visual artist. After years of encouraging people to explore and share their artistic gifts, she realized she must do what she promotes in others. Currently, she enjoys creating with various mediums, and awareness.

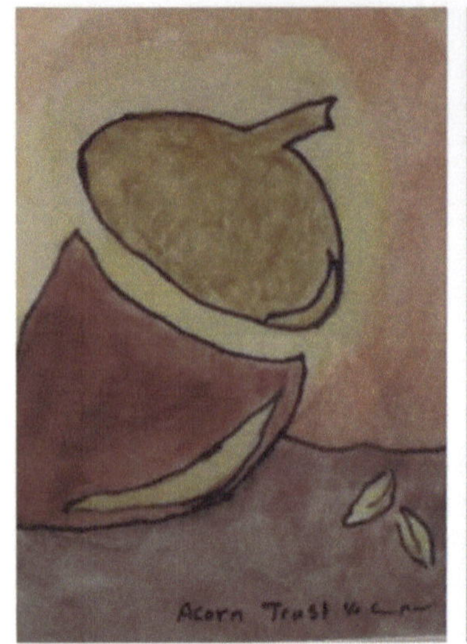

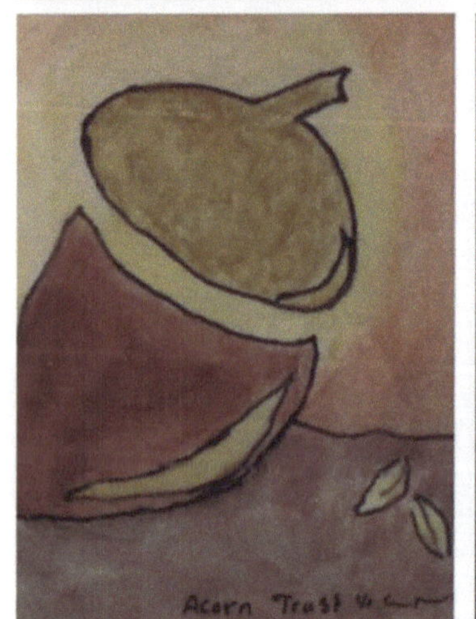

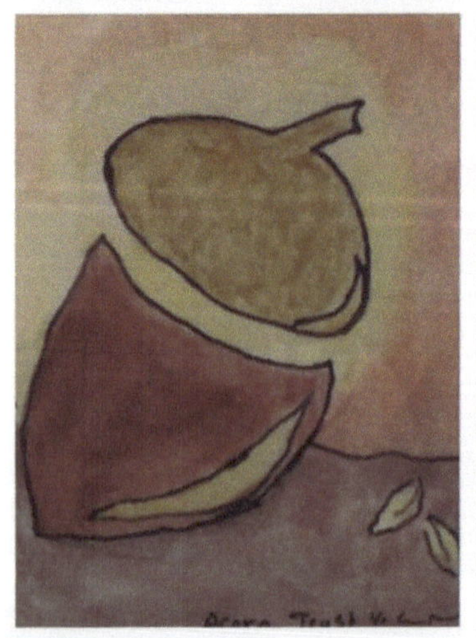

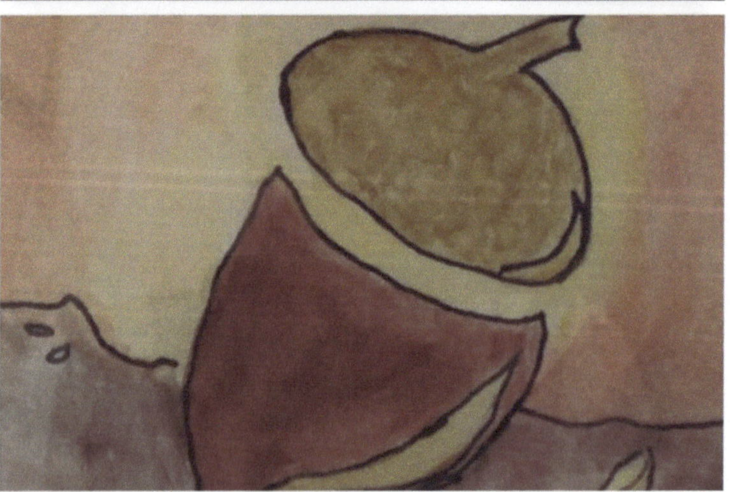

Acorn Trust

"Acorn Trust" is an image based on a poem Esther wrote. Life will have its way with you, perhaps you'll be crunch in teeth, secret buried, or grown tree, but can you just be?

Acorn Trust

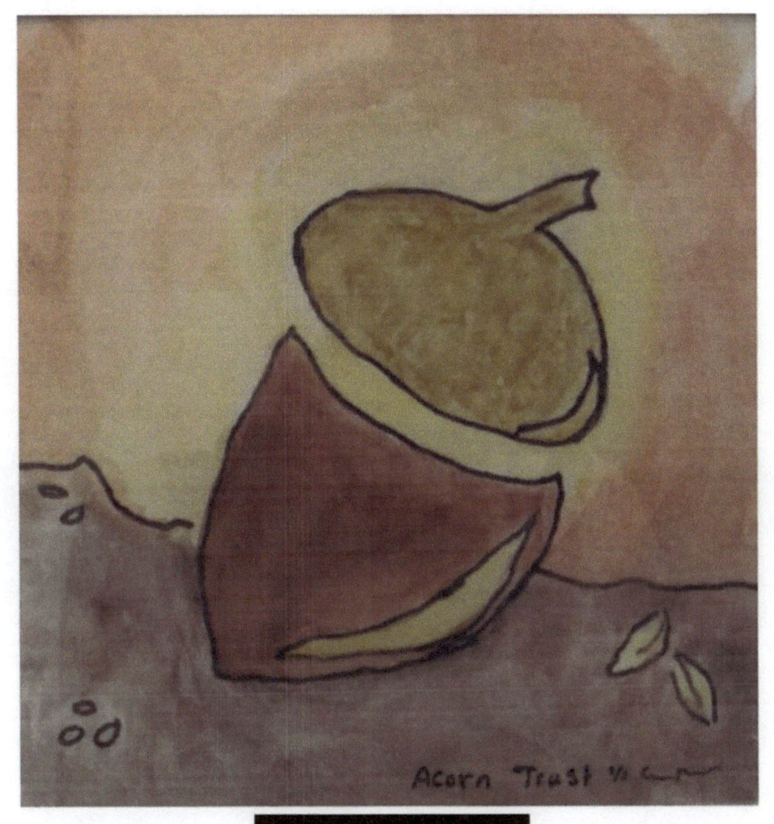

Acorn Trust

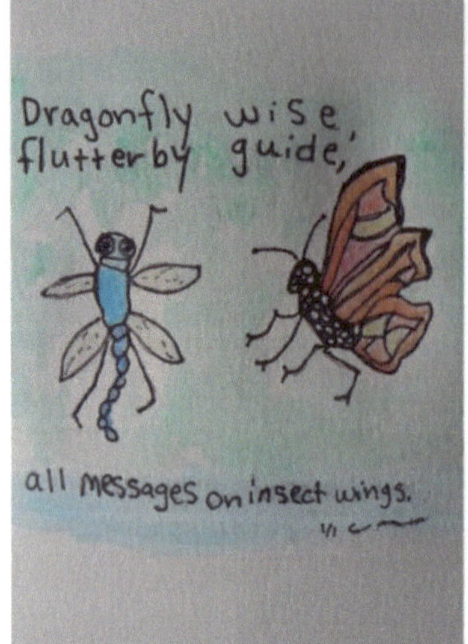

Dragonfly Wise

"Dragonfly Wise" is inspired by a walk surrounded by dragonflies and butterflies, and the idea that we were exchanging the wisdom of the moment.

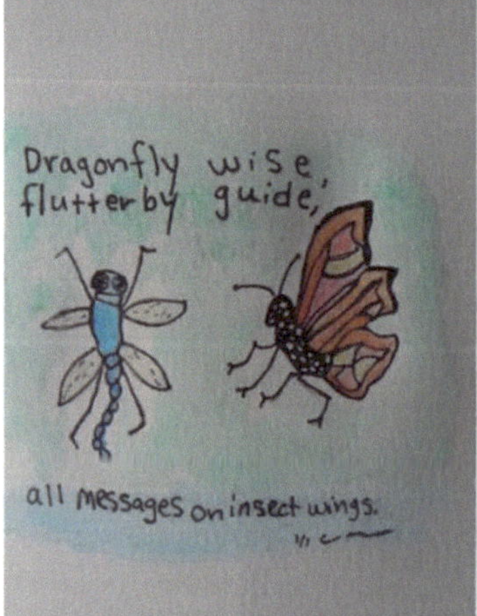

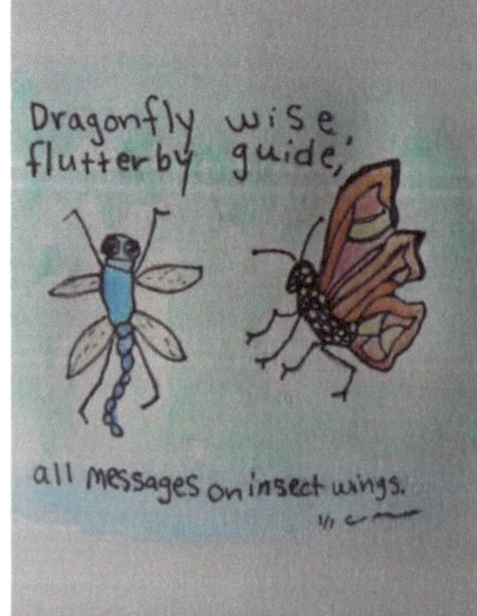

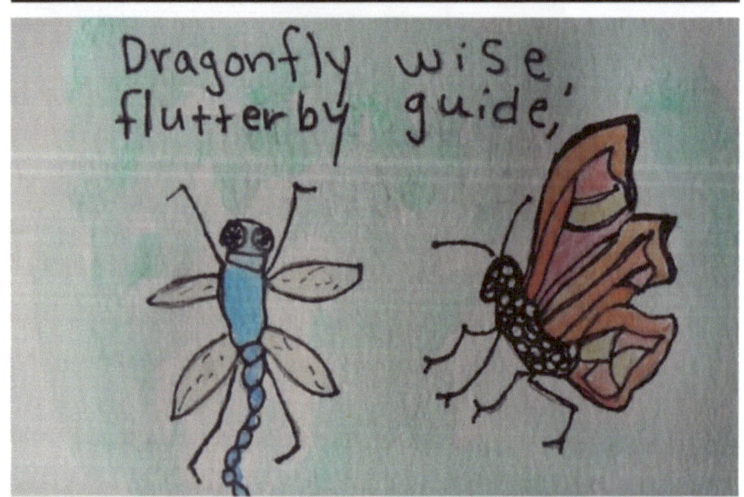

Dragonfly wise

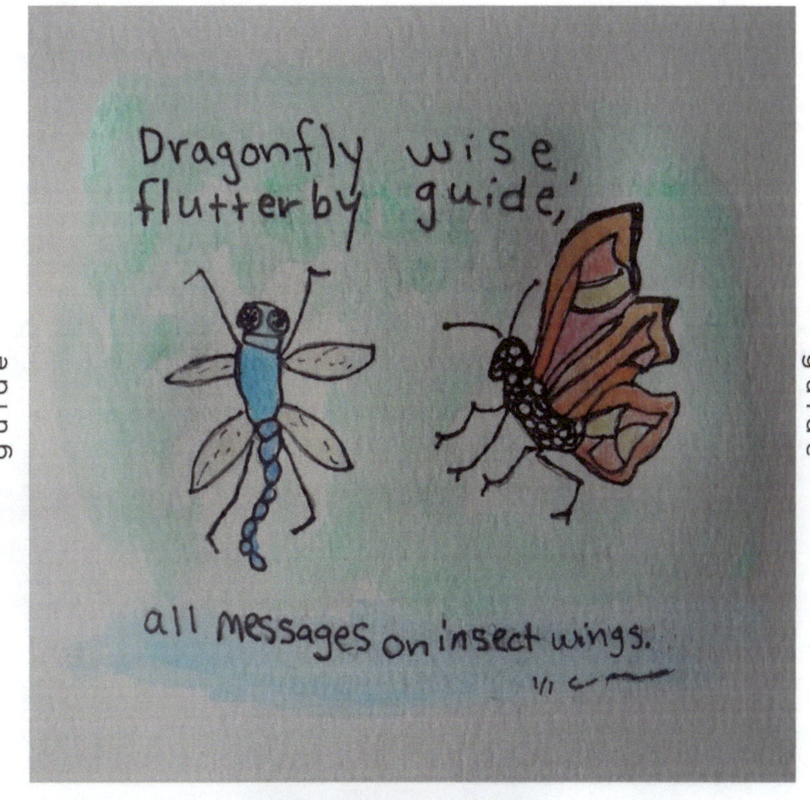

Dragonfly wise

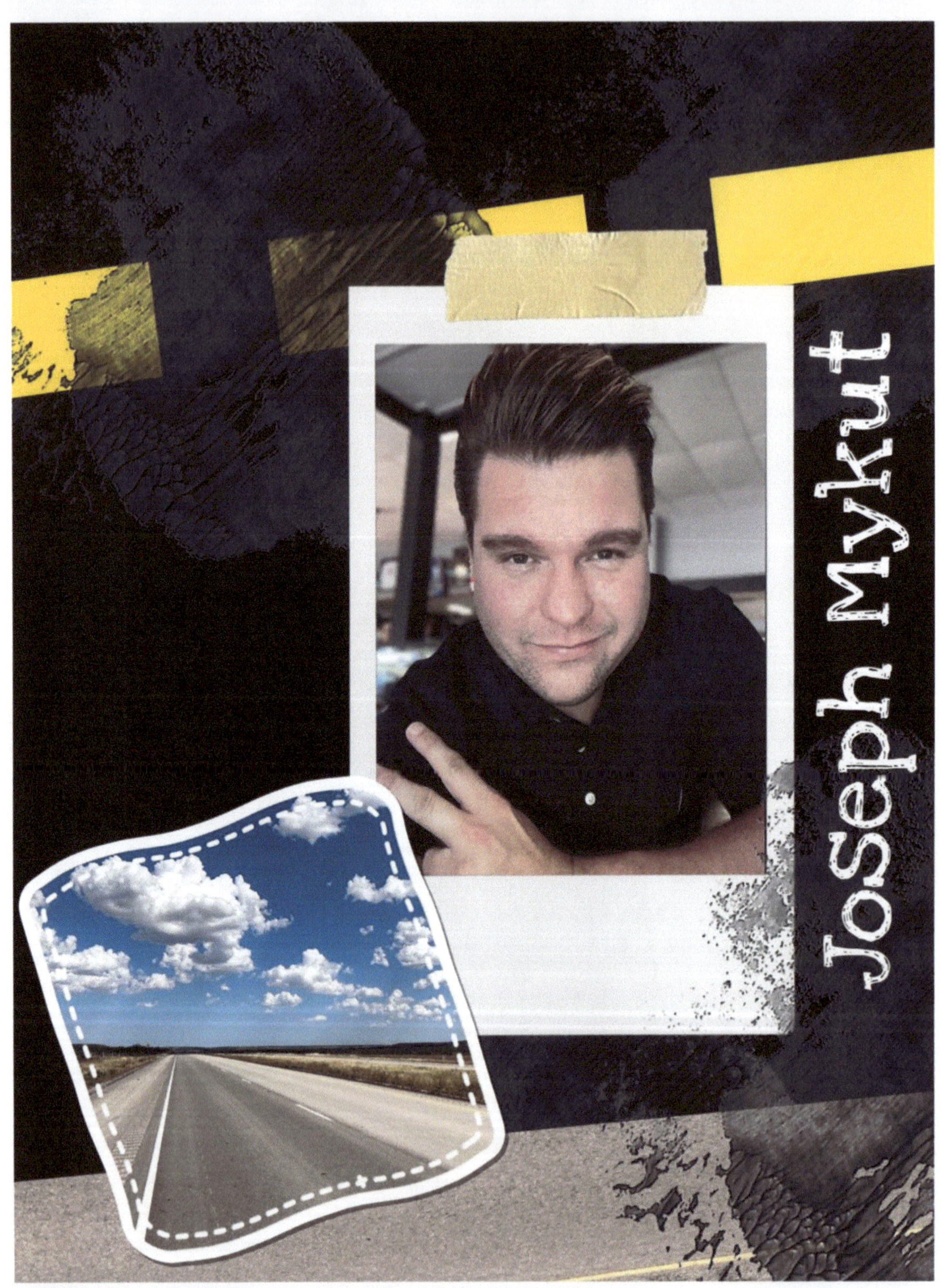
Joseph Mykut

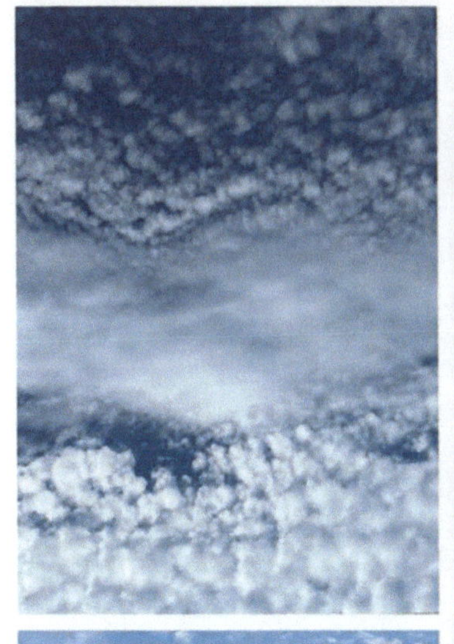

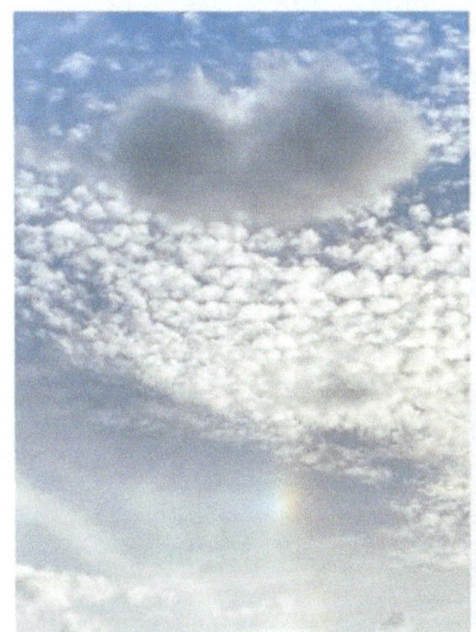

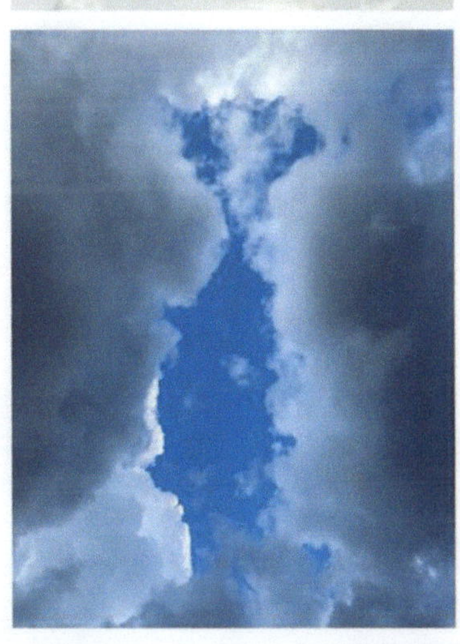

About the Collection

My collection is about the beauty above. Most of us walk beneath one of the most incredible canvasses everyday and maybe take notice once or twice. I can't keep my eyes off the the skies. These photographs are just a few examples of the ever changing empyreal scape hanging just over our noggins. Like a giant etch-a-sketch, the clouds produce endless art from one minute or day to the next. There is something beautiful and terrifying about the world above. The sky can be familiar and friendly or it can be daunting and mysterious. I hope these images captivate the viewers the way they captivated me and give you a new found perspective to the majestic and magnificent skies of our world.

https://cosmiccreationstation.com

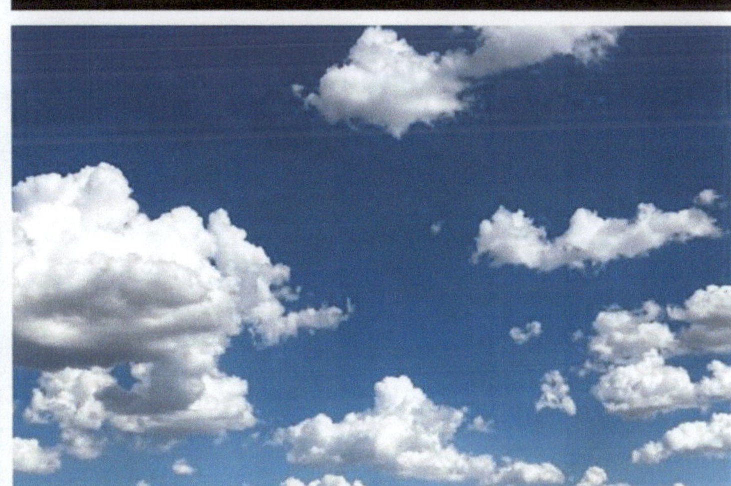

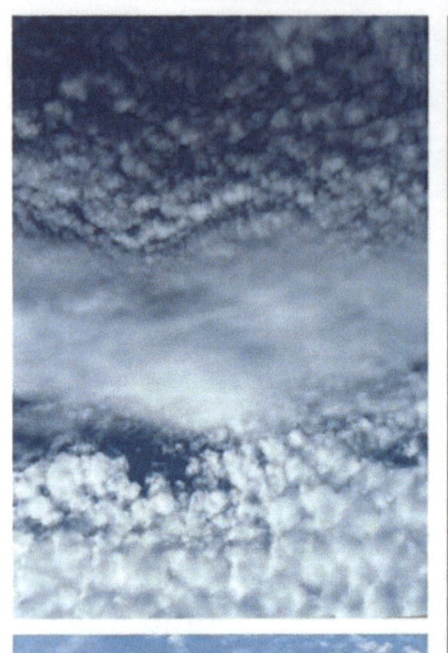

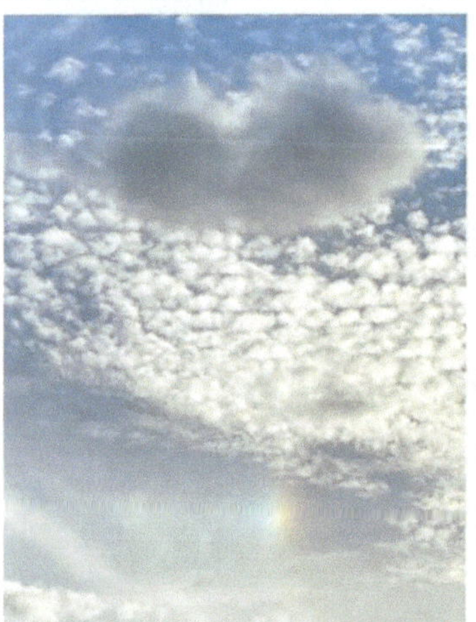

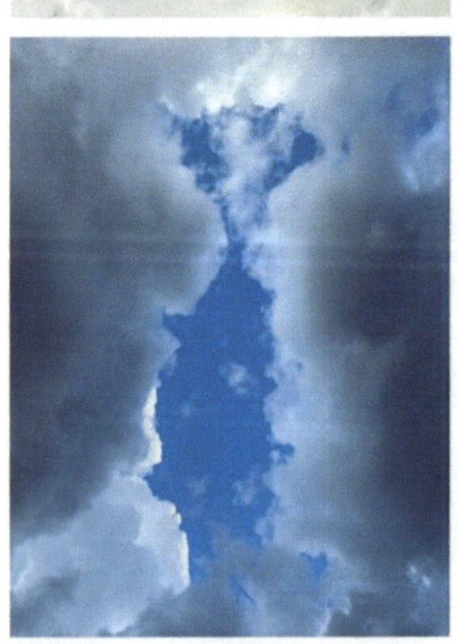

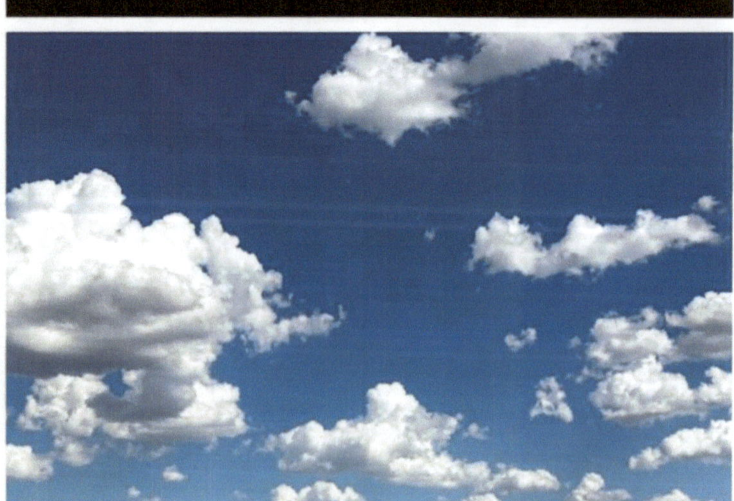

About the Artist

Joseph Mykut is from Alabama, USA. Their art and photography is published in the "3 Amigo Ink and Splatter, The Lonely Soul in the Darkness Anthology" as well as their children's book, "Beautiful Boy." Joseph loves photography and capturing images in unusual places and circumstances. Their style is eclectic yet humble, looking for grandeur in the ordinary.

https://cosmiccreationstation.com

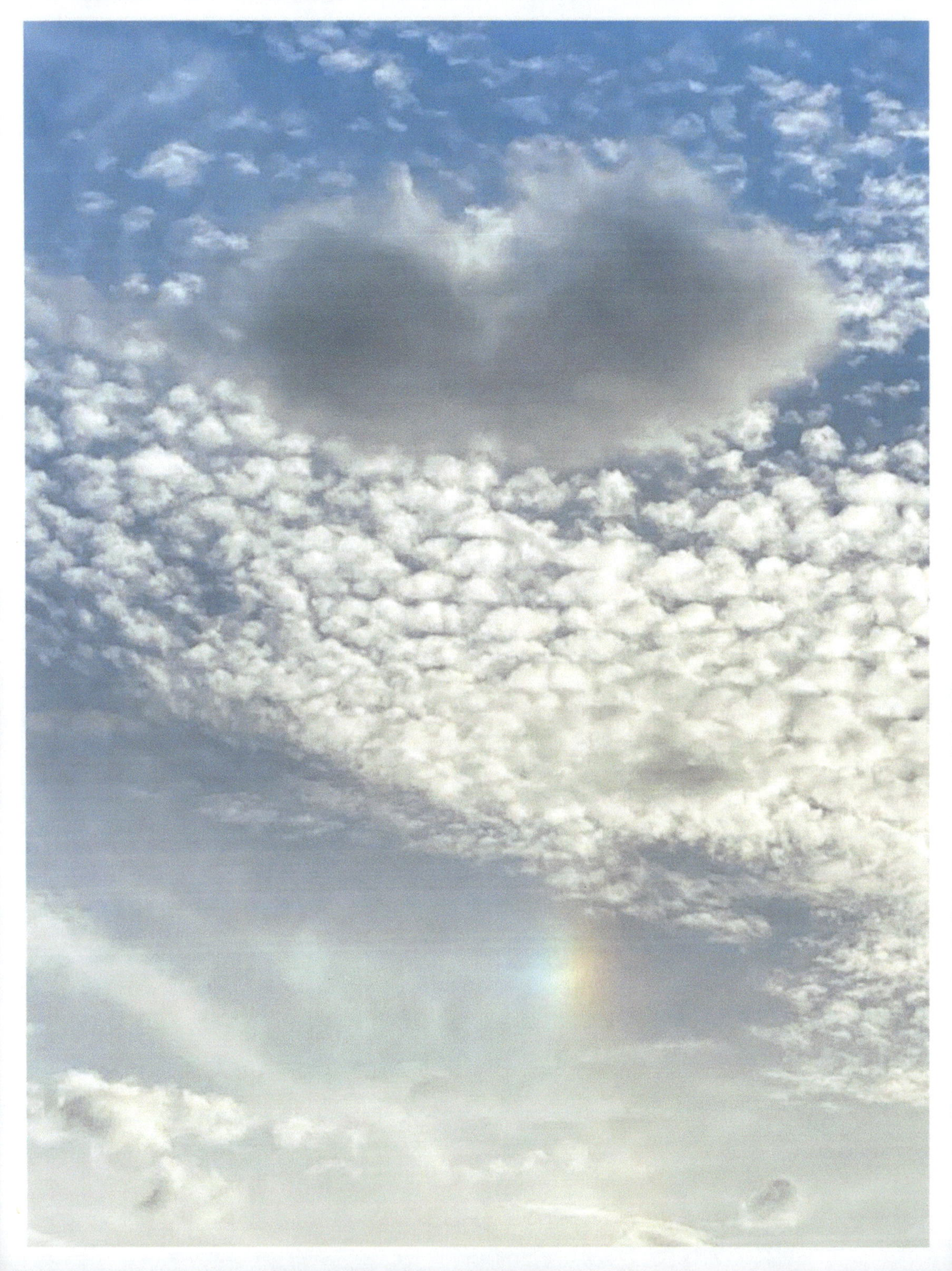

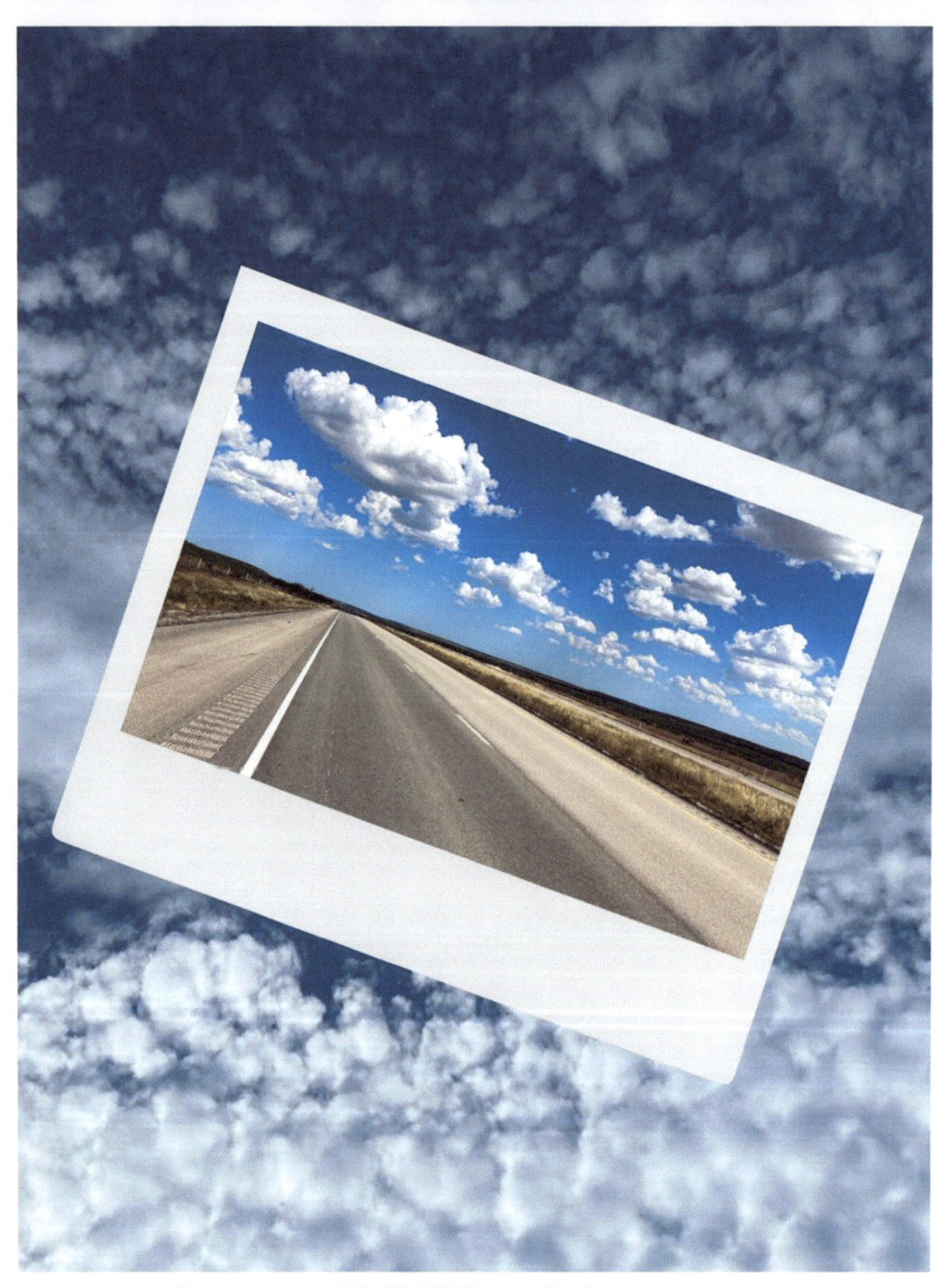

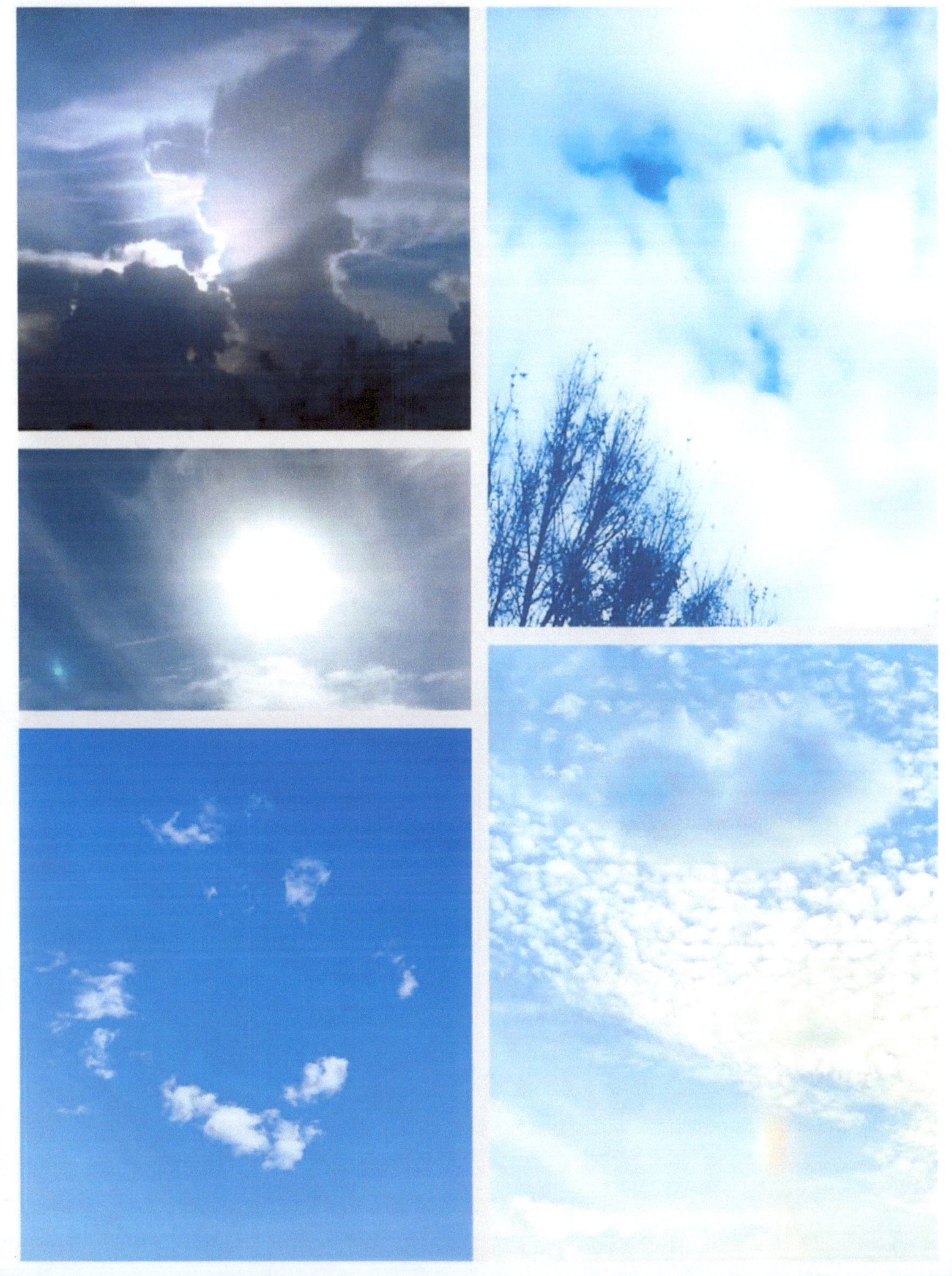

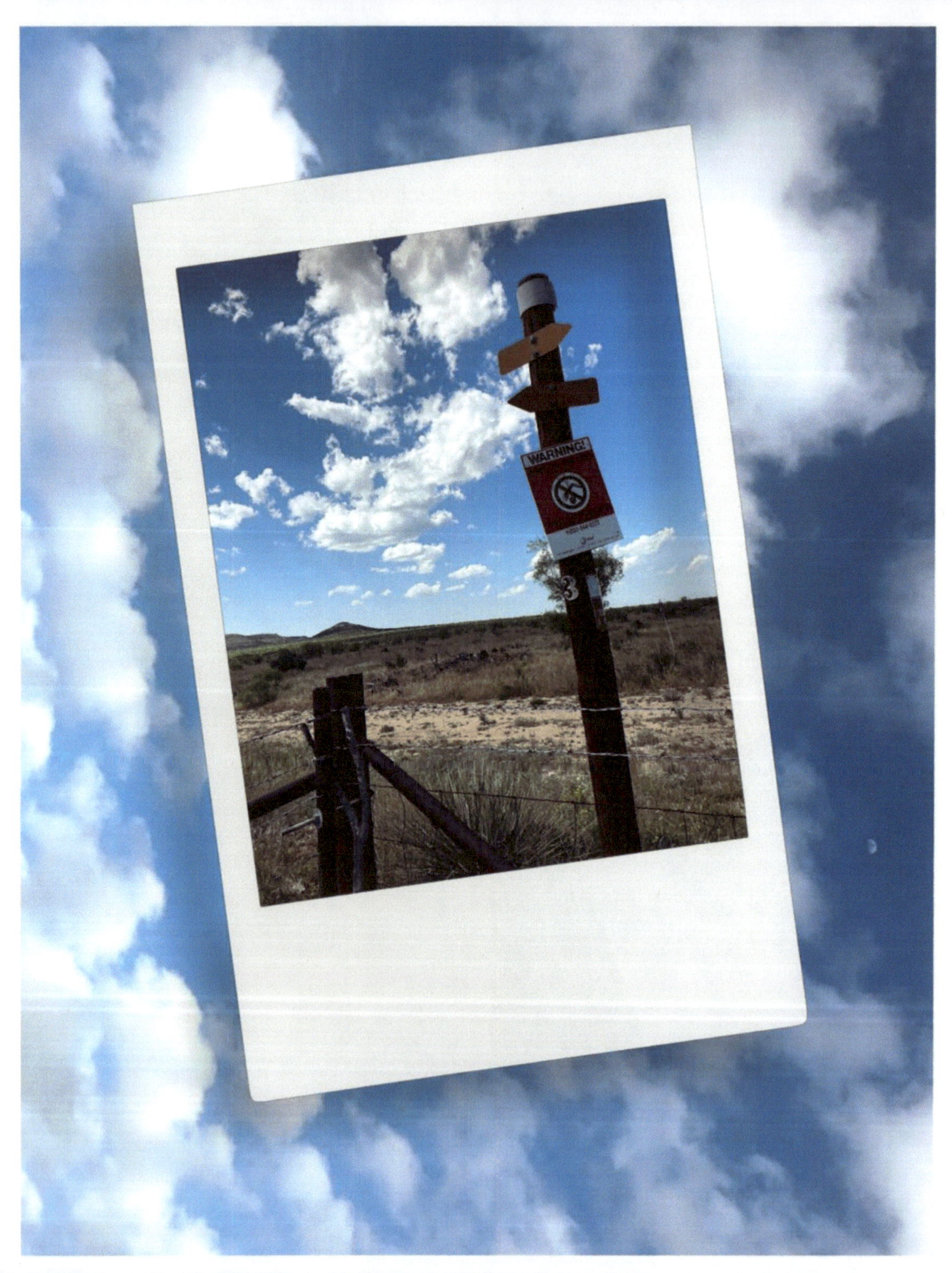
WARNING!

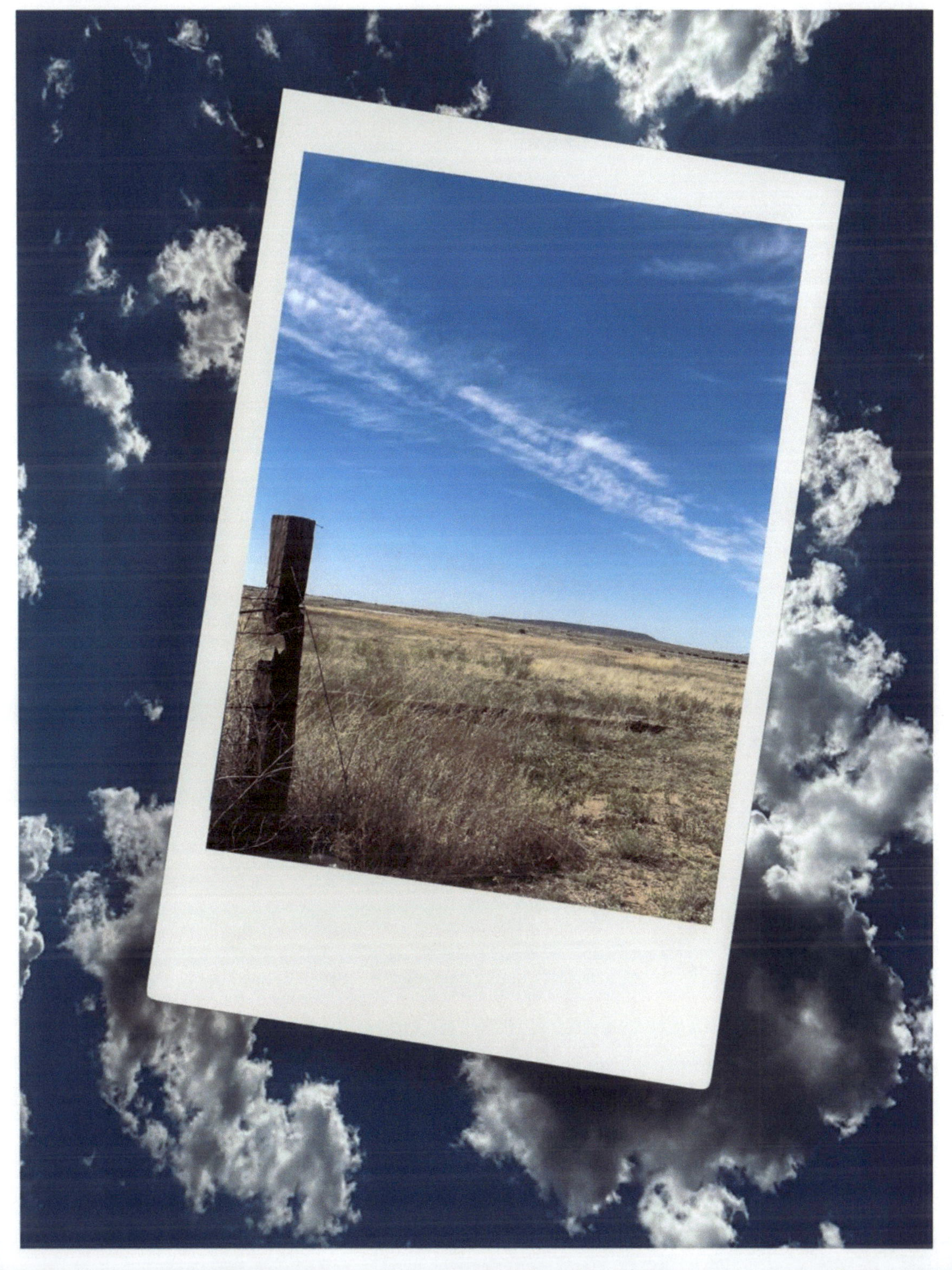

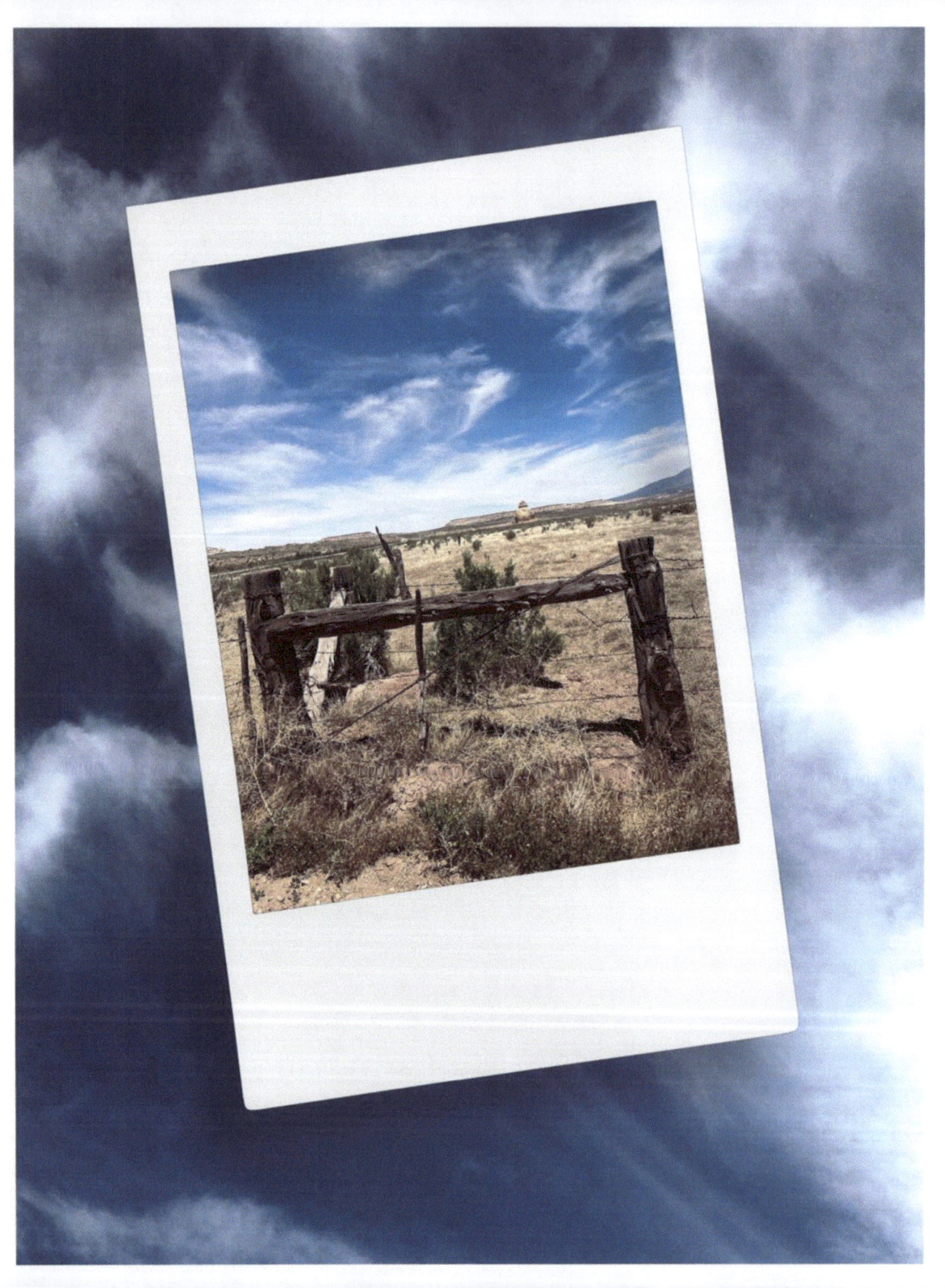

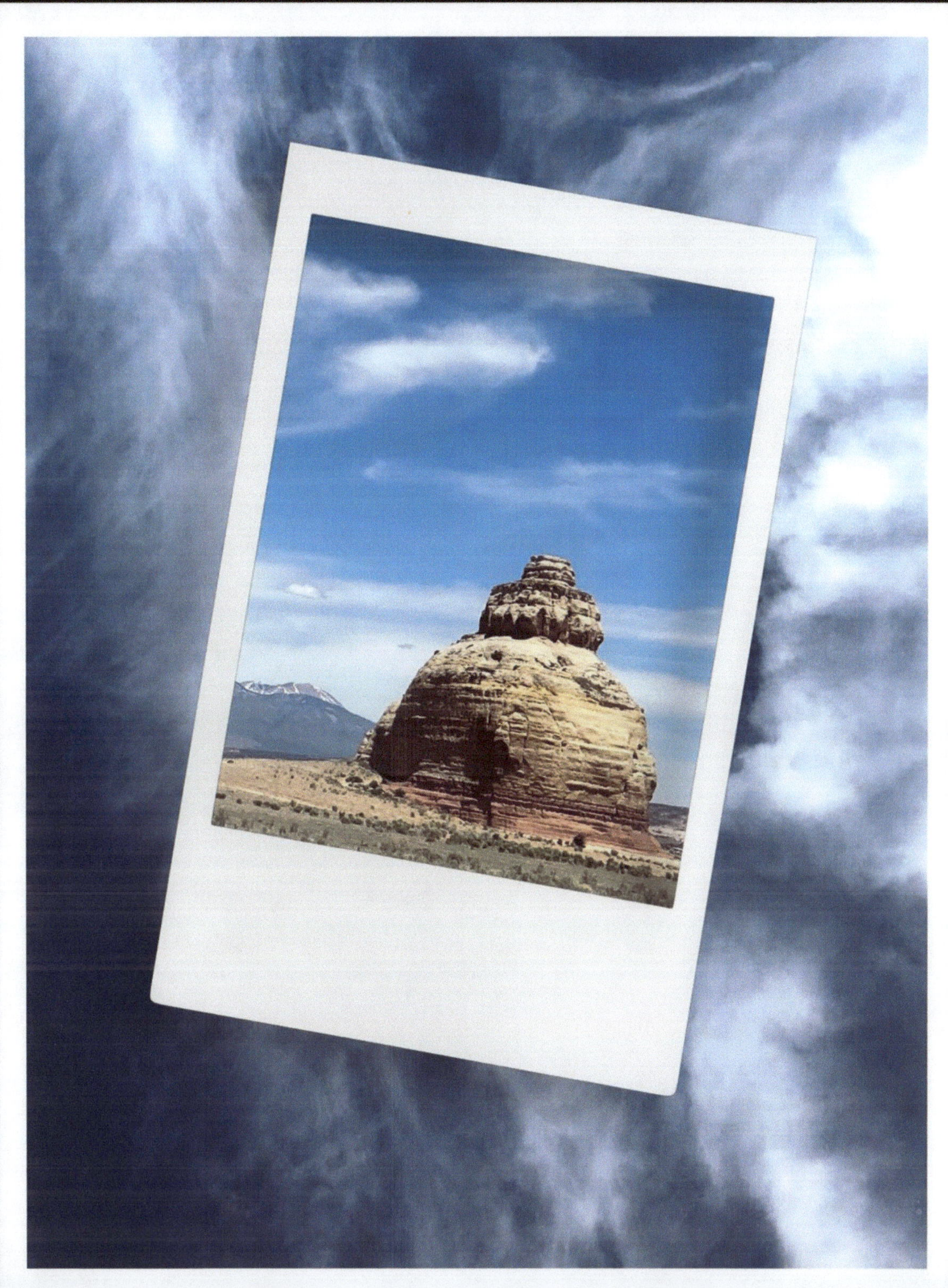

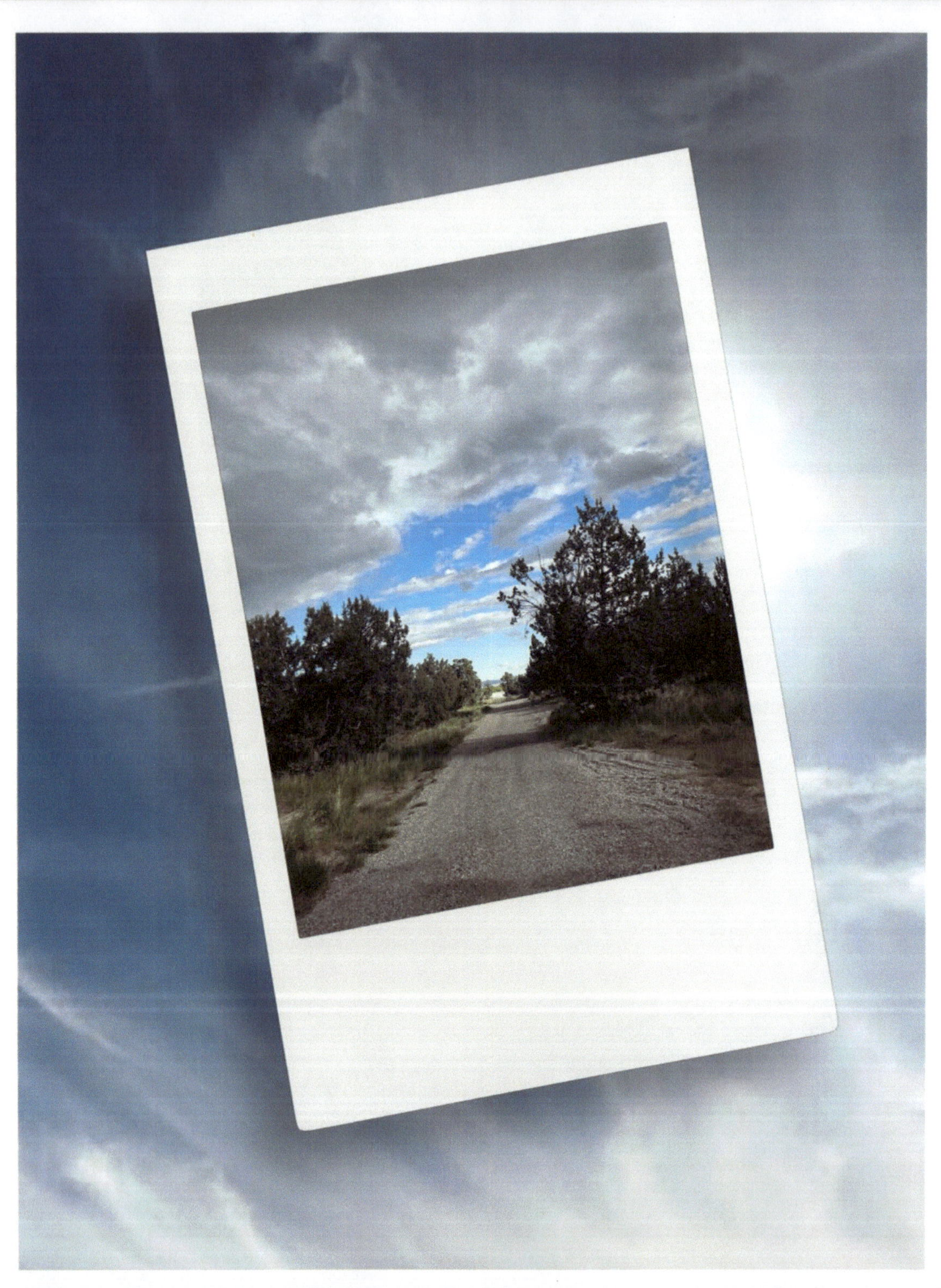

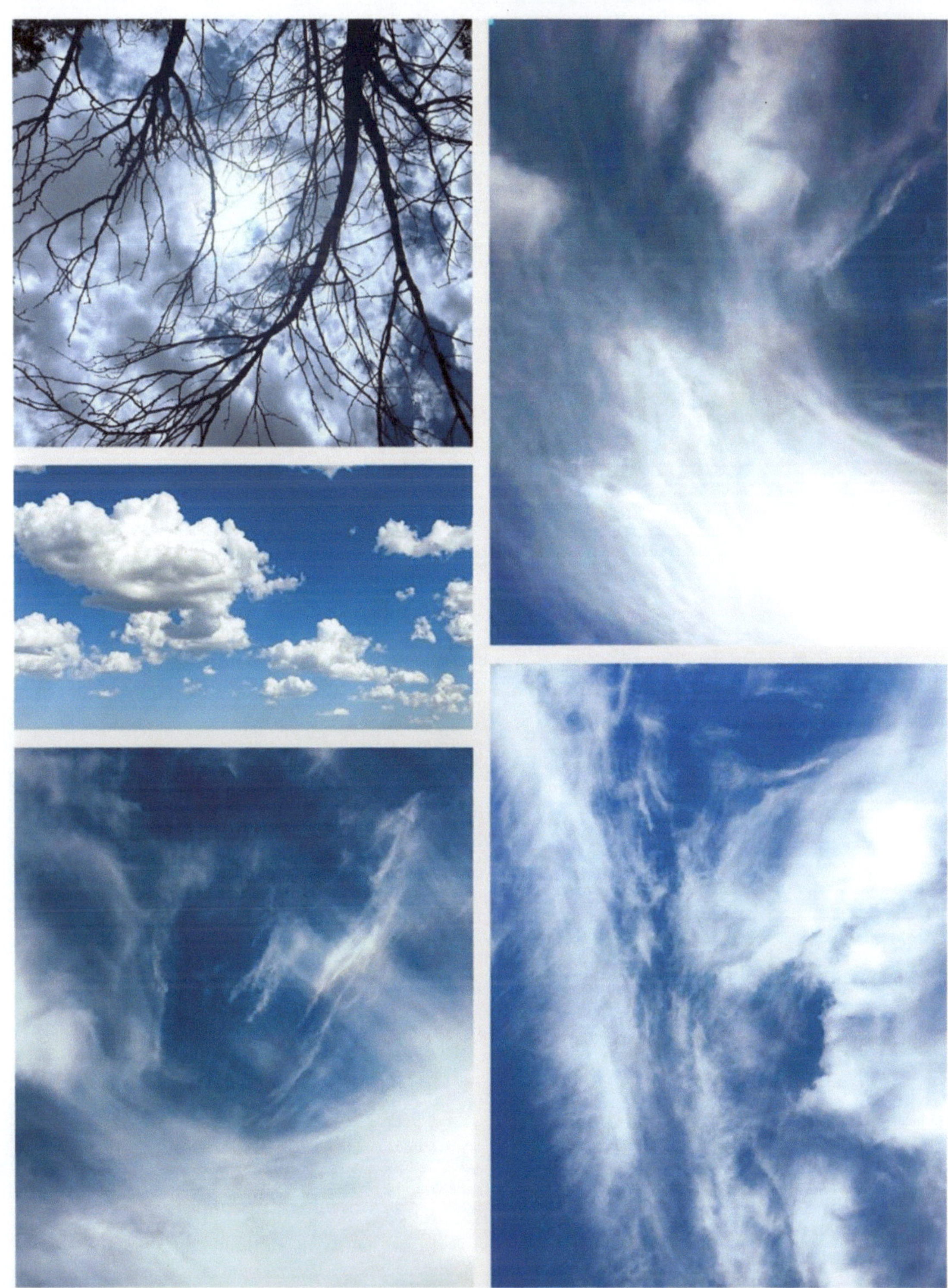

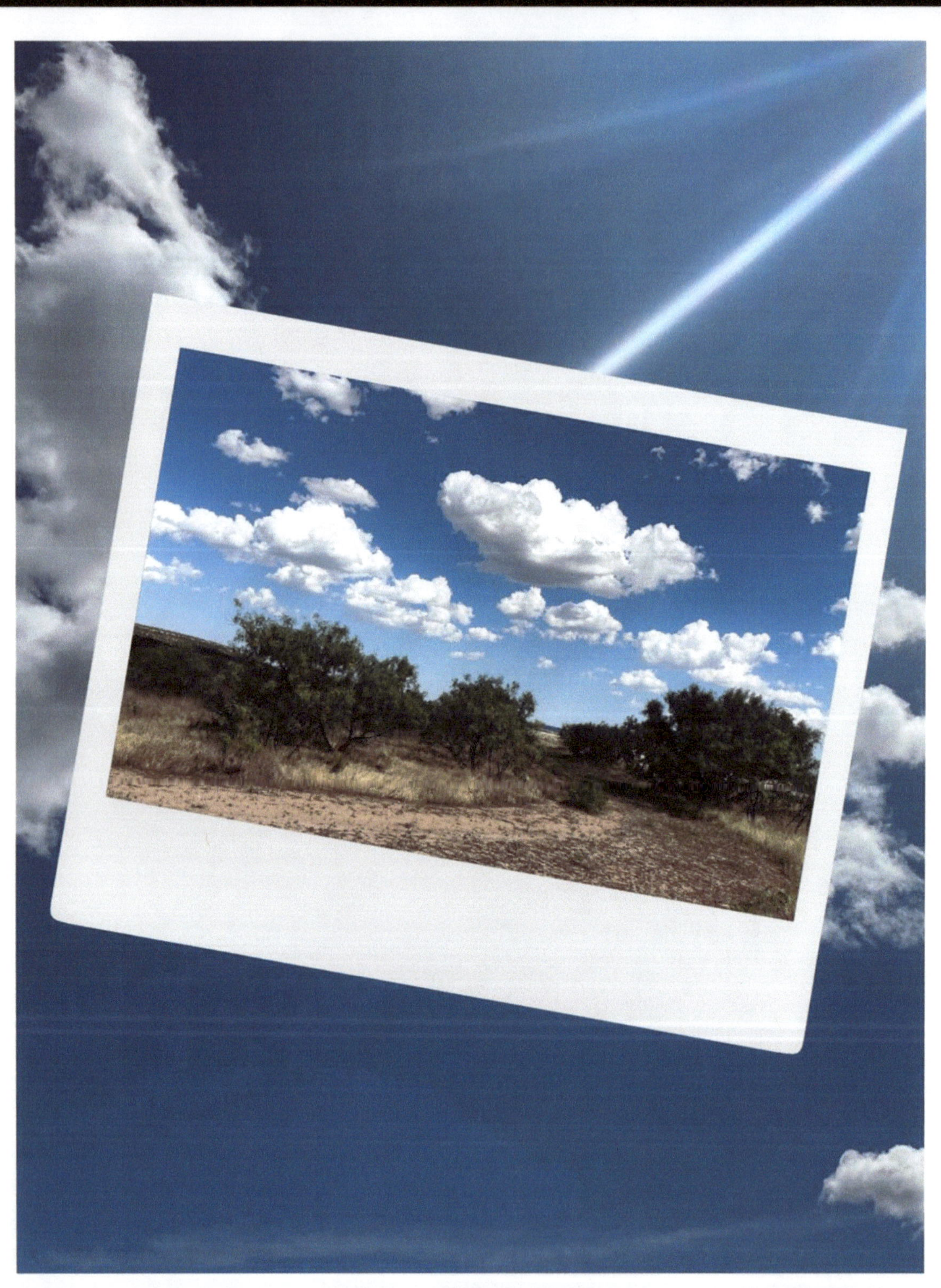

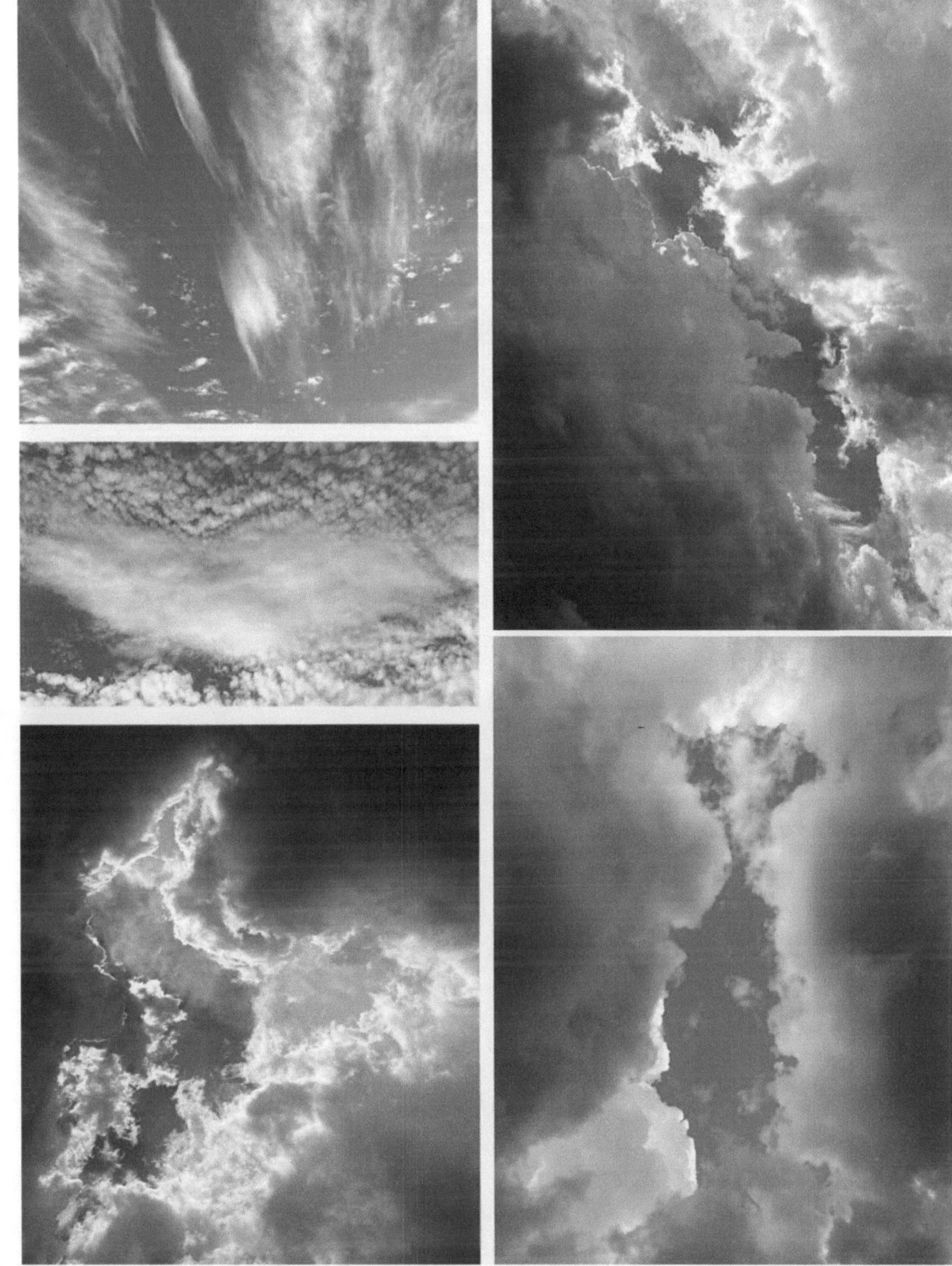

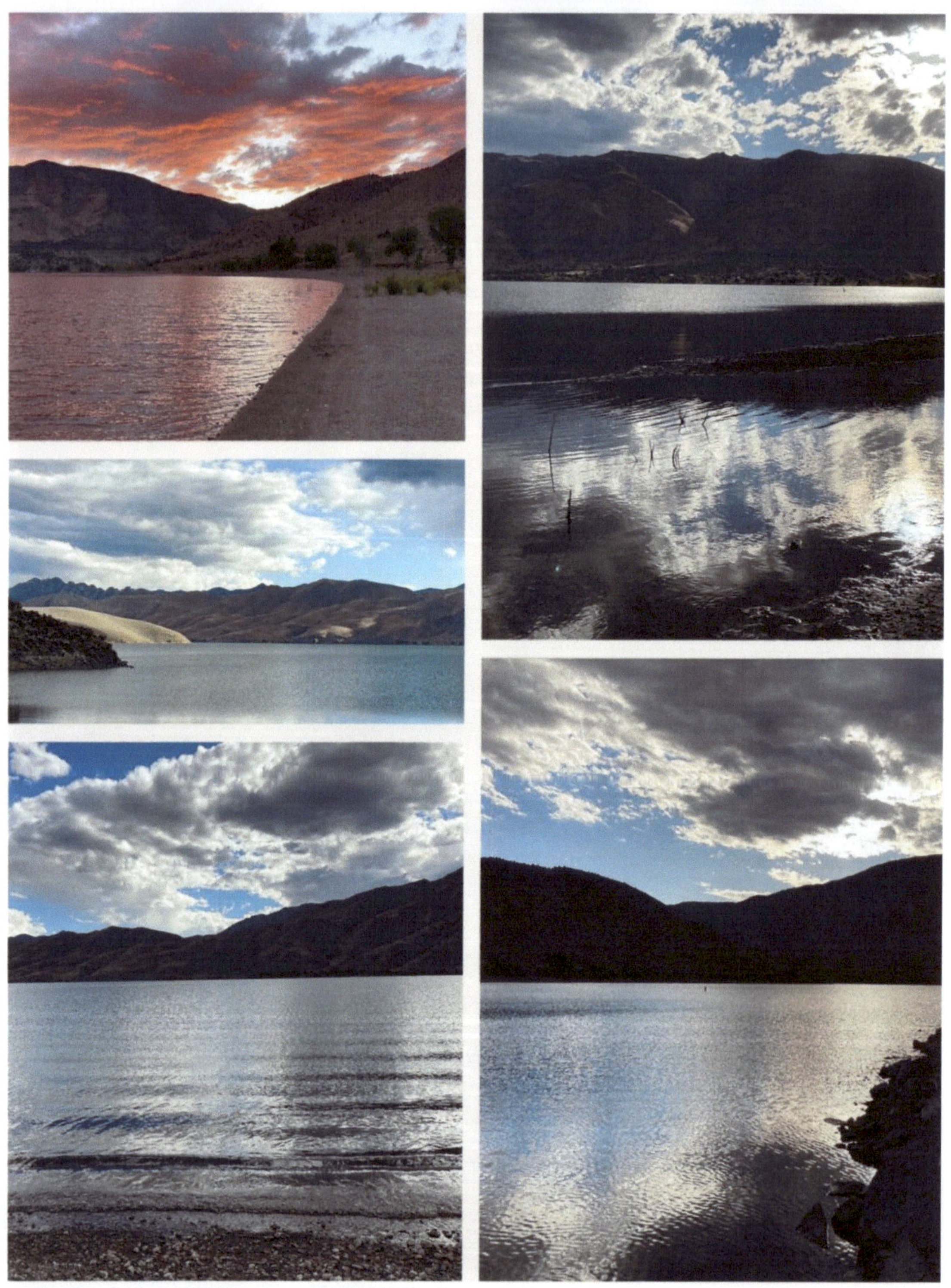

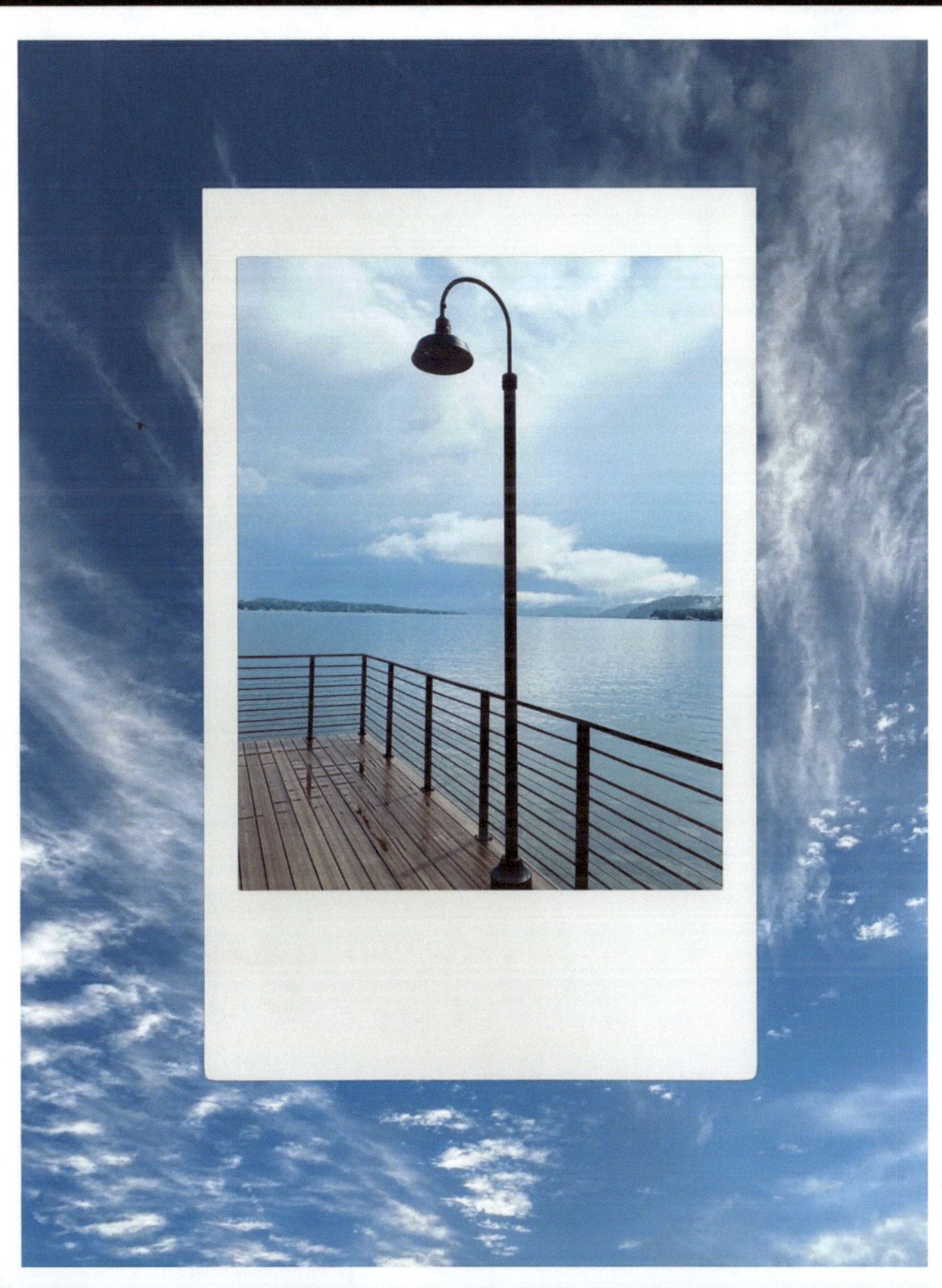

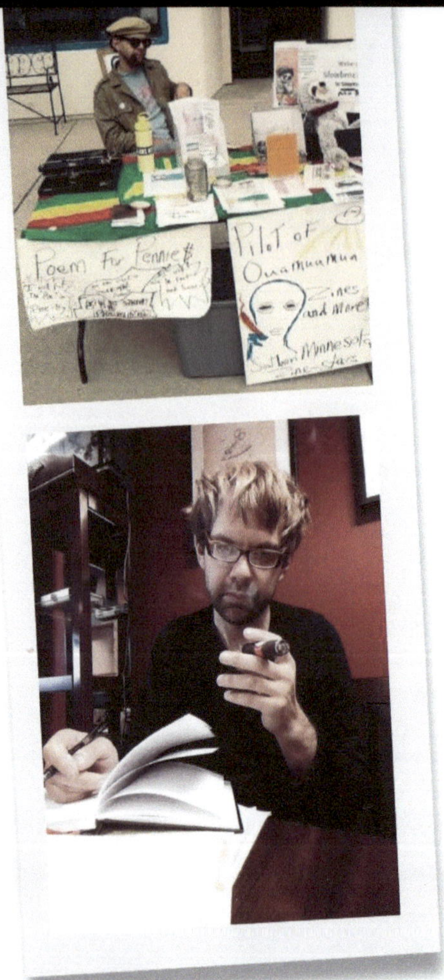

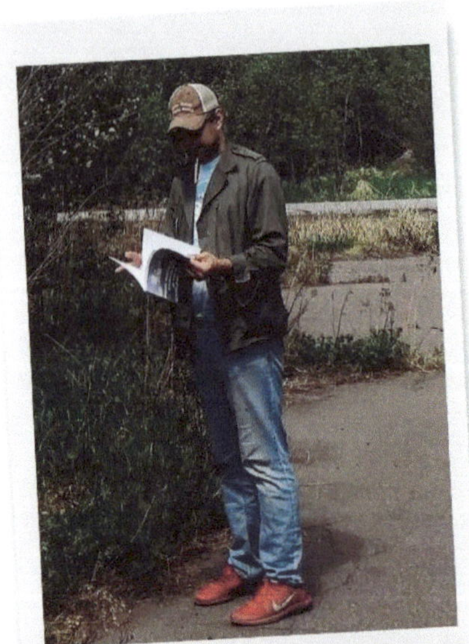

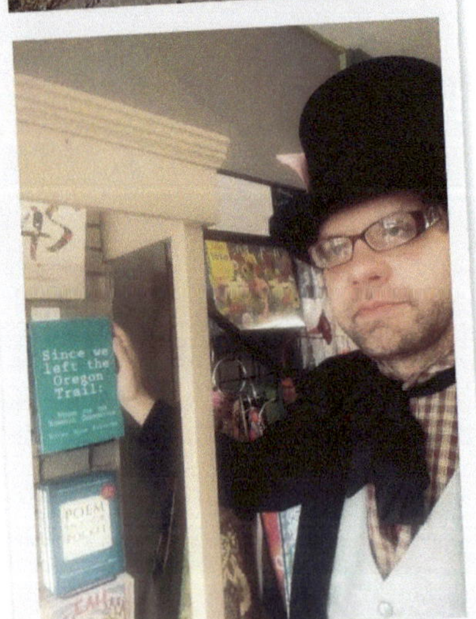

Lucas Alan Dietsche

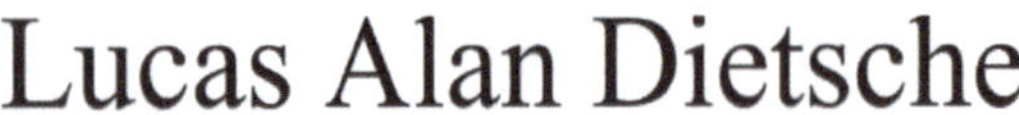

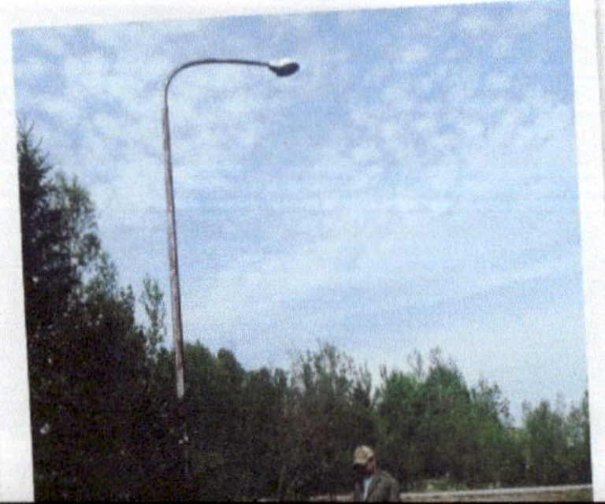

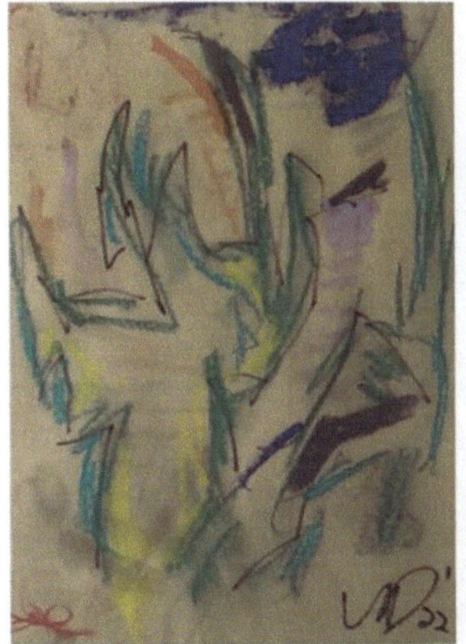

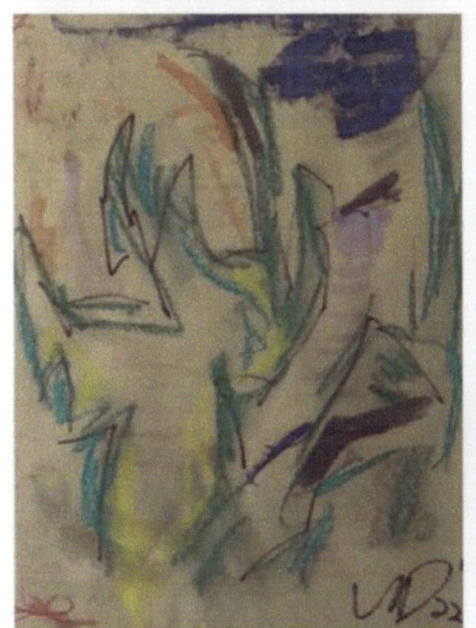

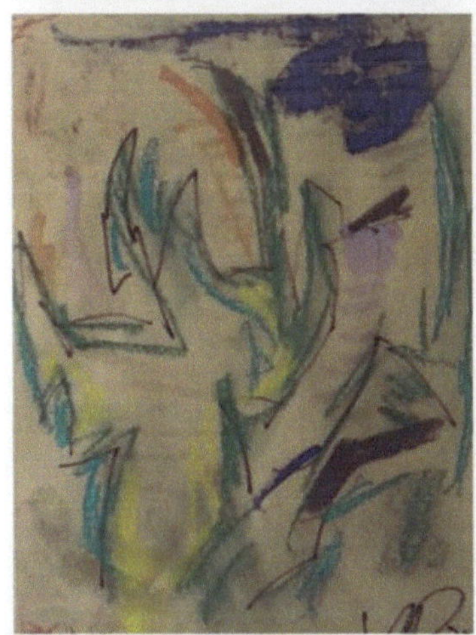

About the Artist

Lucas Alan Dietsche is a PhD student of Art, Theory, Aesthetic and a poet-builder/imaginanian without any equal caliber of his contemporaries. Inspired by dada, post-modernism, surrealism, and modernism, he pulls and plucks out of the multiversal to disrupt and critique banality and convention.

email at lucasdietsche81@gmail.com

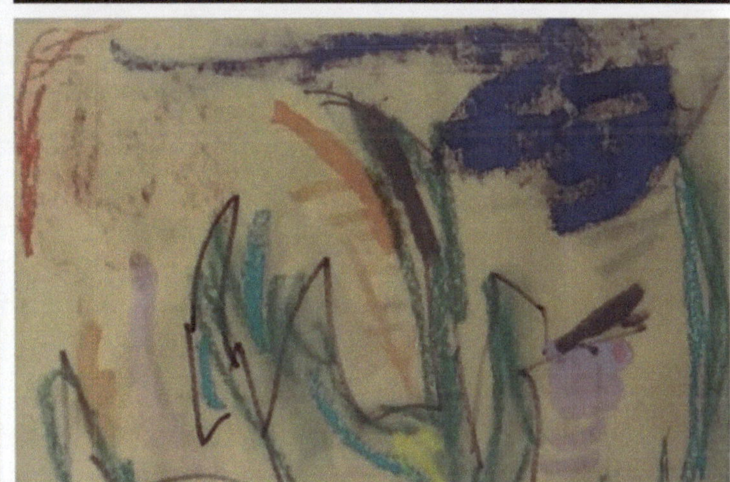

"For GODS Throw Away CHILDREN"

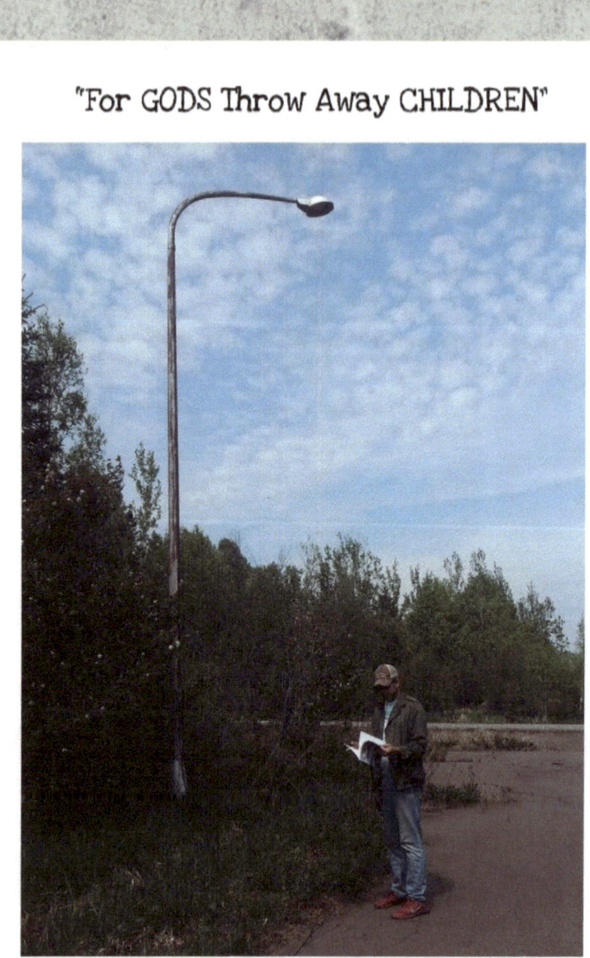

Taconite Harbor, MN

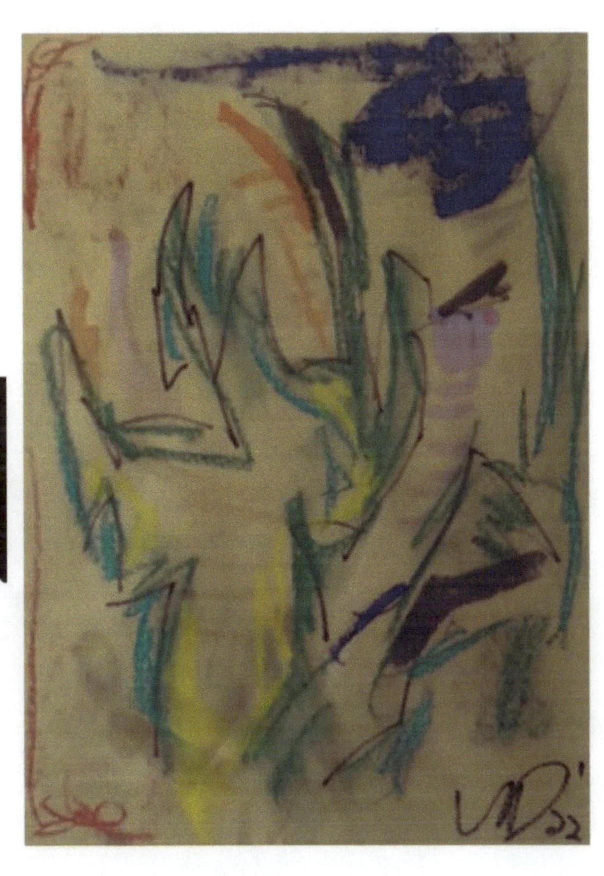

" i could'nt wait to die to sell
this for 50,000 dollars."

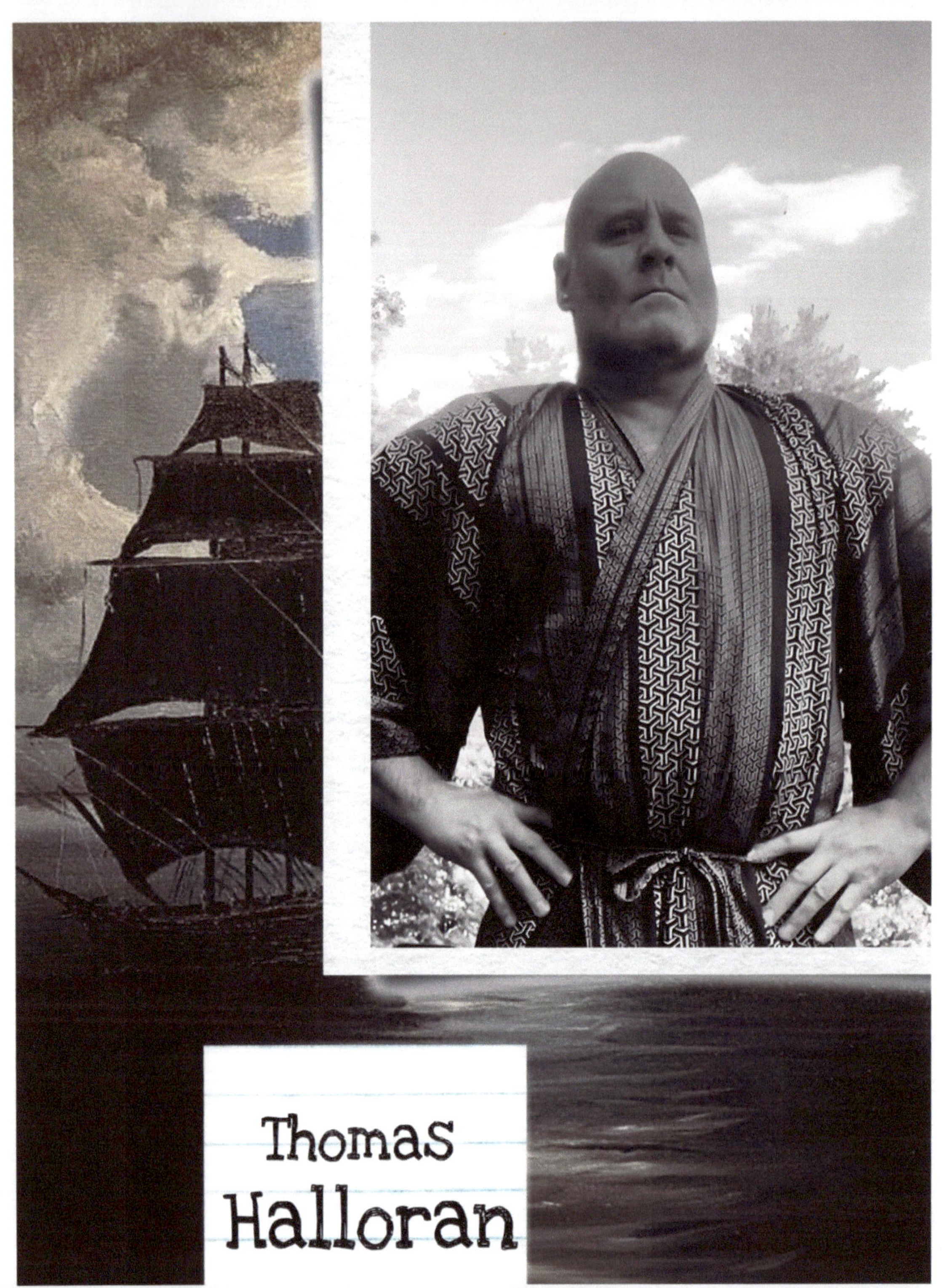
Thomas
Halloran

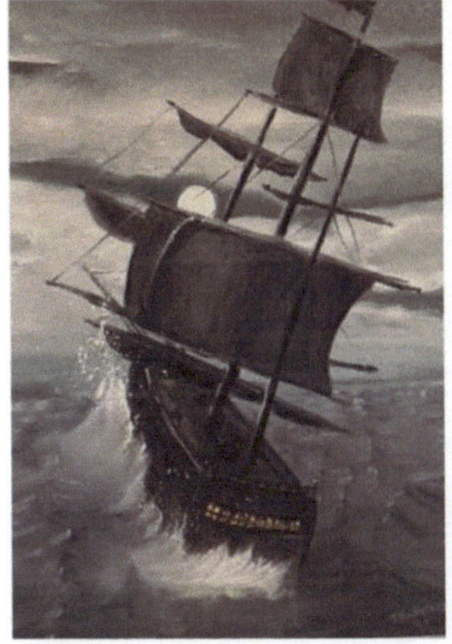

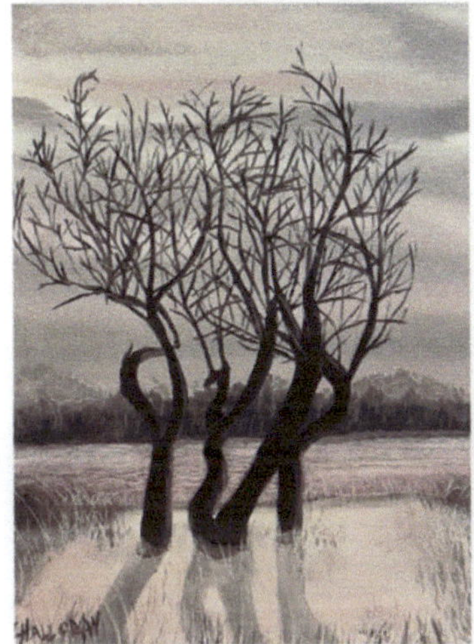

About the Artist

Thomas Halloran

Professor of aesthetics

bingeful ascetic

Crisis Intervention Specialist

Contrarian Thinker

Jujiteiro

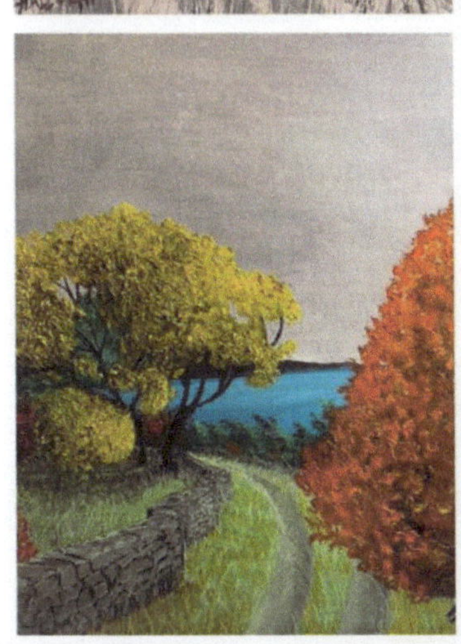

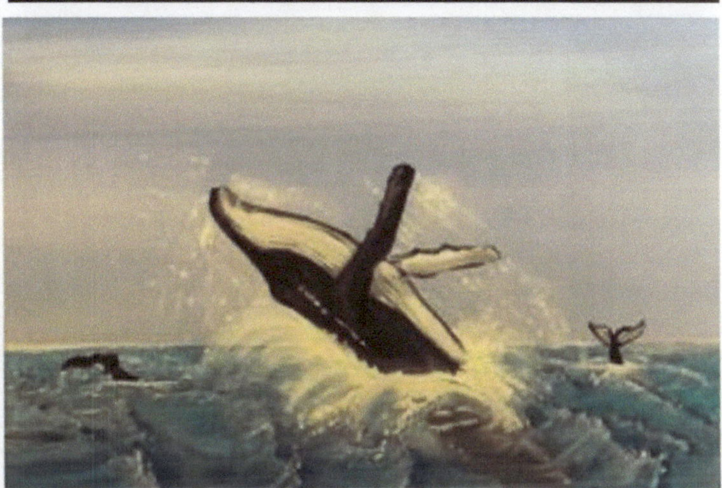

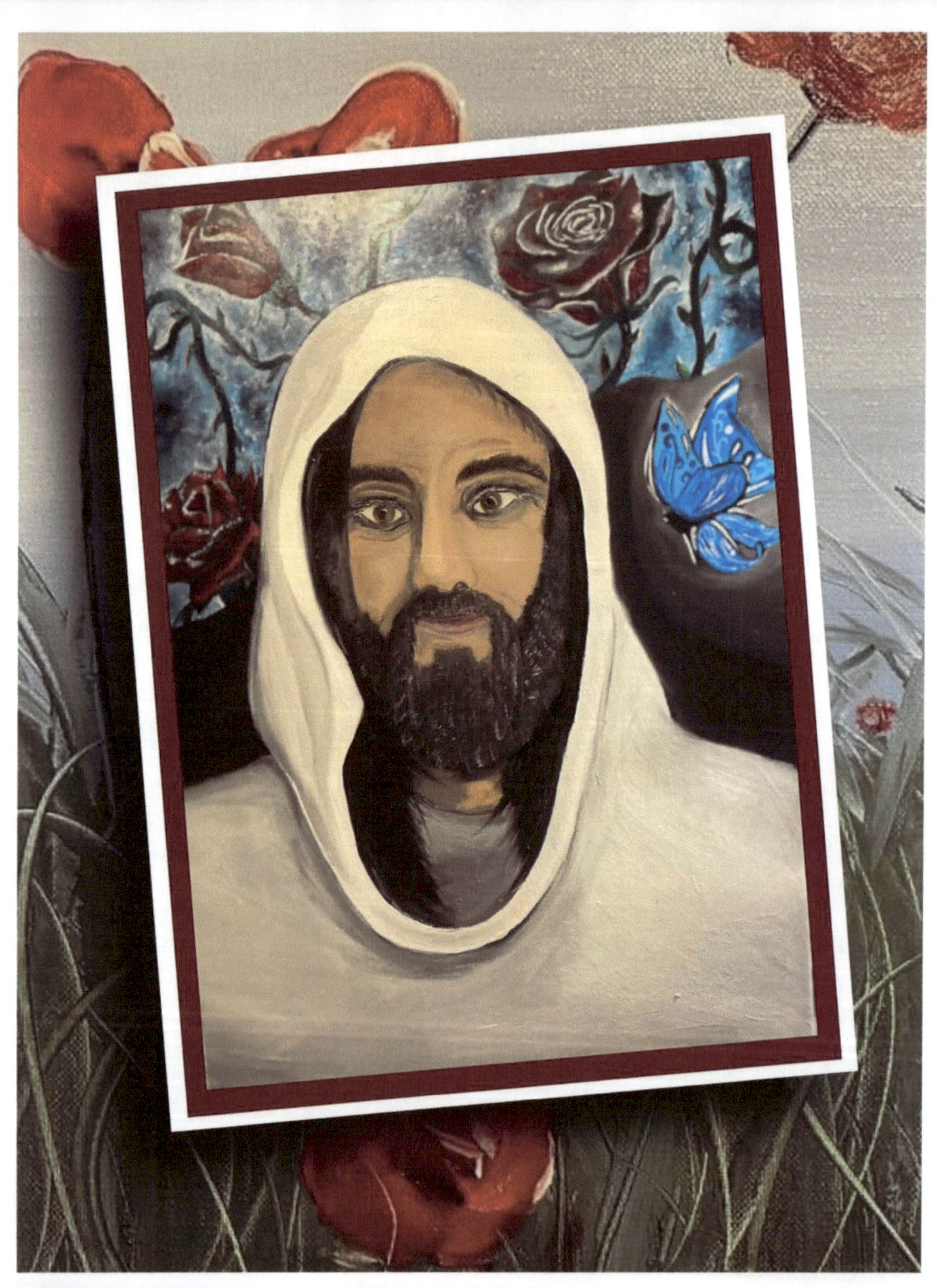

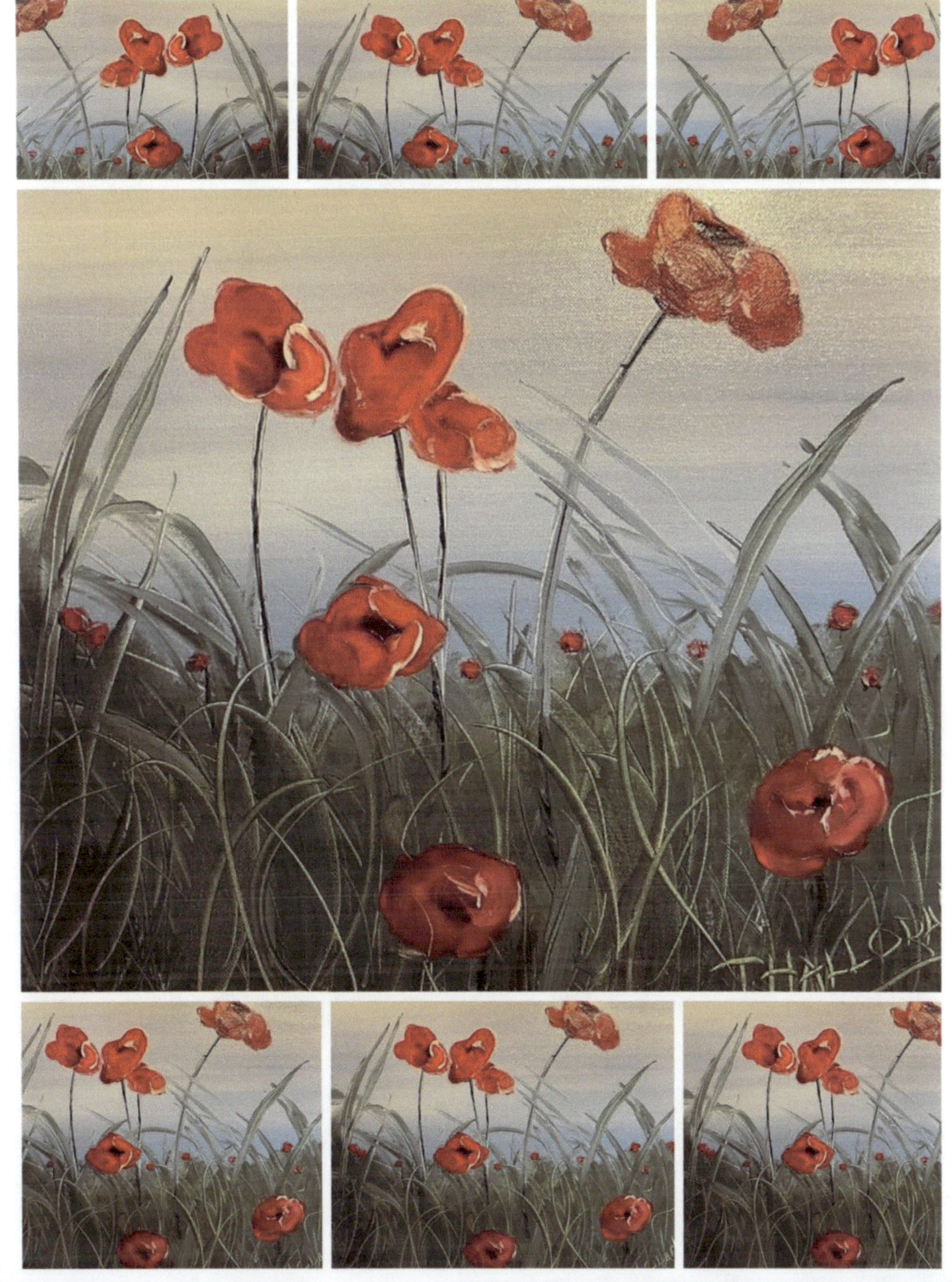

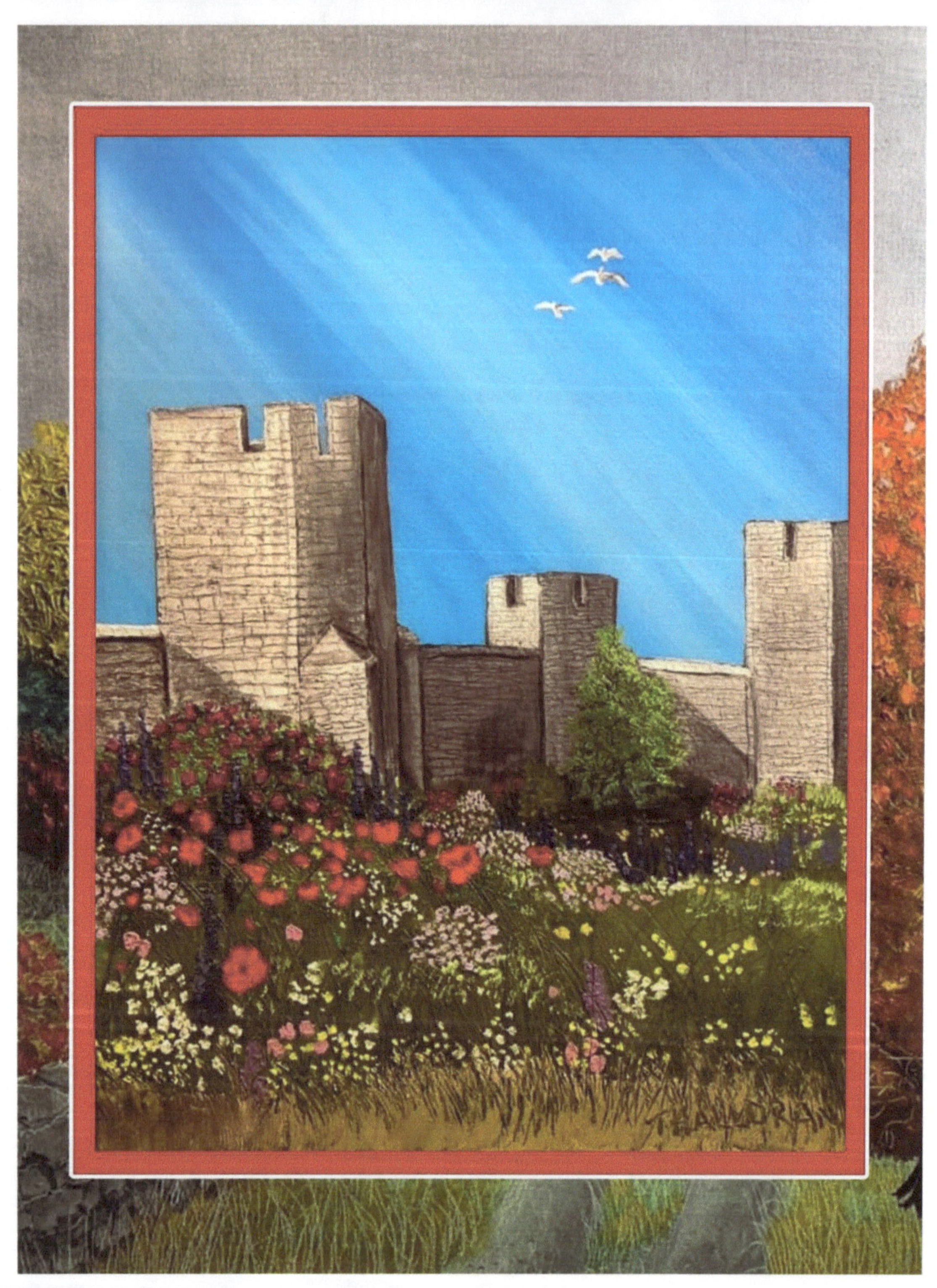

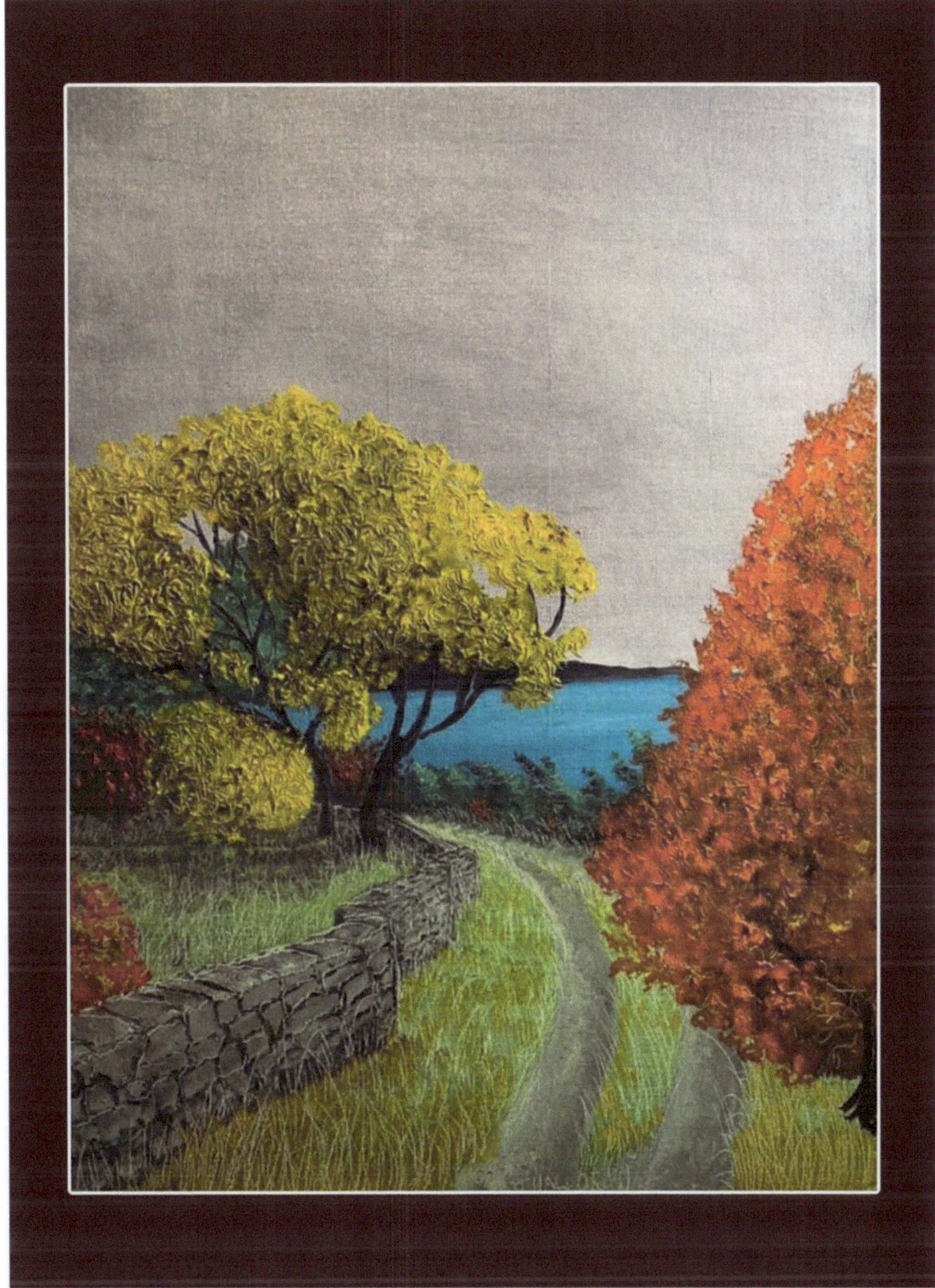

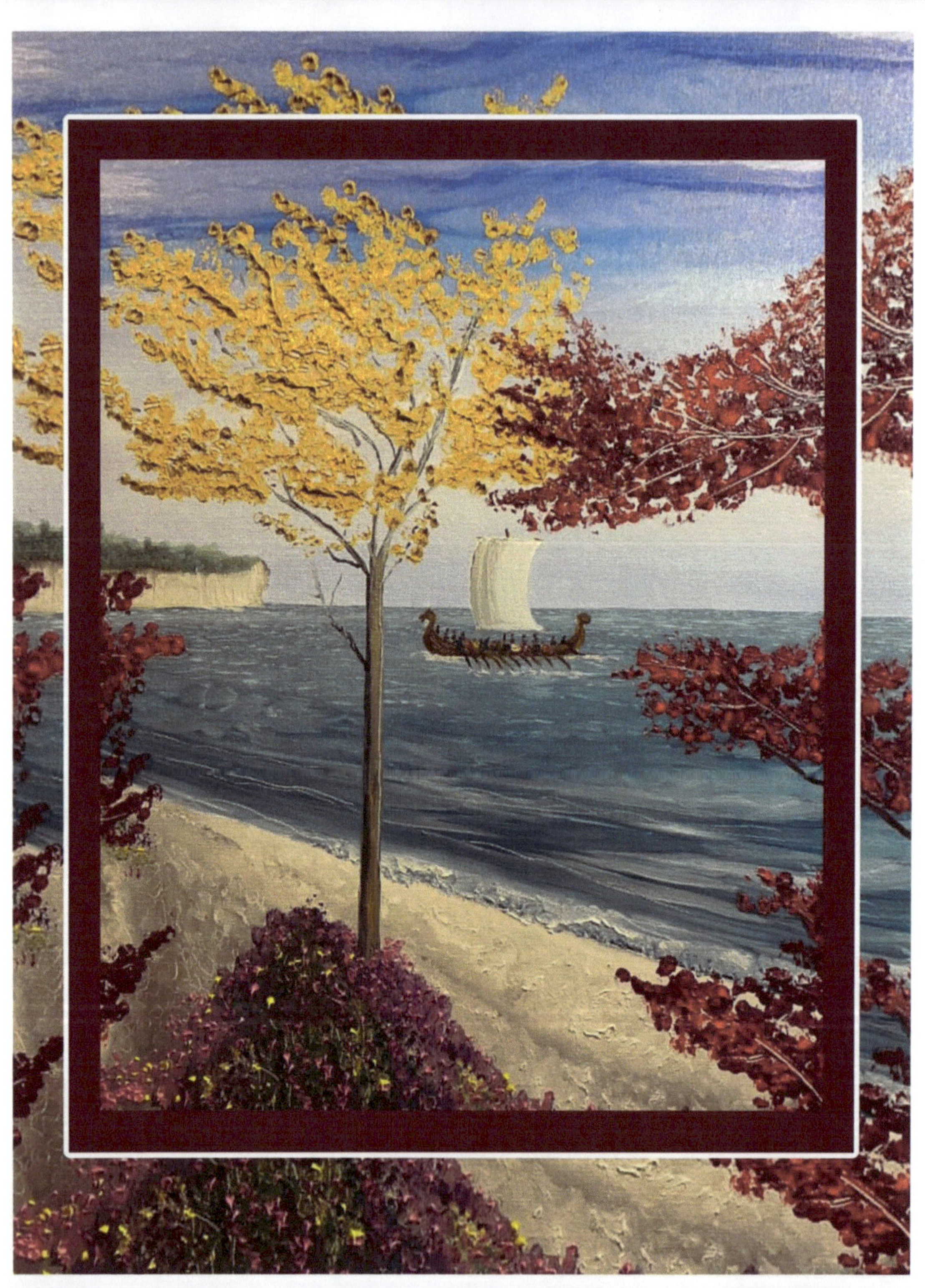

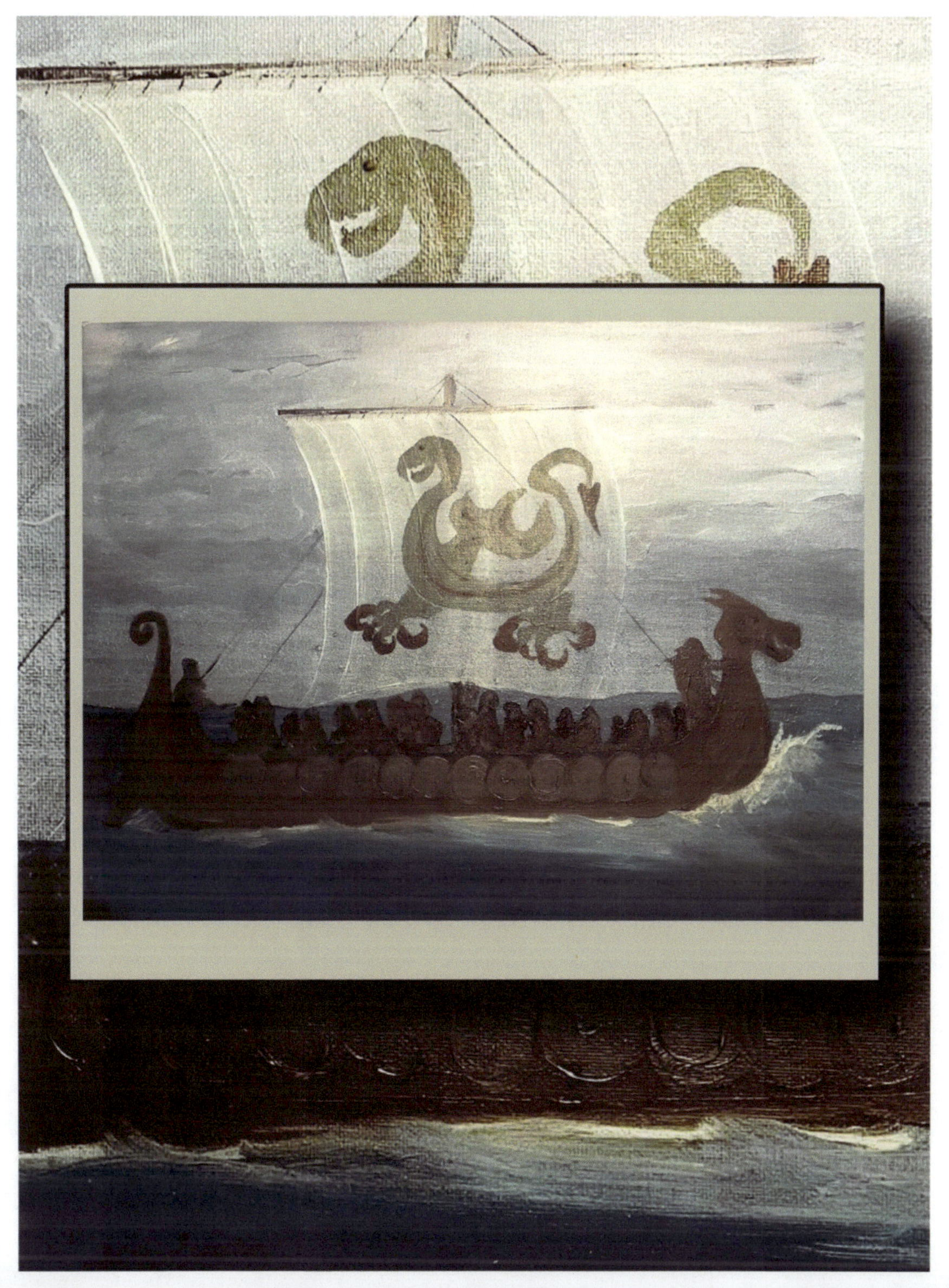

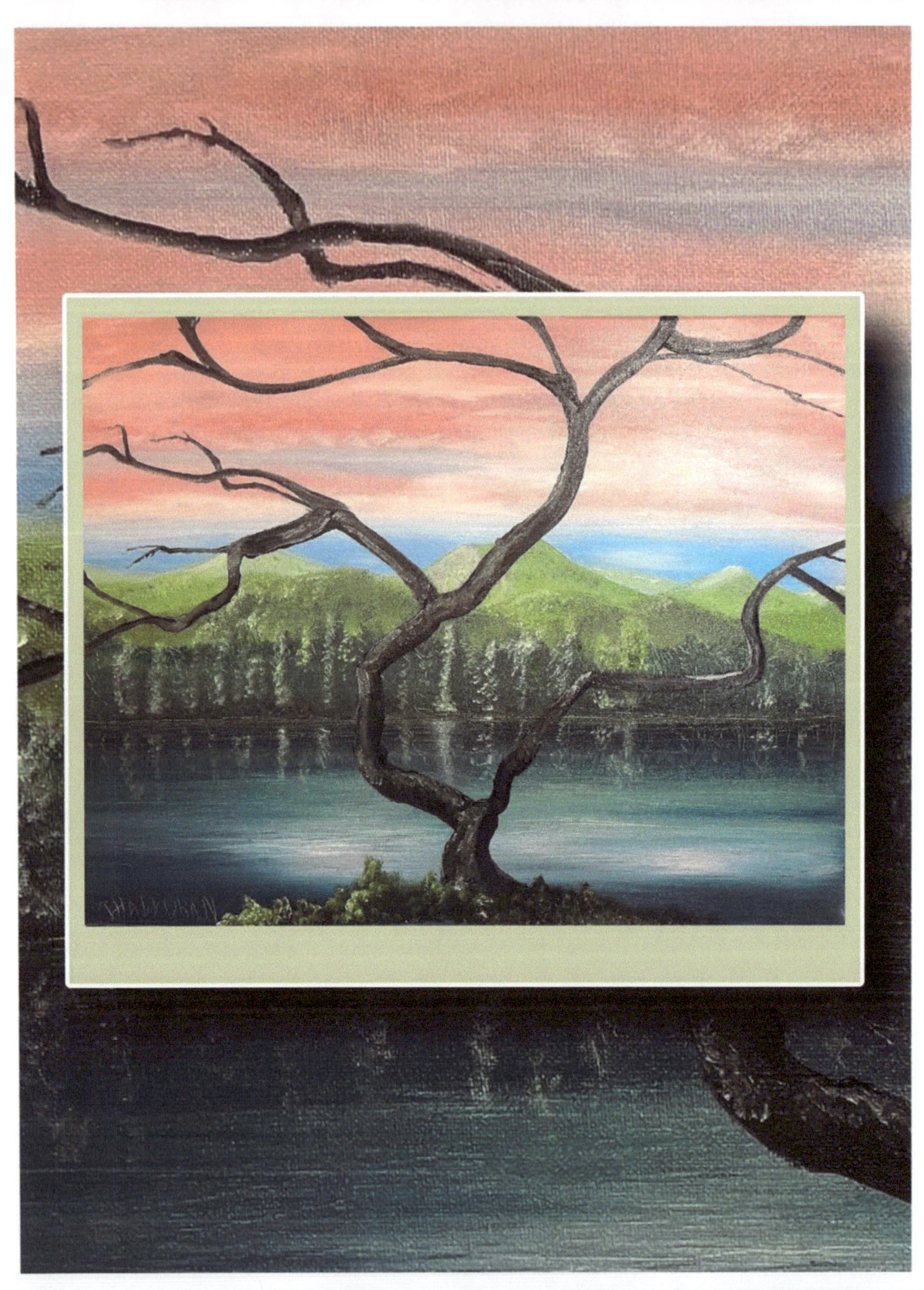

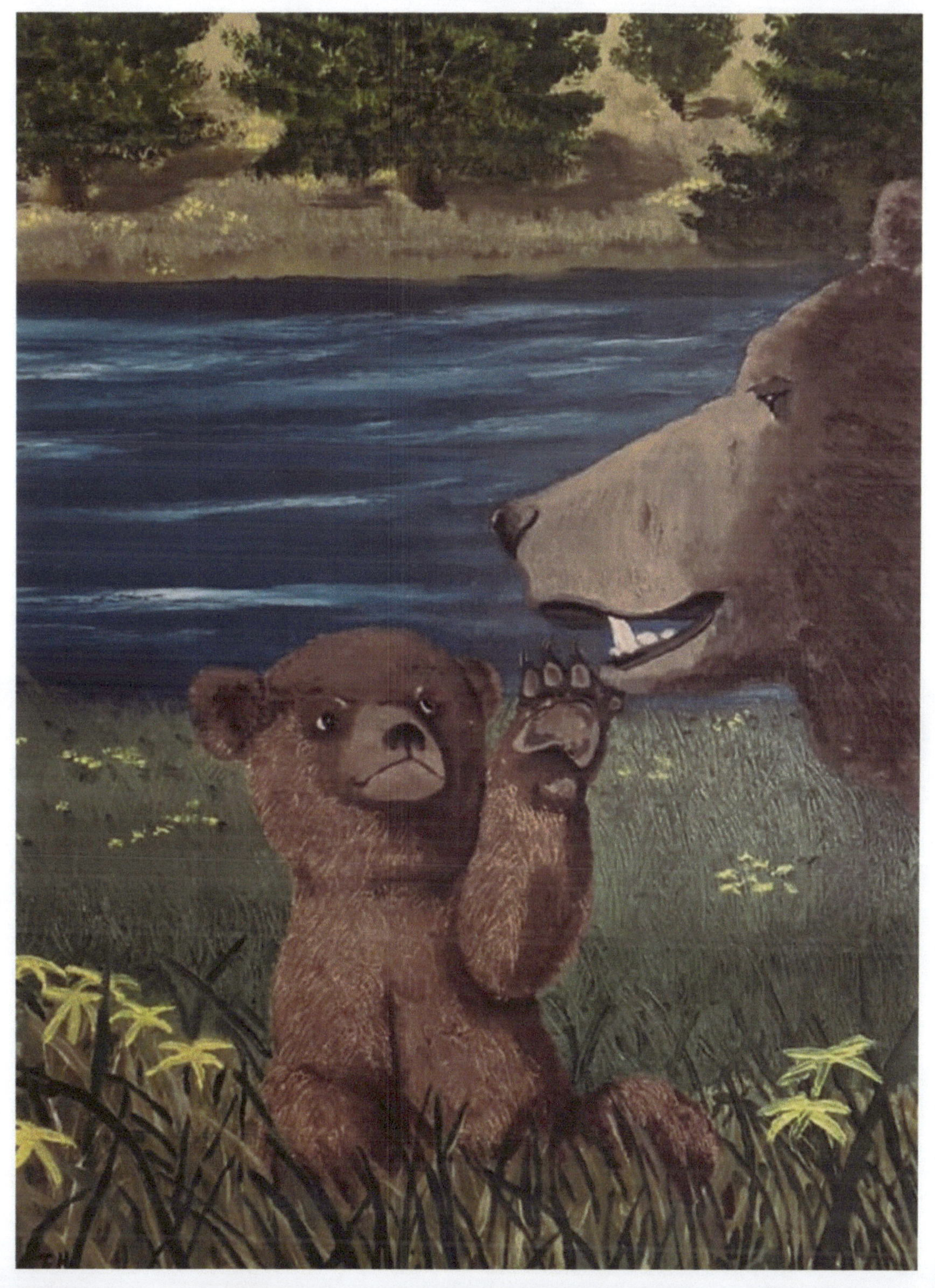

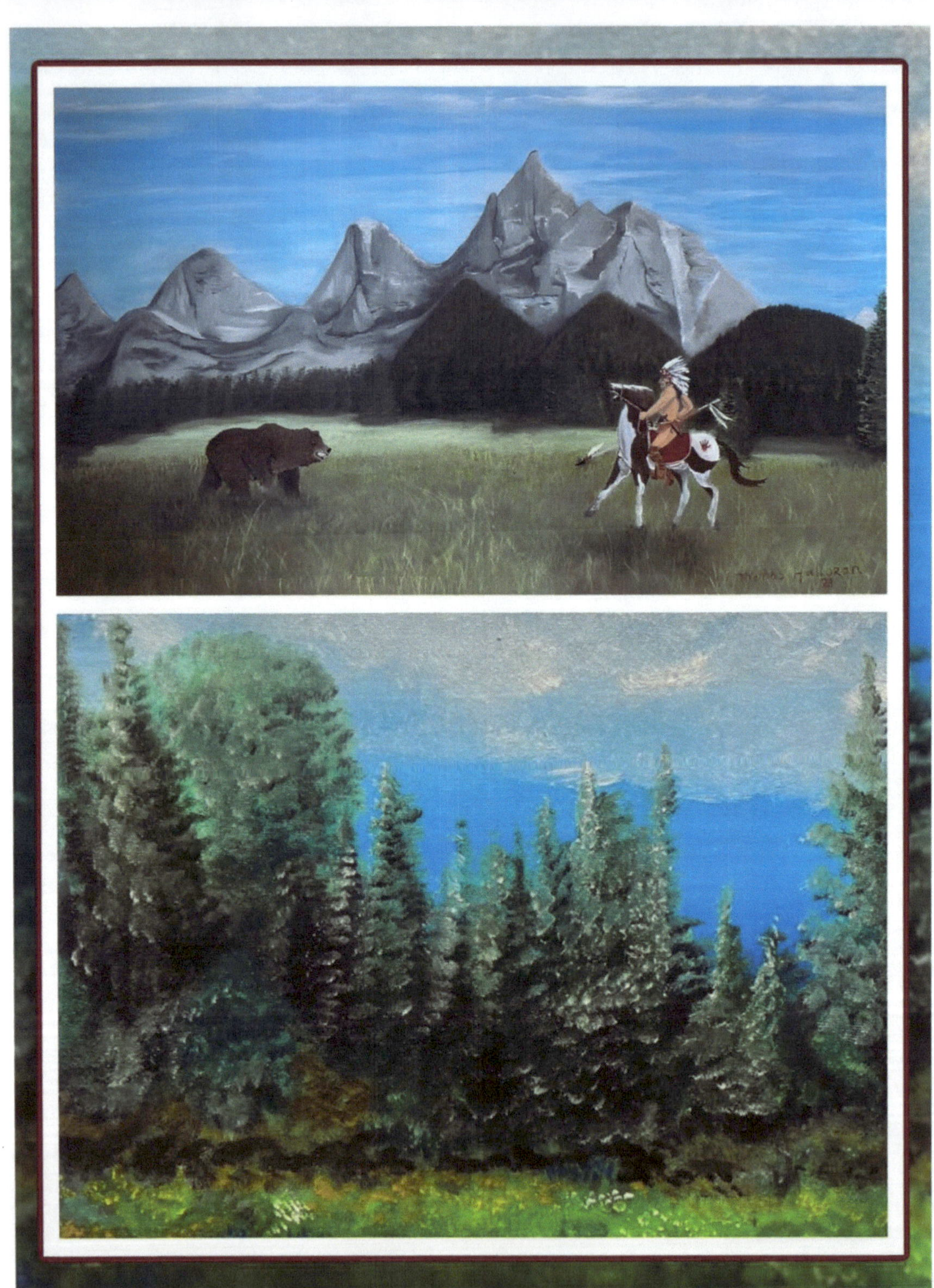

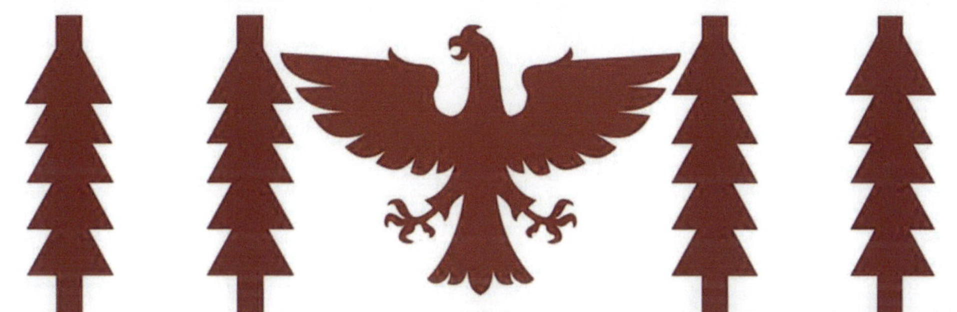

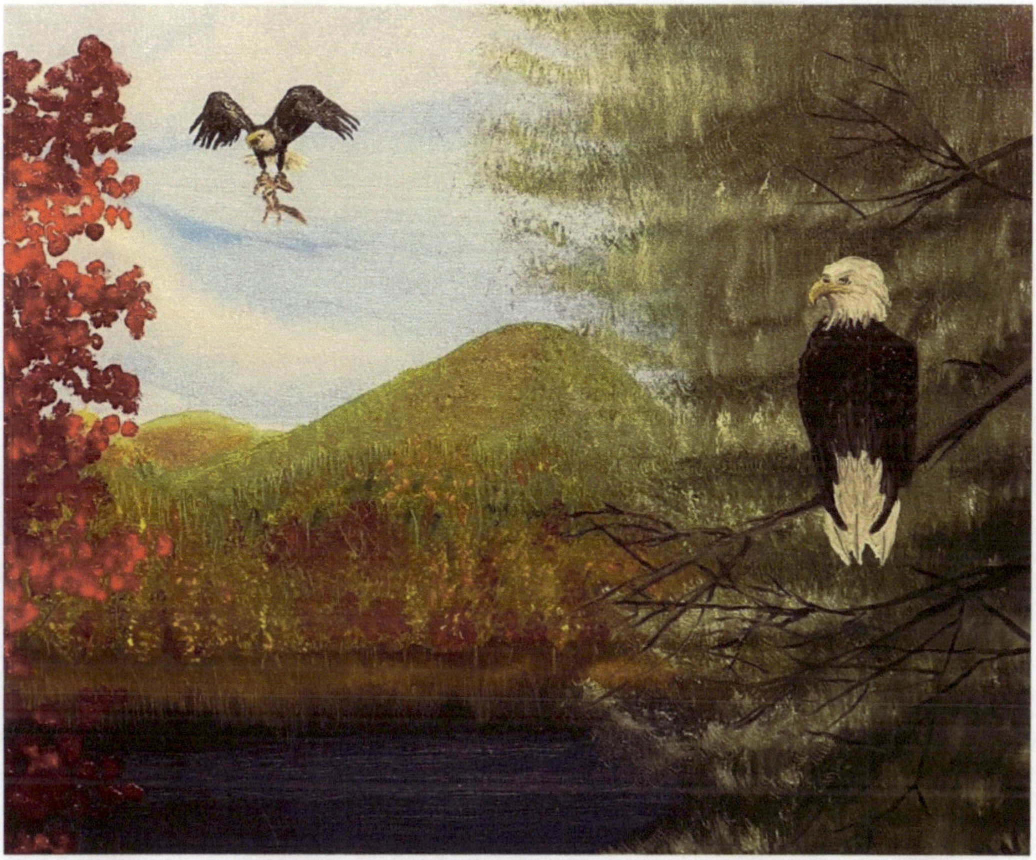

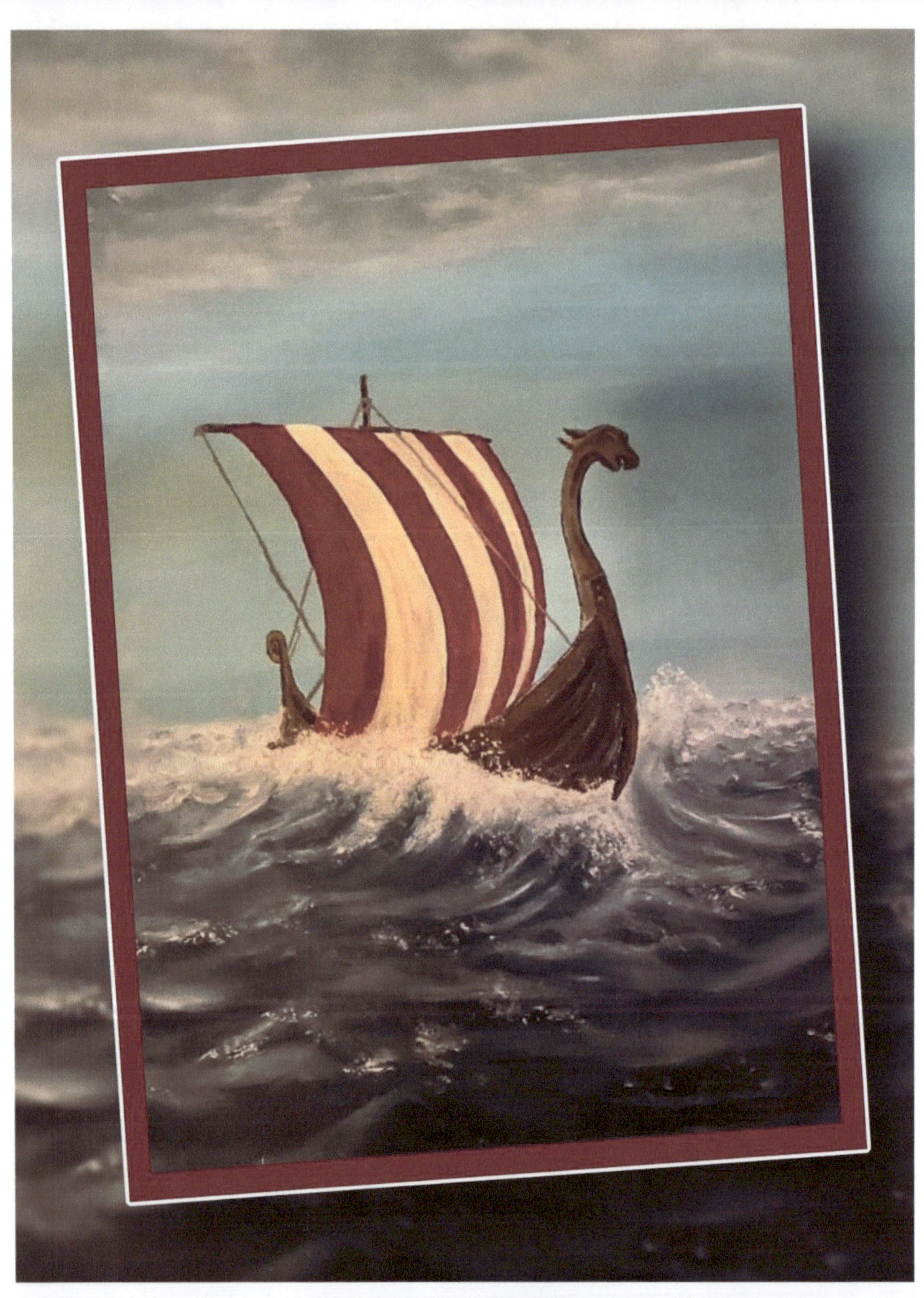

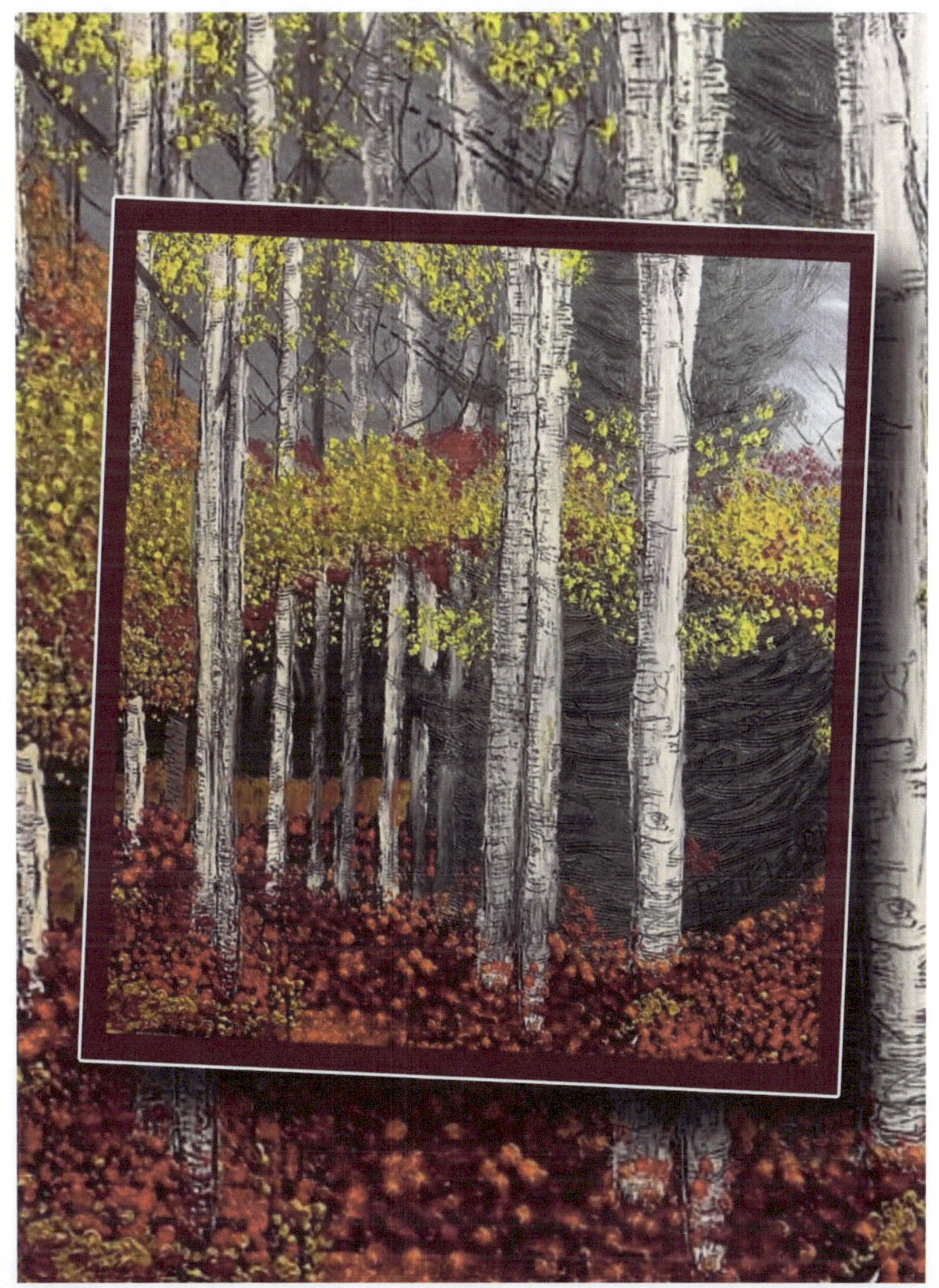

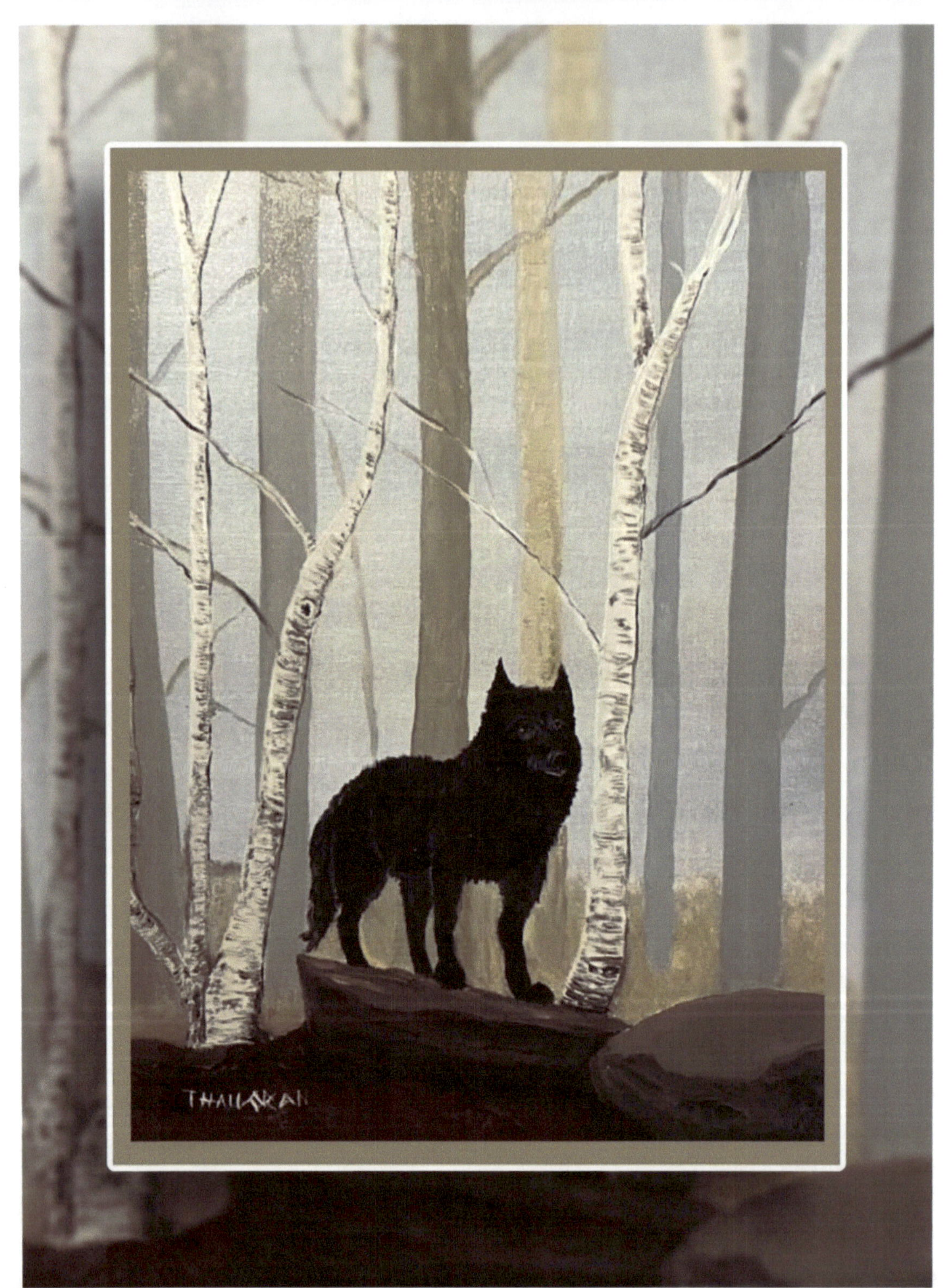
THAILAKAN

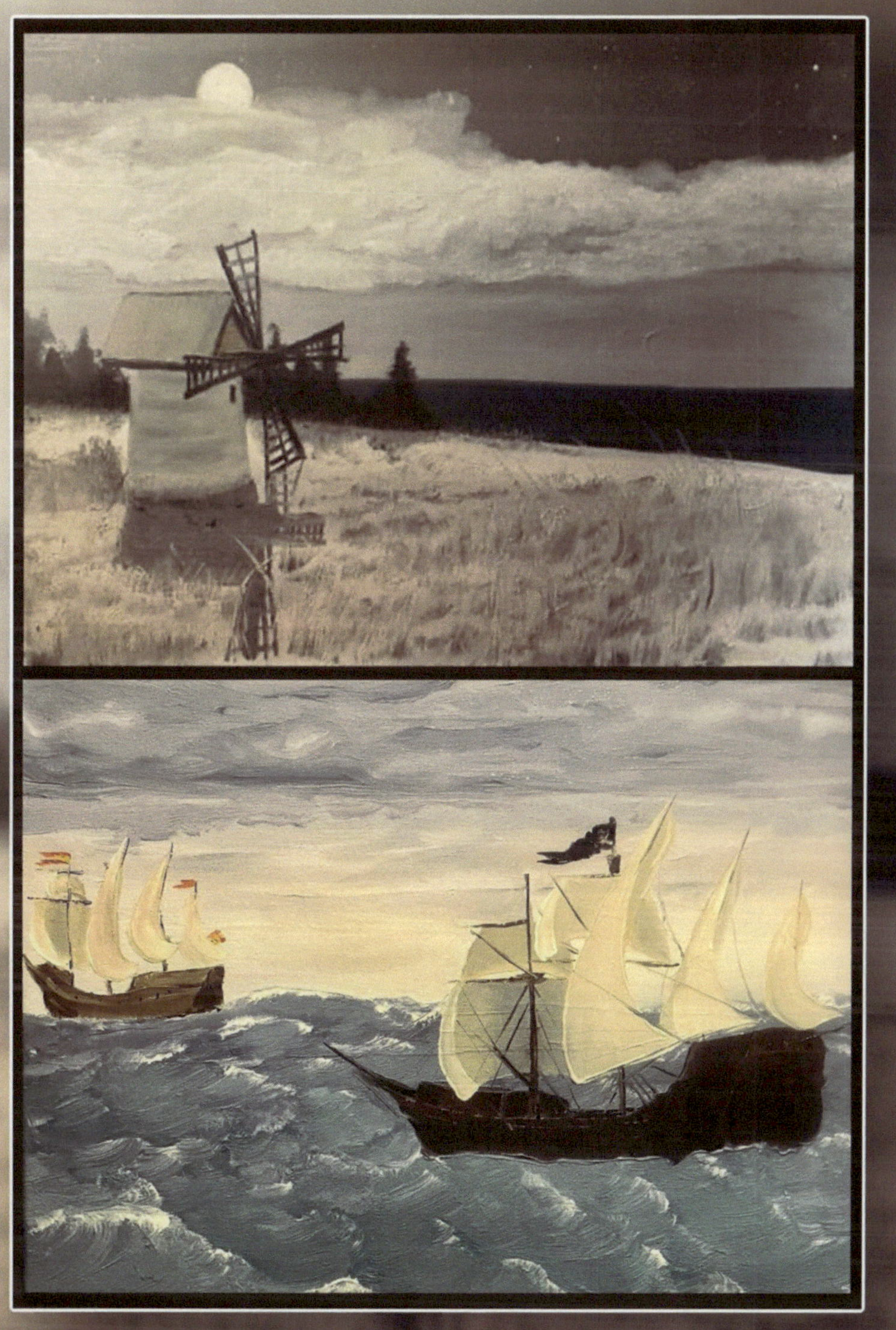

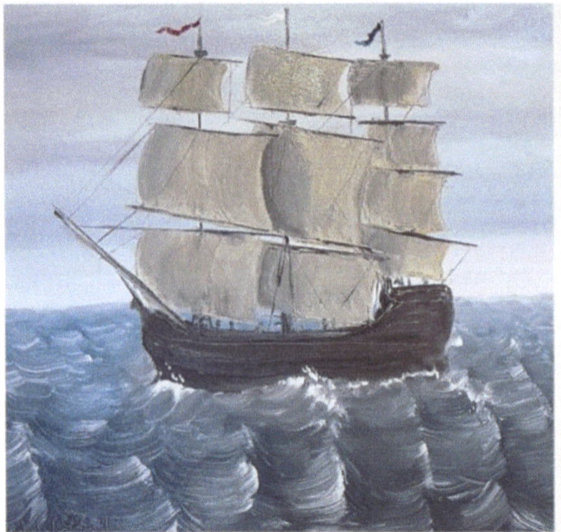

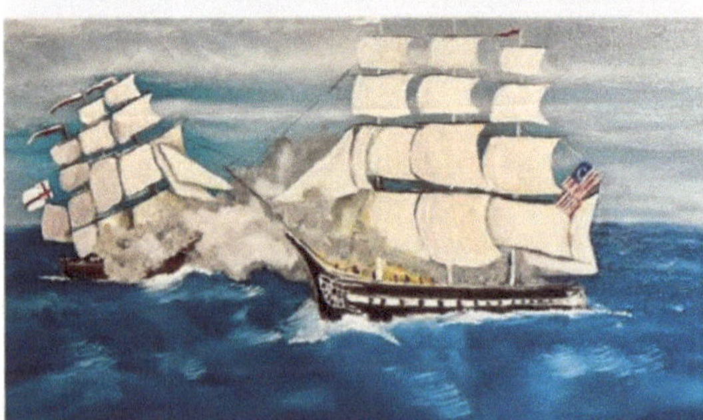

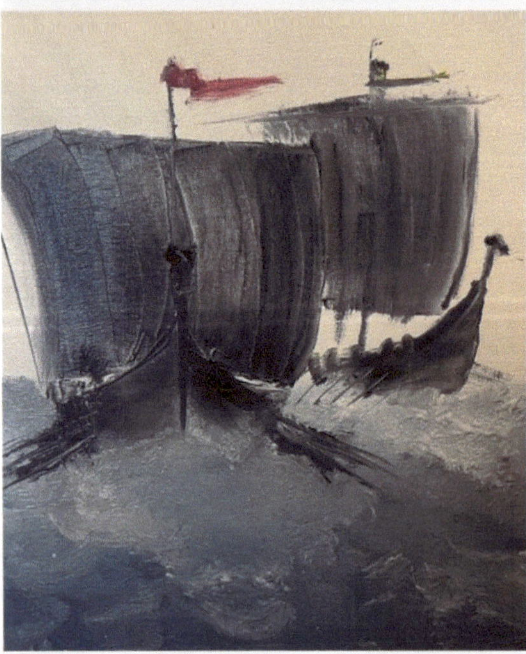

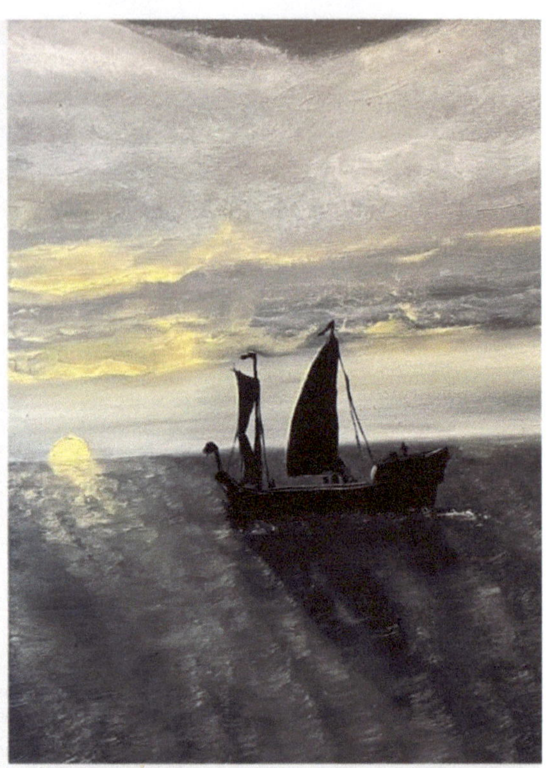

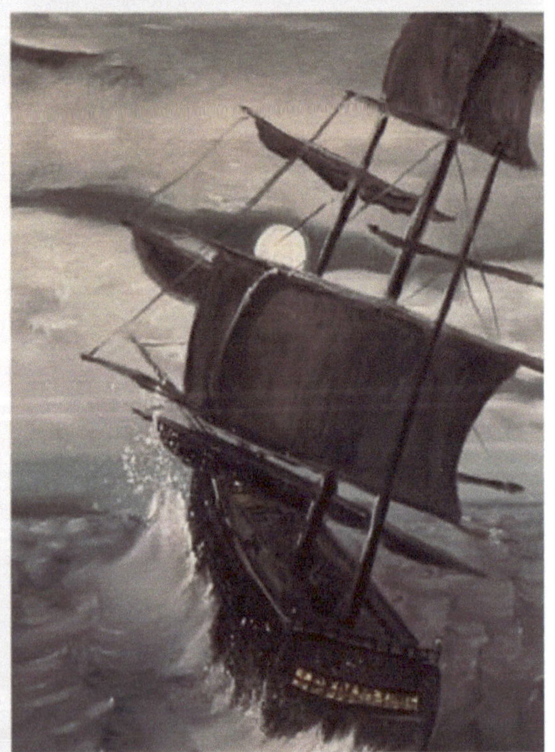

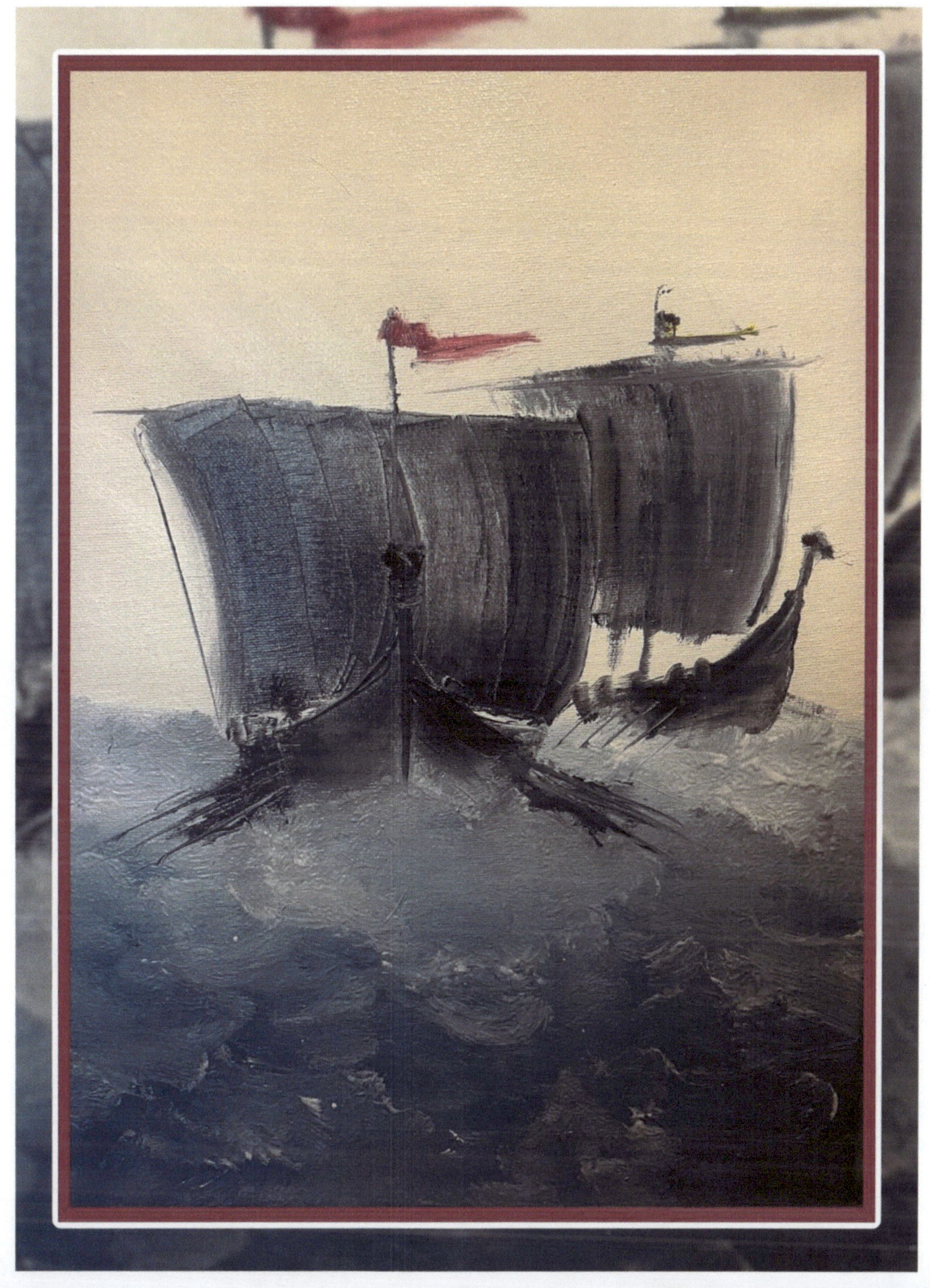

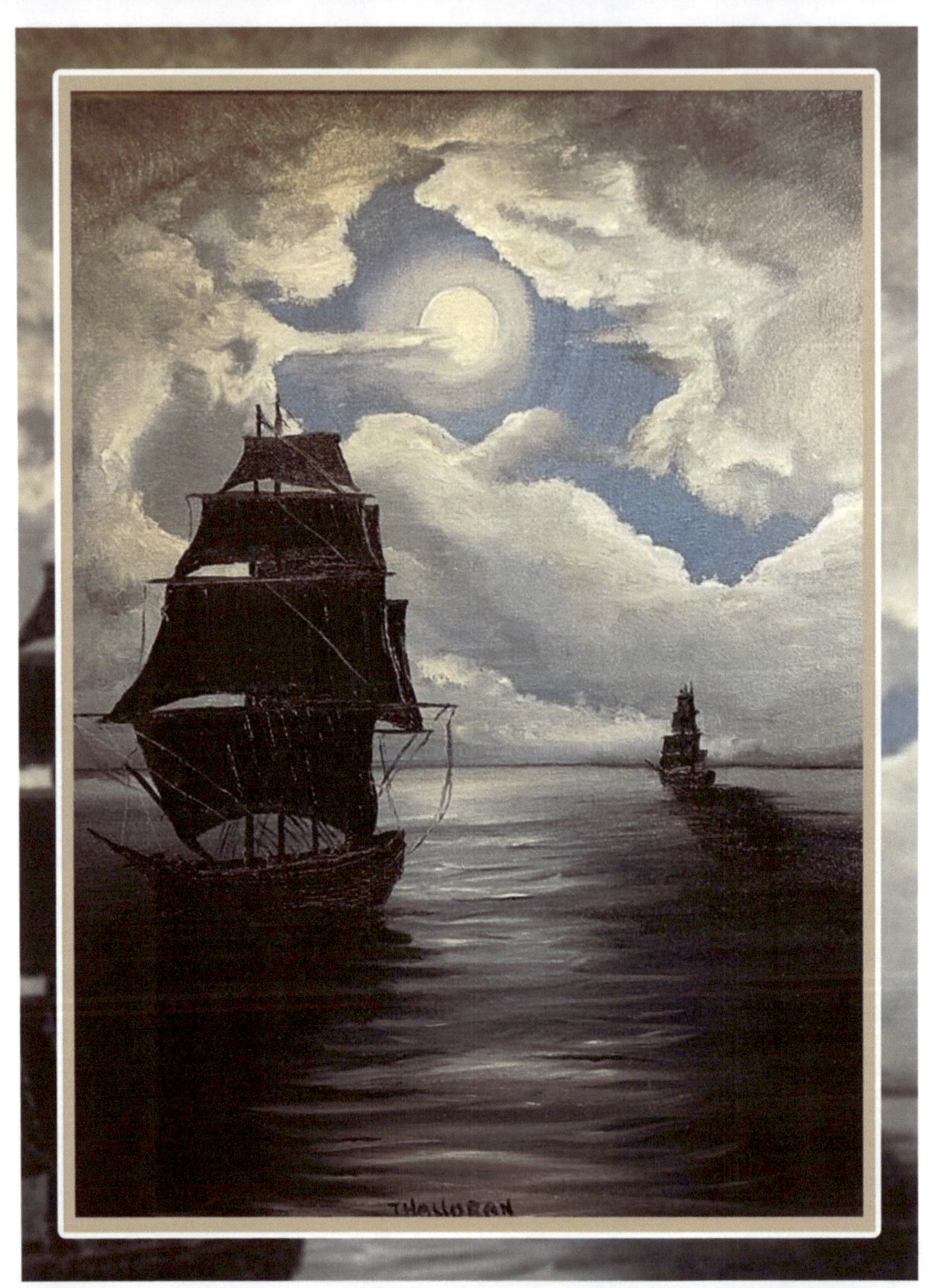
THallorn

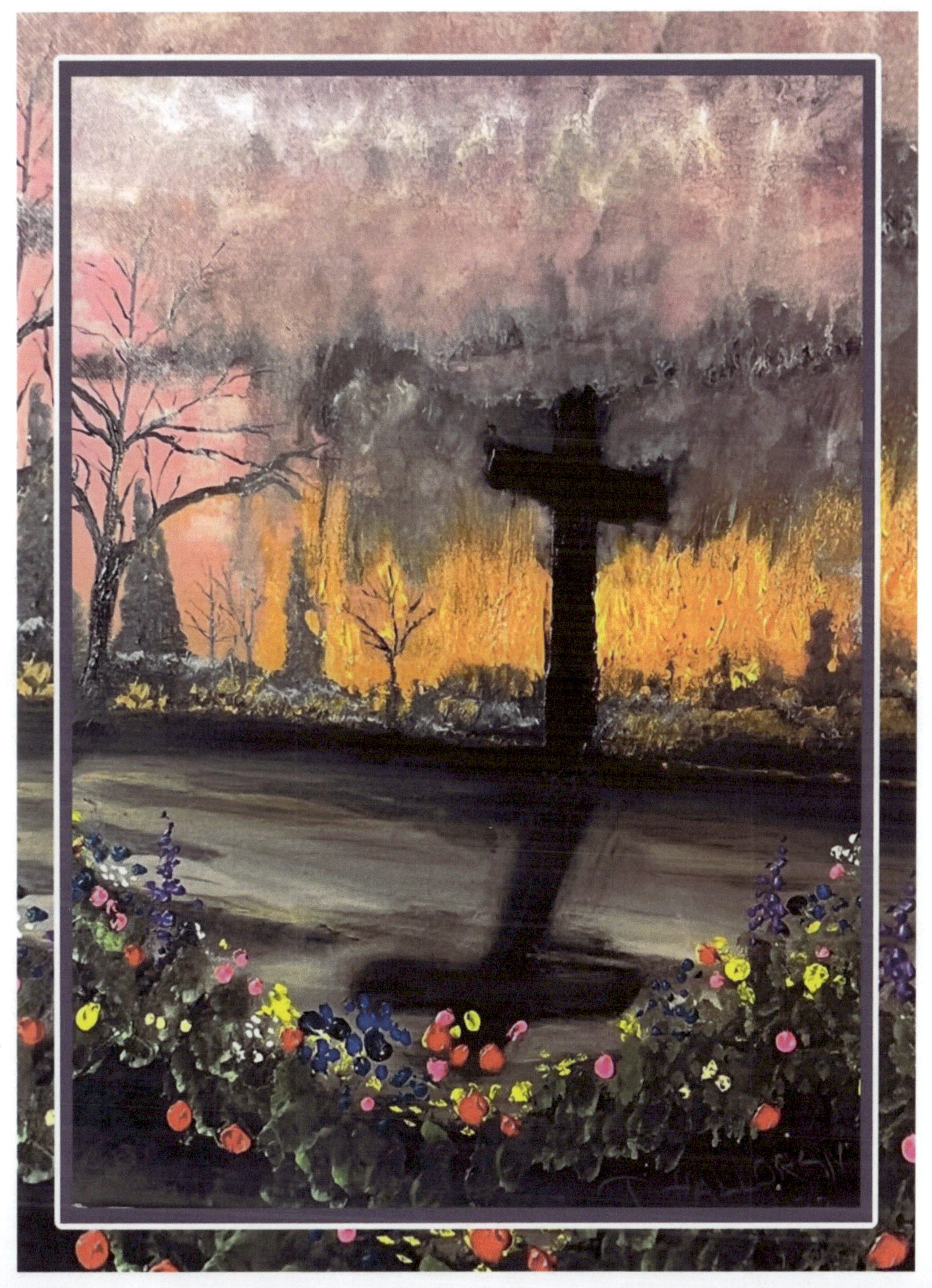

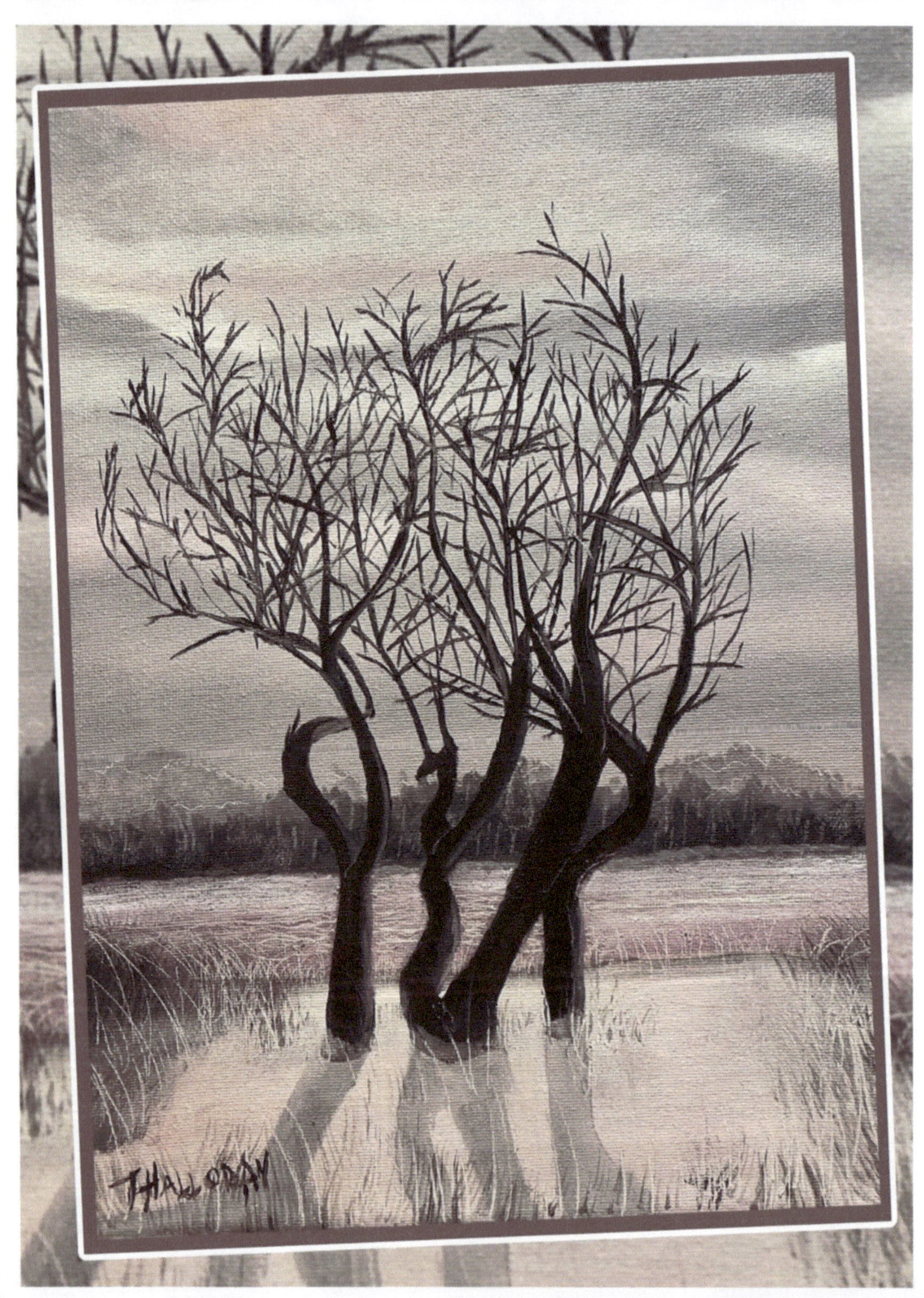
THALLODAY

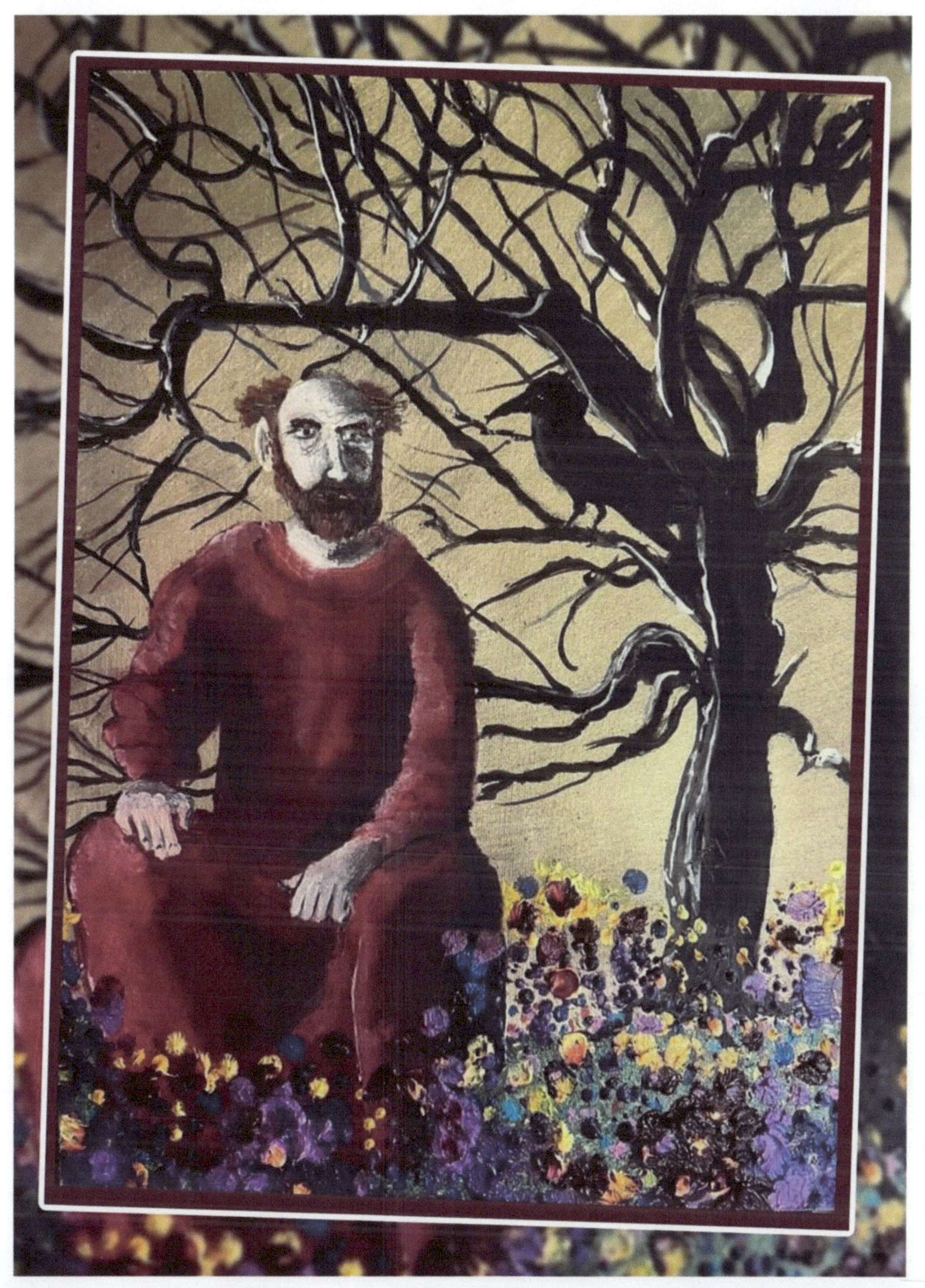

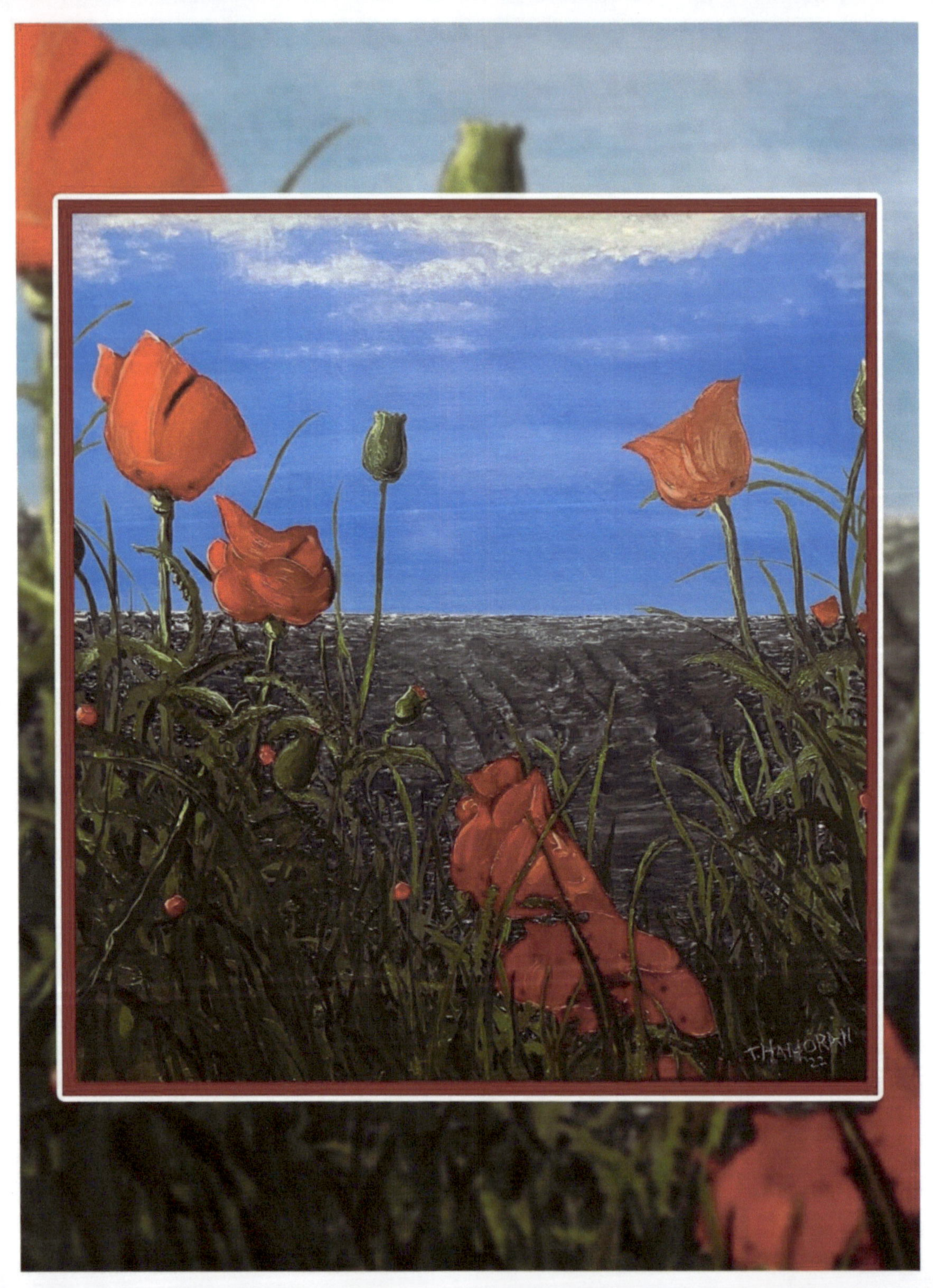

T.HALLORAN
'22

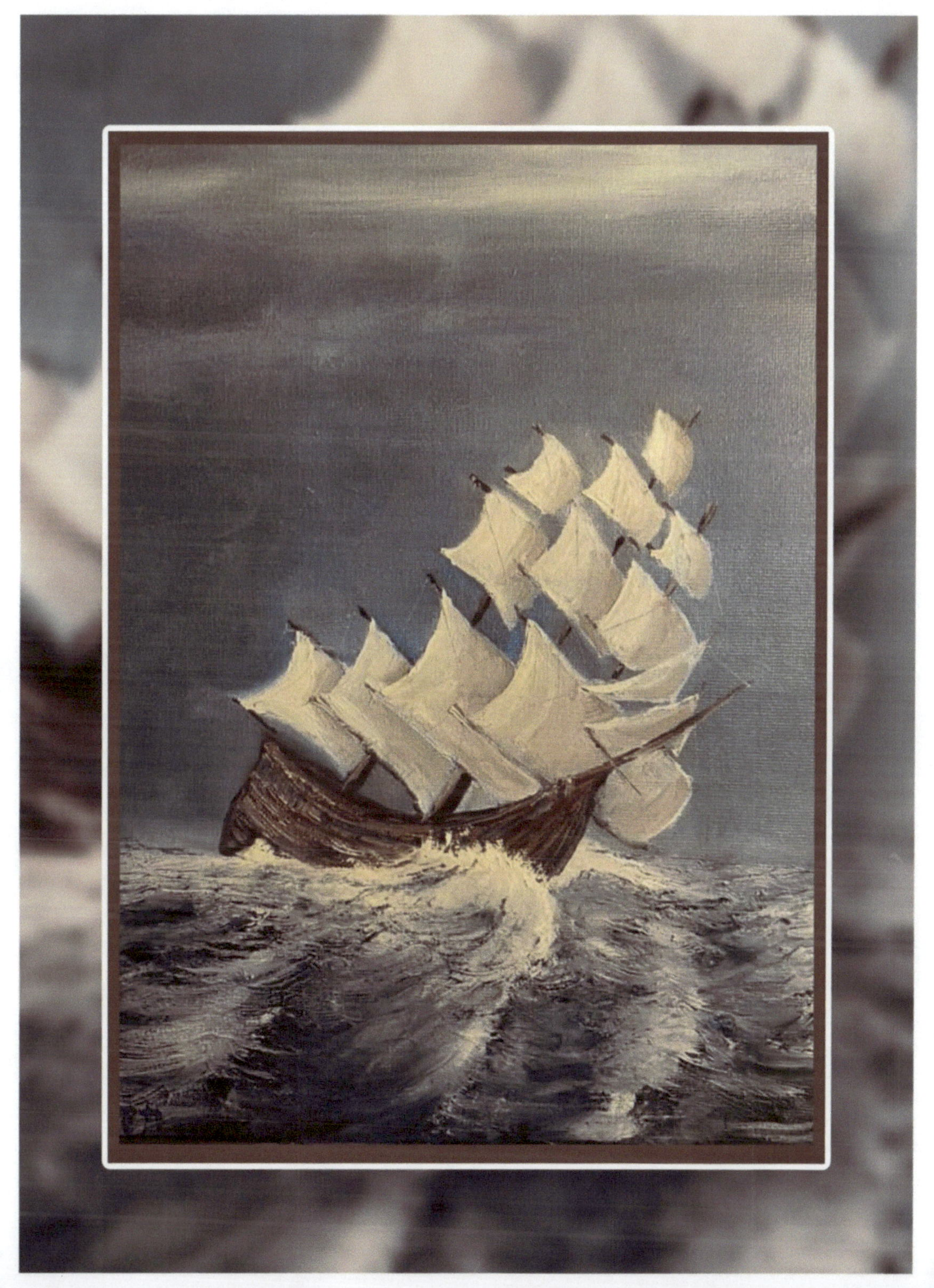

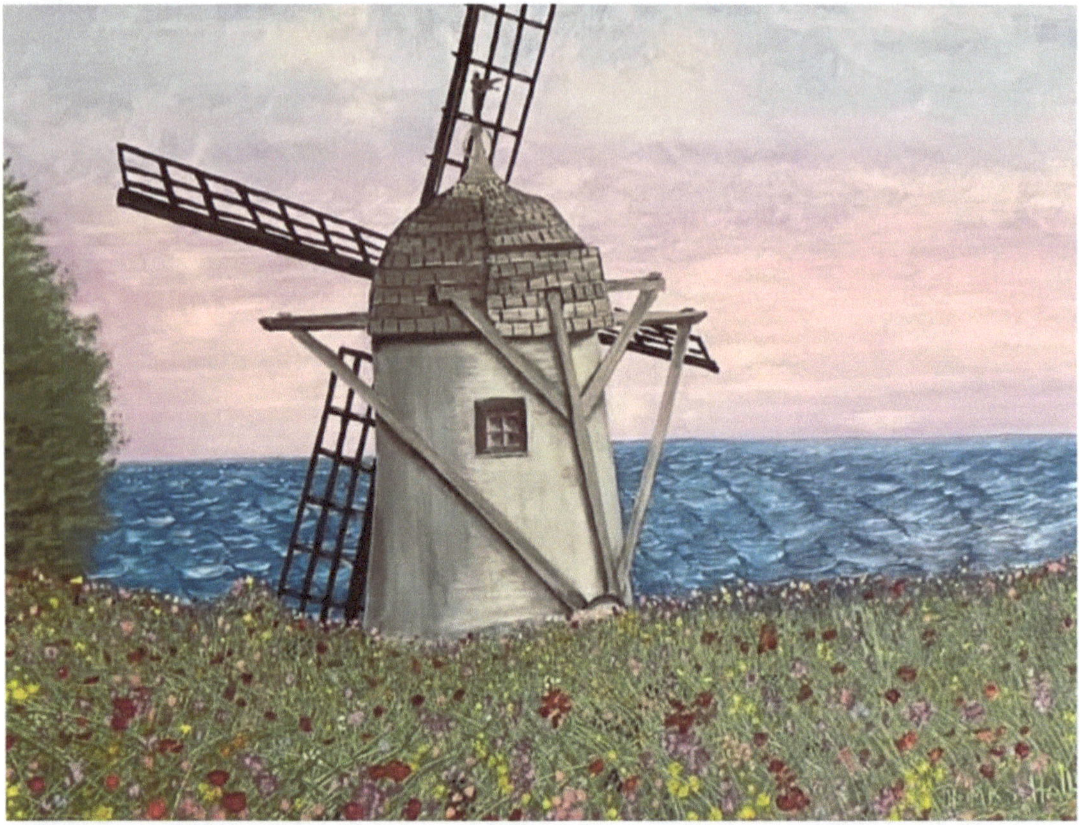

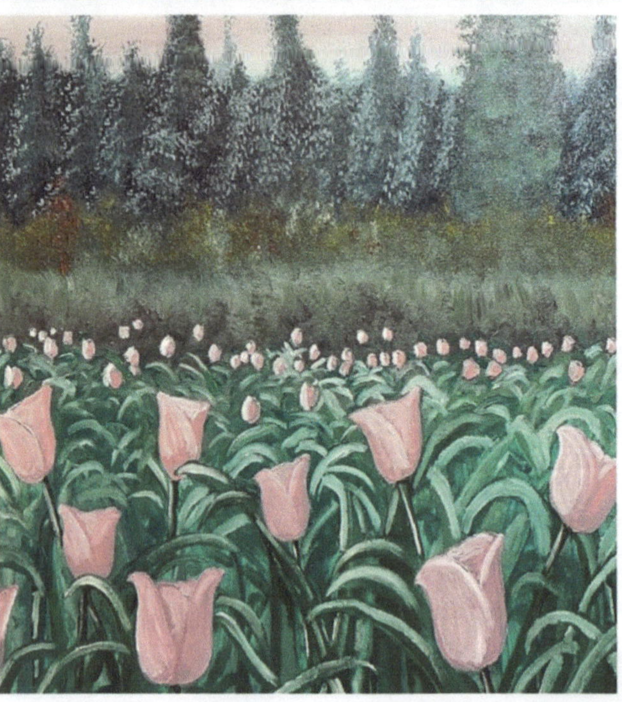

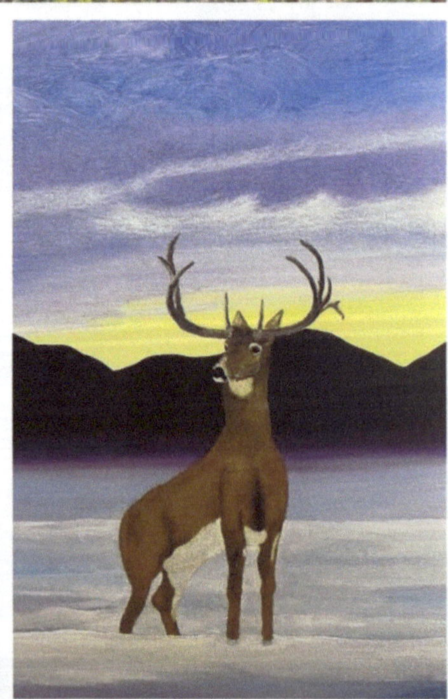

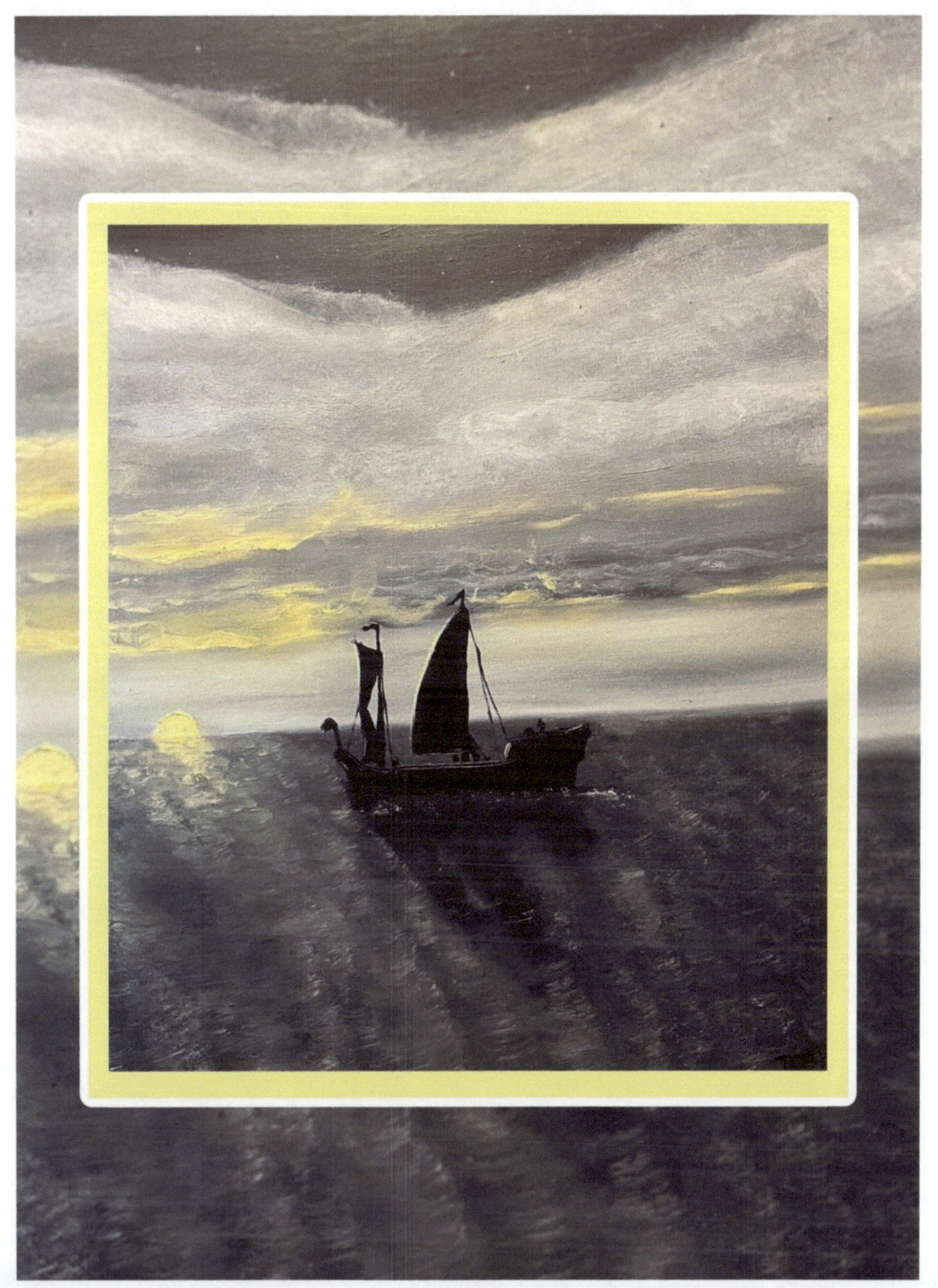

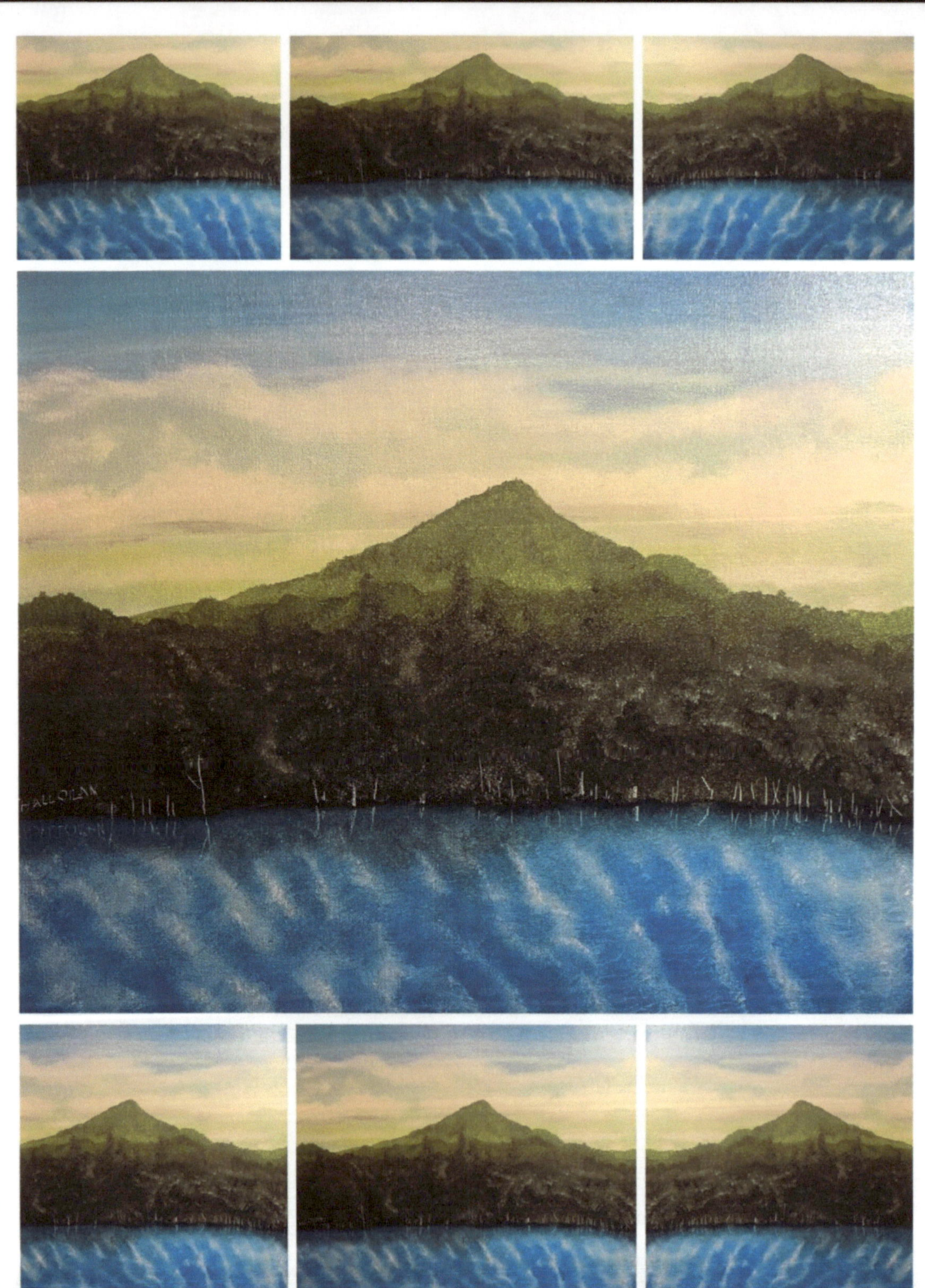

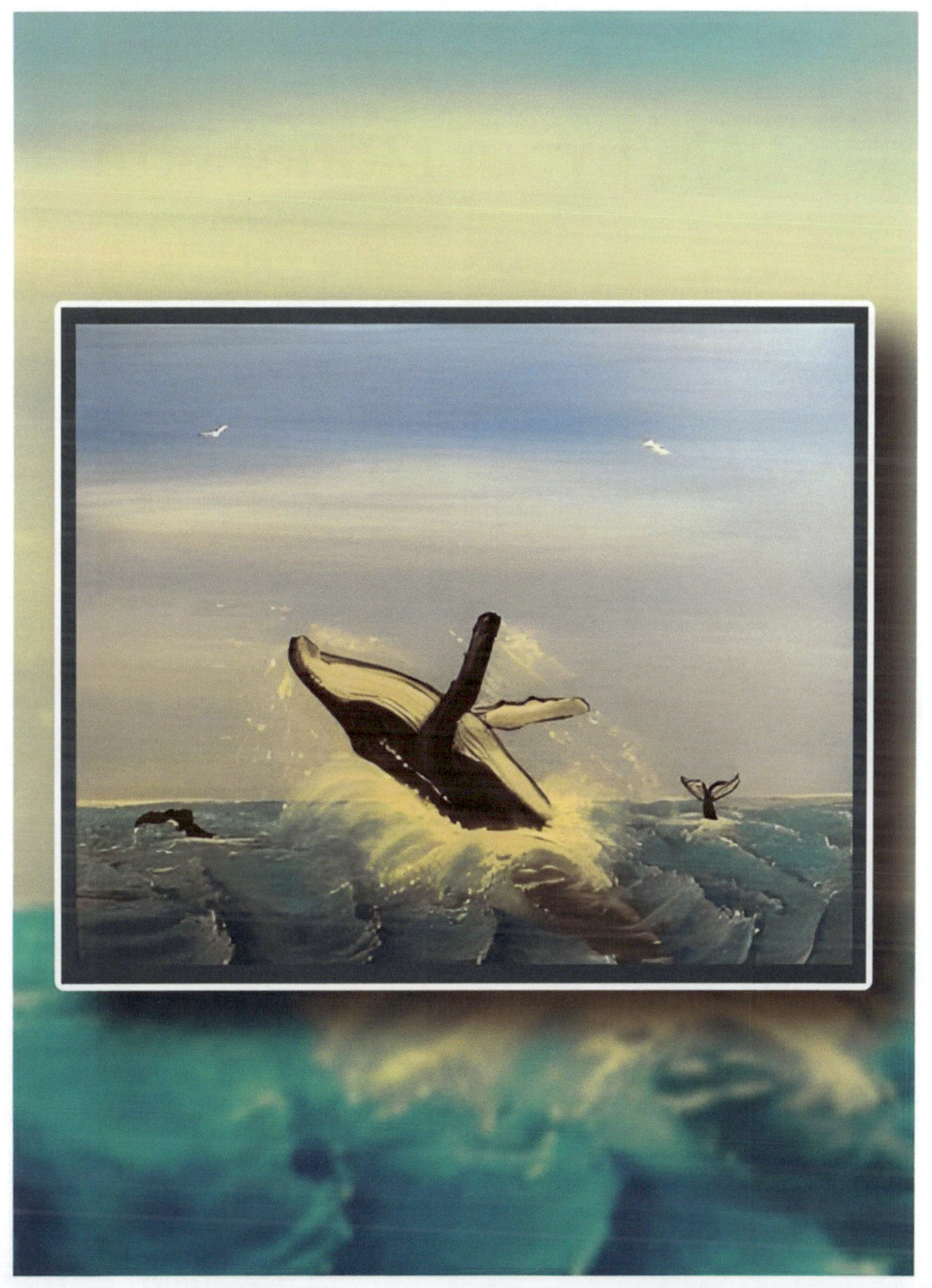

More from
I Ain't Your Marionette

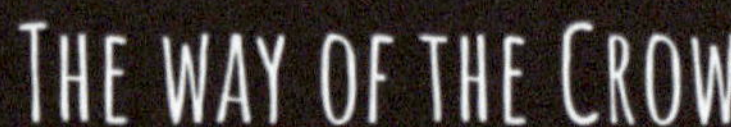

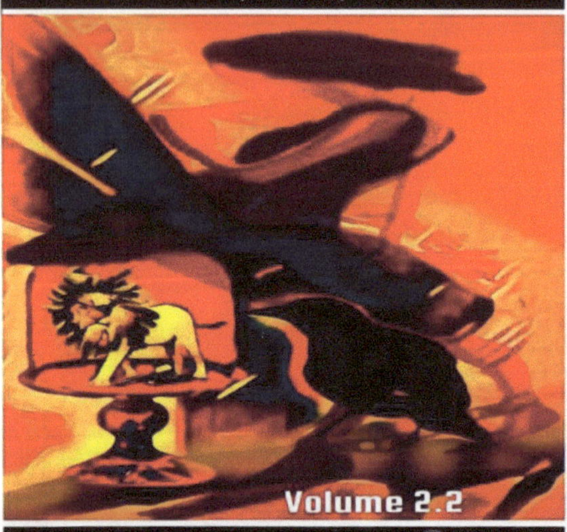

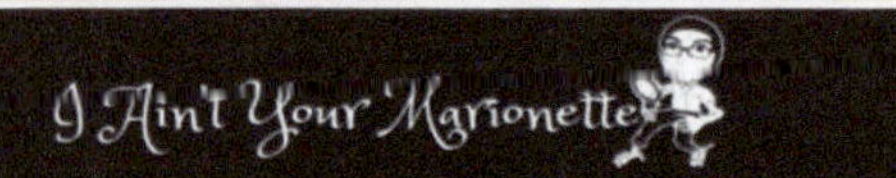

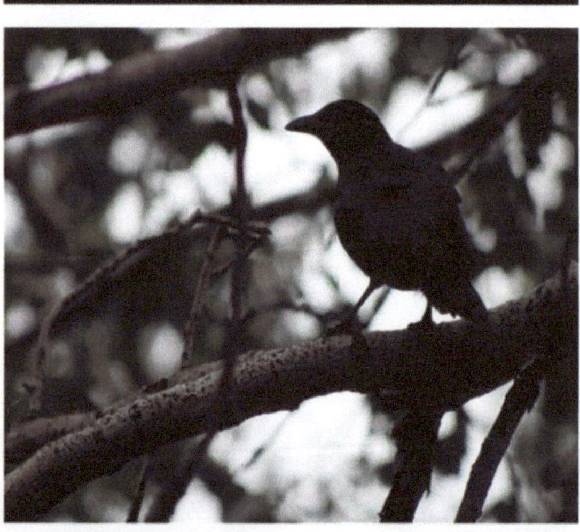

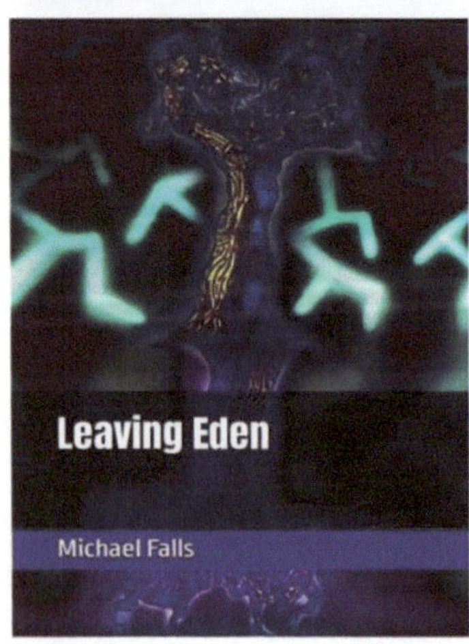

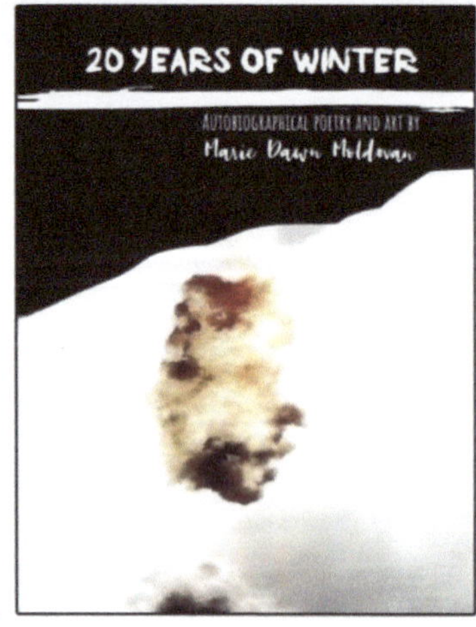

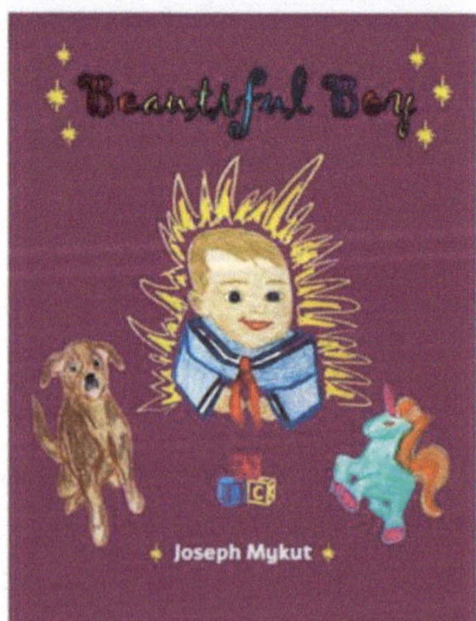

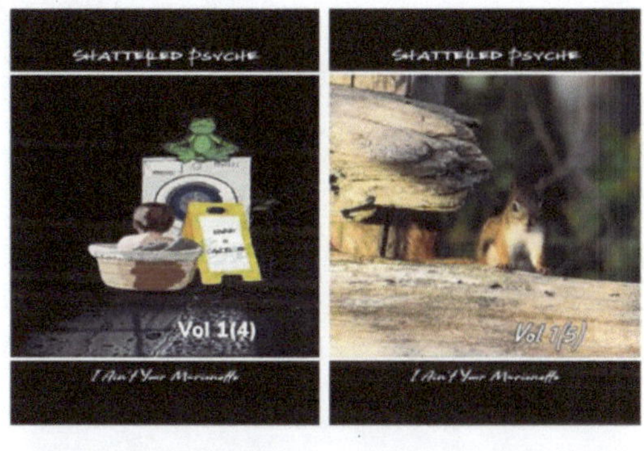
SHATTERED PSYCHE
SHATTERED PSYCHE
Vol 1(4)
Vol 1(5)
I Ain't Your Marionette
I Ain't Your Marionette

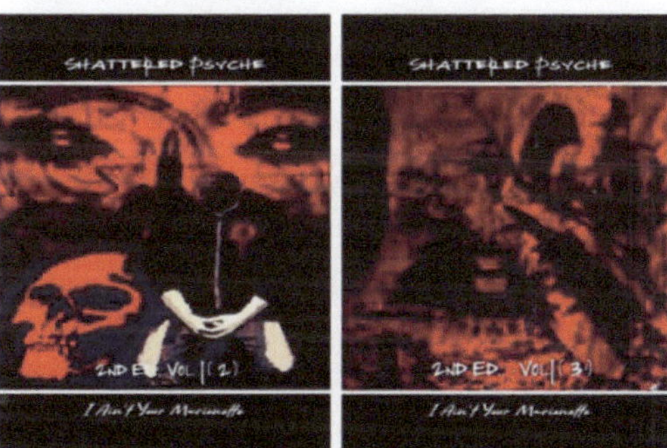
SHATTERED PSYCHE
SHATTERED PSYCHE
2ND ED., VOL 1(2)
2ND ED., VOL 1(3)
I Ain't Your Marionette
I Ain't Your Marionette

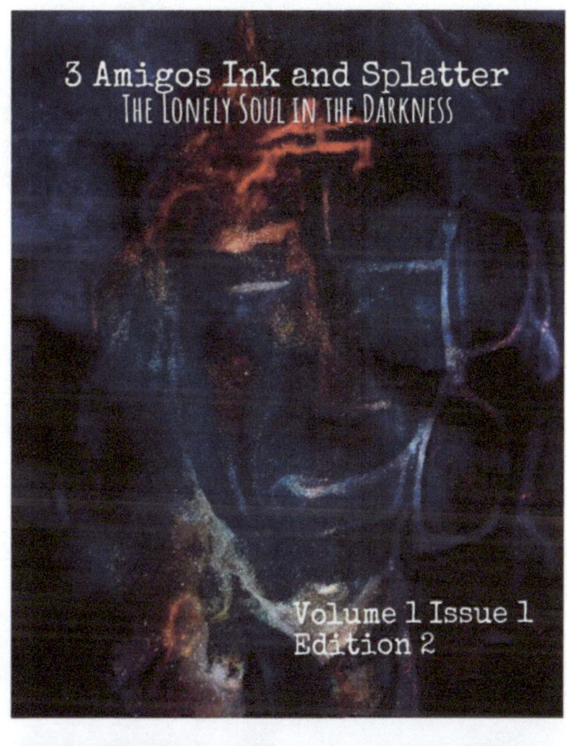
3 Amigos Ink and Splatter
The Lonely Soul in the Darkness
Volume 1 Issue 1
Edition 2

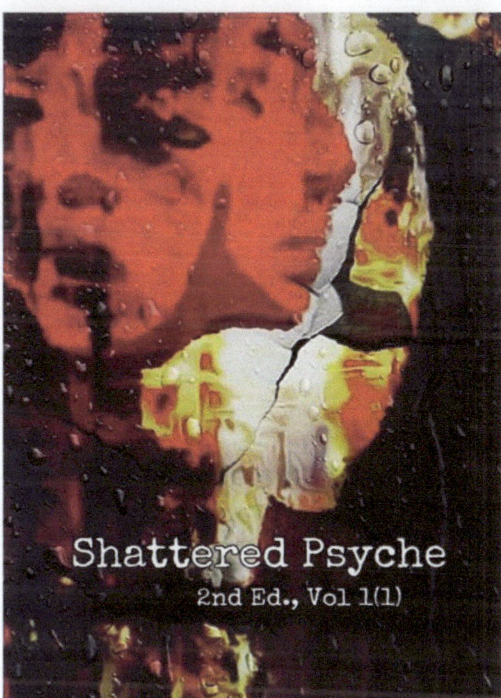
Shattered Psyche
2nd Ed., Vol 1(1)

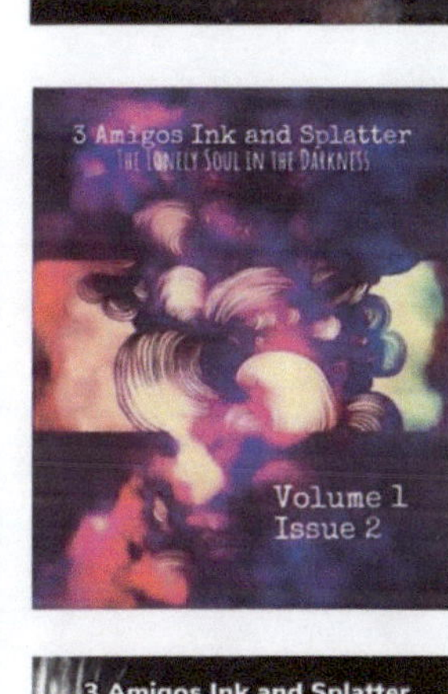
3 Amigos Ink and Splatter
The Lonely Soul in the Darkness
Volume 1
Issue 2

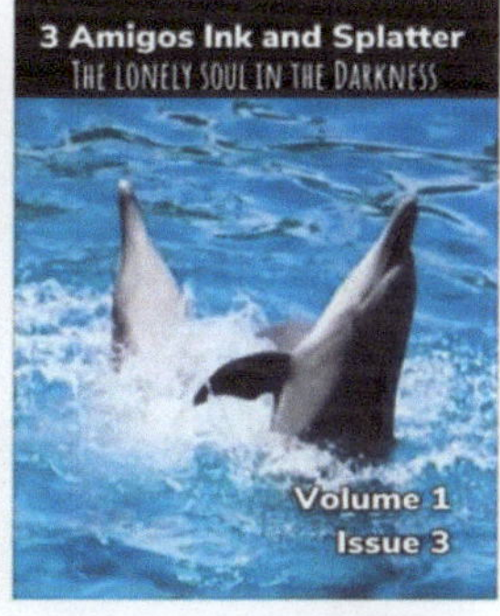
3 Amigos Ink and Splatter
The Lonely Soul in the Darkness
Volume 1
Issue 3

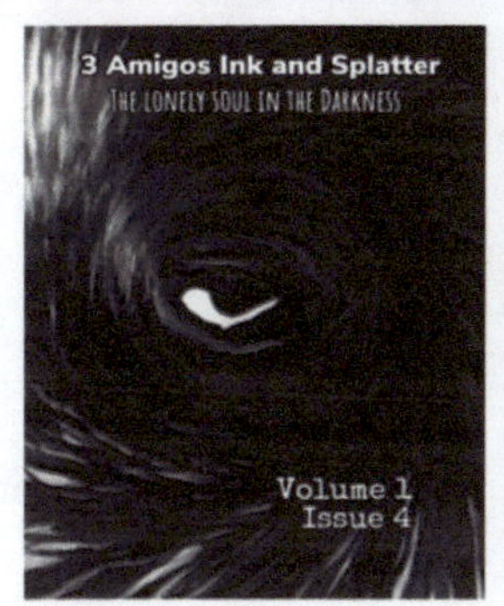
3 Amigos Ink and Splatter
The Lonely Soul in the Darkness
Volume 1
Issue 4

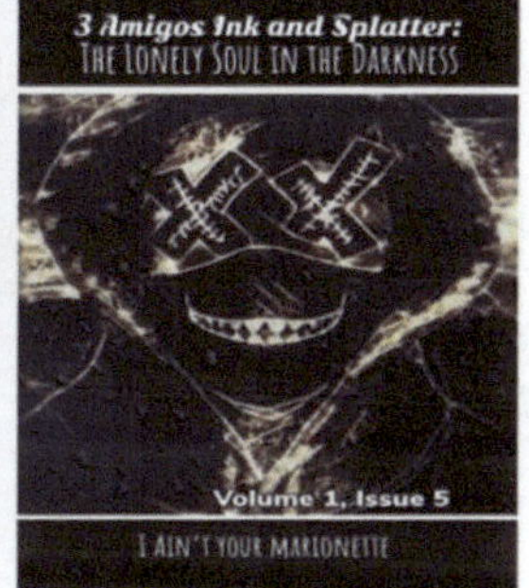
3 Amigos Ink and Splatter:
The Lonely Soul in the Darkness
Volume 1, Issue 5
I AIN'T YOUR MARIONETTE

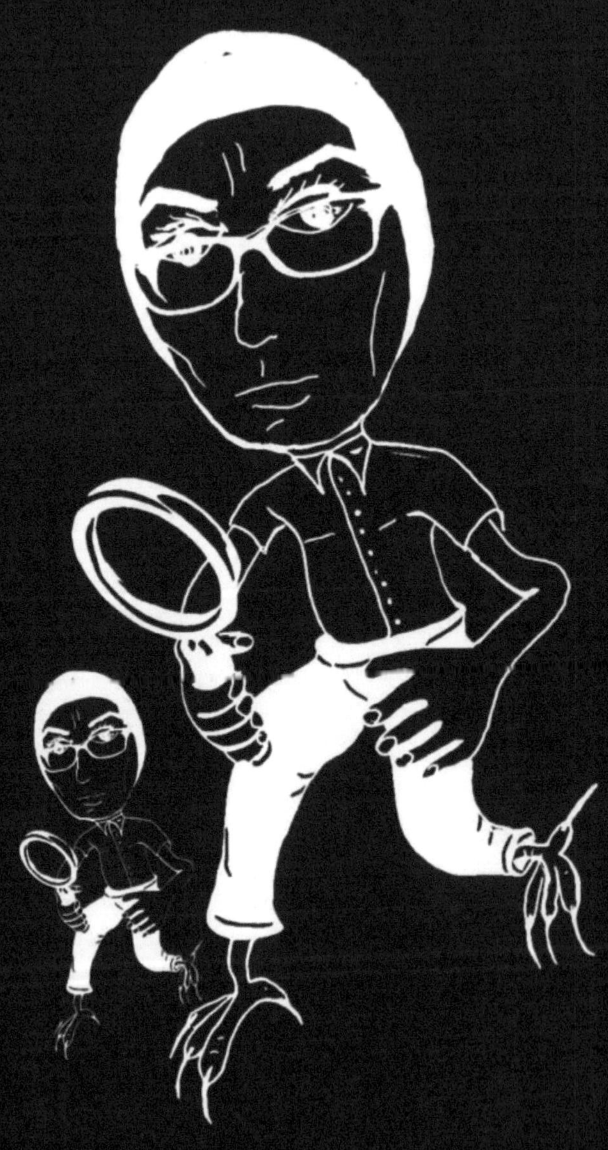

THANK YOU